DEAD CENTRE

Clean evidence of
the damage Ottawa
does.
Good luck at City Hall.

DEAD CENTRE

HOPE, POSSIBILITY AND UNITY FOR CANADIAN PROGRESSIVES

JAMEY HEATH

John Wiley & Sons Canada, Ltd.

Library and Archives Canada Cataloguing in Publication

Heath, Jamey
    Dead centre : hope, possibility, and unity for Canadian progressives / Jamey Heath.

Includes bibliographical references and index.
ISBN 978-0-470-84073-3

1. Progressivism (Canadian politics). 2. Political parties—Canada. 3. Social values—Political aspects—Canada. 4. Canada—Politics and government. I. Title.
JL195.H42 2007   324.271   C2007-900148-3

Production Credits
Cover design: Ian Koo
Interior text design: Adrian So
Wiley Bicentennial Logo: Richard J. Pacifico
Printer: Friesens

John Wiley & Sons Canada, Ltd.
6045 Freemont Blvd.
Mississauga, Ontario
L5R 4J3

Printed in Canada
1 2 3 4 5 [FP] 11 10 09 08 07

Contents

To Jo and my nephews.
And Chantal Hébert, Rick Smith and Brian Topp.

Introduction

IN JANUARY 2006, Canada elected its first neo-conservative prime minister, Stephen Harper. He won with 36 per-cent of the vote. A country that had just stayed out of the Iraq War, ratified Kyoto and embraced equal marriage for lesbian and gay people suddenly had one of the most right-wing leaders around.

Something's not quite right. How did Harper come to lead a country that wants to be more progressive? And how could an election when 64 per-cent of people voted progressively leave us stuck with *him*?

As we ponder, we should ask what we do when we are anxious, which is the question that really keeps progressives apart. I can hear Bob Rae now, saying the answer's simple: Liberal majority government, to get that branch-plant Republican out of 24 Sussex Drive. That's what you might be thinking, too. And wondering why this thick New Democrat doesn't get it and keeps up with the partisanship that split the vote to begin with—and let Harper win.

Which brings me back to what we do when we are anxious? I know why Harper's at odds with me: he's reckless on global warming, too unquestioning towards George W. Bush and doesn't really want a federal government around. So why weren't New Democrats nicer to

Liberals so we never had to worry about him, I can hear you wondering. Why the last-minute Harper hate-fest now?

And that's the rub. New Democrats did try and stop him. Ridings that elected Conservative MPs in 2004 elected New Democrats in 2006, and people don't join the progressive party because they want to help the neo-conservatives. Sometimes, Liberals need some harder questioning because, with so much at stake, glib one-liners—Stop Harper! Vote Liberal!—might not be the most strategic advice.

Harper doesn't frighten me because of who he is or the party he belongs to, but because of what he does. Global warming and current Republican foreign policy are scares. And the growing gap between have-more and have-less has some worrisome consequences, too. Now let's check the record. Under Liberals, Canada's greenhouse gas emissions rose faster than in Bush's America; Liberals—not Harper—began the imbalanced mission in Afghanistan; and who else was in office as basic income support programs were abandoned?

But Harper also clarifies what we want by often doing what we don't. Each stand he takes makes progressive values clearer, and with more people believing in more progressive things, possibility may follow. So as we suss out what we think of all this, we should ask if it really is true that the Liberal Party is as progressive as it portrays—and if this can't be the time we try to realign politics.

Pollution didn't become a frightening issue just as Harper entered the Prime Minister's Office, and poverty should have been a concern well before he did. That's why what we do when we are anxious sums up the progressive tragedy we've seen and makes the progressive rethink we've put off more needed now than ever. Because as pollution grew under Liberals, progressives had more than the usual two options:

- Vote for a governing Liberal Party and hope for actual pollution cuts.
- Vote for the NDP to elect more NDP MPs, perhaps with a balance of power.
- Vote for the Green Party, either to encourage more debate or to maybe elect an MP one day.

- Help non-partisan environmental groups pressure governments and parties.
- Get out of polluting Canada, and let Quebec come up with its own plan.

That's a progressive mess, looked at one way, but an opportunity looked at in another. But we have more options than Liberals let on. It's true, I'm not a fan of the Liberal Party of Canada, but for reasons beyond that they wear red buttons and I prefer orange. It's because it masquerades as progressive, in much the same way Enron passed as profitable: looks good on the surface, but don't scratch too deep. Eventually, the rot catches up and another in the cycle of Liberal defeats takes place.

Those defeats are now more likely than not as politics enters possible realignment. For so long, it was just natural that Liberals would win. They had a power base in Quebec, then the right split, and our governments became more predictably red. But the Liberal Party has now lost Quebec in seven straight elections, and along the way managed to convince us of its hegemony when in fact it's long gone, now facing a united right.

Instead of this being a time to fear in Canadian politics, it could be a time to hope and take advantage of what's presented itself. And hope versus fear—what we do when we're anxious—sums up the tragedy of a progressive country being stuck with Harper. Surely, with politics in flux and a broken Liberal Party we can have a broader progressive rethink than why we didn't all just Vote Liberal to Stop Harper in 2006.

Make no mistake. I think that Canada would be a lot better off with a lot fewer Liberal MPs, and that the party has not served us well. The centre's dead, doesn't deliver progressive victories voluntarily and often looks a lot like Rome before it fell: swilling around in the fat indulgence of a one-party state, drinking the rich wine of hegemony; sadly, with many progressive Liberals trapped within, watching pollution and poverty grow, along with the rest of us.

In part, *Dead Centre* is about the NDP, and I'm not ashamed of that. Canada's done well by the NDP, and we're the kind of country we are, in part, because of the reforms it demanded—and then won. It is not a fringe voice in federal politics, but mainstream on every issue that we often use to describe what Canada stands for. But it's also imperfect and needs the kind of change that growth brings.

Liberals and New Democrats both have their icons—Tommy Douglas and Pierre Trudeau—and what they managed to win before often shapes what we think now. To a degree, there's a fight about which one of them stands higher, but instead of debating which one's the Greatest Canadian, our rethink could try to bring them both into the same kind of party. To Liberals, the answer is clear, and we should formalize what's often been perilously close to a one-party state. Just vote Liberal, they advise, and all will become well again. We have to Stop Harper, after all.

True. But if we only ever pick up the story exactly where Liberals want, without taking a broader look at what happened before, we'll keep being pulled by the Liberal Party's chain. A broader look is needed, for the progressive rethink that's overdue.

Progressive people do feel anxious about what Harper could do to our climate and country, but voting Liberal or not doesn't really sum it up; nor was voting Liberal that dandy an idea facing some fairly daunting challenges heading our way. Manufacturing jobs are evaporating. And the British government says global warming will cost $7 trillion—worse than both world wars and the Depression put together.

Why didn't Canada's "progressive" government commission that report, five years ago? Liberals didn't lead when the world was looking for it—under "lefty" Jean Chrétien, or the more rightward Paul Martin—and the possibility of Harper making things worse wasn't the only thing of bother in 2006. A credible case could be made that Liberals are frightening on the environment, too. But my, wasn't that Chrétien–Martin fight fun. The pollution? Not quite such a blast.

Now we're asked to forget all that and pick up the story where it suits Liberals. Maybe it's just me, but perhaps the Liberal Party of Canada hasn't earned the right to be trusted on what's the most strategic spot to start examining global warming. And perhaps the new Green Party leader, Elizabeth May—a prominent environmentalist during the last decade—also shares some responsibility for us not doing better, for validating policies during the Liberal years of going backwards. She herself says Brian Mulroney is our greenest PM ever, so why, in the 2006 election, did Liberal suddenly become synonymous with the environment?

May wasn't alone in feeling anxious. Union leader Buzz Hargrove was, too, and determined to stop a Conservative government. He campaigned three times with Paul Martin—the same Liberal who wouldn't protect pensions, and who left most unemployed workers without Employment Insurance. Even the venerable activist Maude Barlow chimed in, despite Liberals making the trade deals she'd long worked to improve worse at every turn. If Harper winning is a bit odd, what to make of progressives campaigning for Liberals going backwards?

Barlow, Hargrove and May joined the Think Twice coalition in the 2006 election. Some call it a Liberal front group, others say it was a genuine attempt to stop a neo-conservative taking office as leading lefties took to the TV to urge people to Stop Harper. And Vote Liberal, as fear trumped hope during a time of anxiety.

With non-partisan progressives playing larger roles, thinking twice about Think Twice is fair game. Unless we ask why policies get worse and why debate's slipped more towards the right, the possibility that's here can't be realized. Canada wasn't the only country to vote in the Americas in early 2006. Chile had an election, too, and elected the progressive Michelle Bachelet as president. It's becoming quite a parade across the Americas as world politics are blown by progressive winds more and more. Sometimes, moderately in Europe, Chile or New Zealand; other times, radically in Bolivia or Venezuela—but there is a very good example, right next door.

Most of our fear of Stephen Harper is that he's like George W. Bush. Perhaps, the people most like us—progressive Americans—have some pointers, facing similar neo-conservative enemies.

Progressive Canadians are often accused of anti-Americanism, but that's nonsense. We're not anti-American, but anti-Republican Party, in which we've got plenty of company in almost every corner of the world. Democrats, however, most progressive Canadians can relate with—and progressive Americans have some tricks they can share.

Chiefly, a two-sided debate that lets civil rights activists, environmentalists, progressive business people, workers or anyone who thinks Bush is dangerous to push together. They might not all like the Democratic Party, but they all dislike Bush, and if we want to enjoy elections where we can co-operate more, we should use this period of flux to get them.

Dead Centre is unabashedly inspired by one brilliant progressive American, Berkeley professor George Lakoff, who in 2004 wrote *Don't Think of an Elephant: Know Your Values and Frame the Debate.* It urged progressive Americans to fix the frame on which political debate took place so they could win more often.

But it doesn't work here, because we have two-sided debates in a multi-party system—with the biggest "progressive" party being the Liberals. Their record says they're *rarely* progressive and, with politics changing, it's time to create the conditions that let progressives win more from elections. Pierre Trudeau was right. It is tough being in bed with an elephant, and tougher still having its calf in Stephen Harper as prime minister—but instead of doing the usual and building Liberals back up, let's use this time to bring about some possibility.

We're divided about whether that's a good idea, partly because we're stuck in the frame of the Liberal Party. As long as we let it explain what happened, we might end up thinking that the NDP called an early election to kick off the 2006 campaign or somehow helped Harper win during it. Unless we do a bit of probing of the official line, we might end up squandering the possibility before us.

Entering a period of almost-certain minority governments, we've got time for a rethink that bluntly asks if the Liberal line on things isn't more for their benefit than progressive wins. Multi-party democracy could work to our advantage—but Liberals won't let that dirty little secret out, because that could mean we'd start to want cleaning their other dirty little secrets up.

After working for Greenpeace and for a union, I worked in Ottawa for four years with the NDP. New Democrats battle the Liberal line on things every day in the capital, but not until the 2006 election did I realize how strong it really was. Entering the campaign, I had always suspected the Liberals were right about how the 1988 election worked. Again, I hear you asking, so what?

The 1988 election matters today. It was the last time the Liberals had lost, and because Tories won—which isn't the same thing—free trade with the United States came. Most Canadians voted for parties opposed to free trade, and the fact that it passed makes today's progressive division worse. Many lefties blame the NDP; nobody more strenuously than Liberals. The 1988 and 2006 elections are mirror images of each other, and the common link isn't a divided progressive vote between the Liberals and NDP. The common link is that Quebec progressives were divided from their cousins everywhere else.

Figuring out that I'd partly been trained to see politics as Liberals would like was an appalling eureka moment. But positive as well, because working with 1988 veterans such as campaign manager Brian Topp on the 2006 election made me realize that my frame of what happened in 1988 was wrong. I did a bit of a rethink.

This book's about frames, because progressive people are stuck in them. But like our cousins south of the border, around the Americas and in the rest of the world, when we manage to create common frames against which we can all push together—we can win. Not to replace a blue sign with red, or a red one with orange or even for splashing a bit of green about, but to win on the things that matter. So a progressive country doesn't have to hear our Tory prime minister embarrass us by fighting Kyoto in the world—or Liberal ones embarrass us by ignoring it at home.

Part One is about what happened and progressive lessons learned from our icons. It covers the minority Parliament elected in the 2004 election and saw progressive victories in a rewritten budget on the partisan side, and a big win on equal marriage for non-partisan circles—then ended, followed by Stephen Harper's win in the 2006 election. What happened and why isn't as simple as Liberals explain. Letting the Liberal line stick could be risky with so much at stake.

The right had united, the Bloc was strong and growing thanks to scandal, and the NDP kept small by Liberals during the minority Parliament. It was politics' new rules at play and renewed the slide from hegemony that really took hold in 1988. That's Part Two—the possibility that more progressive unity might bring about, and our non-partisan component. These are strategic questions. With politics in realignment and hope possible, too, we should take a good hard look at what Liberals say is true.

We have more options in the years of change ahead. Here's to hoping during times of feeling anxious, and thinking that the progressive country we'd like can be won.

PART 1

THE MINORITY PARLIAMENT AND THE 2006 ELECTION

Progressive Victories, Politics'
New Rules and Stephen Harper's Win

To and From a Dingy Room

O N THE SECOND FLOOR of Parliament's West Block, tucked around the back, is the dingy room where the opposition reads budgets before they become public. It's unspectacular. There are three tables, one for each opposition party, some experts on hand from the finance department to answer technical questions, and the usual assortment of fruit, cookies and bad coffee.

Parties get locked inside without any of the usual trappings, such as cell phones or the loathsome BlackBerry. The budget's contents are perused, parties prepare their response and dutifully line up at the door. Then they race out the moment the finance minister begins to speak in the House. Media interviews begin long before the minister stops speaking and last well into the night.

The budget's path from the dingy room tells the tale of how the minority Parliament unfolded and the 2006 election began. In many ways, it's like a chute for a waterslide that could shape the flow of events to some extent, but never stop water from falling—sometimes rapidly. The water is politics' new rules, borne by Liberal weakness in Quebec. This new frailty, first caused by Conservative PM Brian Mulroney and then by the Bloc Québécois, left Liberals as an unnatural governing entity, no longer in control of their destiny. The mighty had fallen hard and landed far from hegemony.

The 2005 budget was defining for New Democrats in Liberal Paul Martin's minority, and for the life of the 38th Parliament itself. Bounced around by the omnipresent sponsorship scandal and carried by different parties, its trail was often a wild one as an unprecedented Parliament took place. But the budget's prominence only unfolds in time, as disjointed events fuse into progressive victory, disappointment and often high drama.

There are different versions of what happens next, but if progressive people are going to do better than we've done thus far, we'll need a common explanation as to how Stephen Harper came to call 24 Sussex Drive home. If we can't agree on where we've been, it's harder to decide where to go, after all, so Part One deals with how we got into this mess in the hopes we might get out of it with our progressive majority intact. That's saved for Part Two, but before we get there, Harper's win has to be sadly relived, for we're in a spot similar to 1988, when Mulroney was re-elected and made our division worse.

After losing in 2006, Liberals overlook what voters decided, and say the discomfort of opposition benches is theirs because the NDP ended a productive minority Parliament early. Why be original? They blame the NDP for their last loss, too, in 1988. Liberals accuse the NDP of only valuing a few more MPs, while being blithely unbothered by the win of a soul mate to U.S. President George W. Bush. Before determining the next progressive move, we need to see if they are telling the truth. Events need to be seen in order, as they happened, not in reverse.

Liberals like to pretend that Harper teleported into the PMO, starting shortly before the election, but no. His victory was the product of what came earlier. If only the outcome of events, not their cause, shapes lefty analysis, then we will keep being stuck in an unproductive and cyclical loop. As long as progressive thinking is formed by the Liberal line, it's likely better for their hopes than ours.

The two aren't as interchangeable as Liberals would like. Their kind of progressive government left Canada the third-worse industrialized country on global warming emissions, and the gap between have-more and have-less grows each day. We can do better in a country as progressive as ours, and Liberals' assurances that, don't worry, they'll be back in office soon not only may be untrue, but also unwelcome. Before striving for a Liberal majority again, we need to go back. At least for a bit, because Liberals aren't telling the truth about why Harper is in power and not them.

So to the West Block's dingy room, where the minority began in earnest on February 23, 2005: Budget Day. For the NDP, the path to the budget was as unrewarding as the initial path from it, as politics' new rules that drove Liberals from power didn't start during the minority Parliament. Instead, they moved through it, sometimes to the dismay of progressive people, and renewed their assault on Liberals in 2004, two decades after the long slide from hegemony began.

After the 2004 election, Jack Layton's first as leader, the NDP came up one seat shy of the balance of power. It was a cruel blow of fate. With three Liberal minority Parliaments since the 1960s all pleasing progressive Canadians a great deal, expectations were high. Unlike previous Liberal minorities, however, the NDP didn't have the formal balance of power this time, in one of many key differences as politics' new rules renewed their grip.

For progressive people, the evening of June 28, 2004 was filled with relief and a sense of opportunity. After a campaign that pollsters wrongly called a dead heat, a minority government was elected. Fond memories made us eager to get to work. The minority, the first Liberal one since 1972, began fuelled with the anticipation of its predecessors. Its life proved short. It wasn't like its forerunners, not only because the NDP lacked a balance of power, but also because the Bloc emerged as the first openly sovereigntist party. Oh yes, and a governing party under judicial review. They all came out in the wash together, and made memory an unreliable guide to how minorities' rules worked, but as it began, the good times of previous Liberal minorities put smiles on our faces.

Under their new leader, Martin, Liberals won 135 seats, well short of 155 for a majority, but a strong minority still. The Conservative Party, reunited under Harper, saw its seats rise healthily to 99, but share of the vote fall by 10 per-cent from the totals of the Canadian Alliance and Progressive Conservative (PC) parties from which it was born. Gilles Duceppe's Bloc equalled its historic high with 54 MPs, while in Vancouver, Chuck Cadman became an Independent MP. In the minds of many, there was a clear progressive majority in the House. Let the good times roll.

The election was a mixed bag for the NDP. It had almost a million new votes—almost doubling support—but the seat count was disappointing. Only 19 MPs emerged, five more than going in, and longtime MPs lost in Saskatchewan. As the electoral system worked its wonders, 16 per cent of the vote resulted in fewer NDP MPs in 2004 than 11 per cent in 1997. Particularly painful was knowing how close it came. For most of election night, the NDP seemed set to win about 22 seats, but as the night wore long at the headquarters in Toronto and rural parts of the West reported results, the last-minute desertion to the Liberals hit home. By morning, the new caucus numbered only 19. It lost a heart-breaking 12 ridings by fewer than 1,000 votes.

Seven of them went Conservative—three each in British Columbia and Saskatchewan, plus Oshawa, Ontario—and had a New Democrat won any instead, the NDP and progressive people would have enjoyed the crucial balance of power. That they were lost as New Democrats voted Liberal to Stop Harper rubbed salt in the wound. By following Liberals' advice, NDP voters elected Tory MPs, and denied a progressive majority—outside of Quebec, at least—the last say on any non-confidence vote.

As it turned out, the Liberals' campaign-ending frenzy for NDP votes to Stop Harper was a double-edged sword. It helped defeat some Conservatives at Liberal hands, but cost New Democrats close races with both Liberals and Tories. This Liberal tactic left Martin more dependent on the House as a whole for his lifeline, rather than the usual minority arrangement where Liberals could count on NDP support. Sweet justice, perhaps, for the Liberal Party but combined with its scandal, it was unlikely to keep a minority going for long.

Despite its feelings about the election's sad end, the NDP was filled with hope about the Parliament, too. New Democrats delivered a lot in previous minorities, notably former leader Tommy Douglas winning universal health care and the Canada Pension Plan in the 1960s with Liberal PM Lester Pearson. A close Layton confidant, Terry Grier, was an NDP MP in the last Liberal minority, where he served with former leader Ed Broadbent, who had returned as an Ottawa MP in 2004. They were among former NDP Leader David Lewis's key envoys to Pierre Trudeau and downloaded their experiences with Layton. He bounded into the party's first post-election caucus meeting filled with ideas on how to get things done.

Soon, most NDP MPs contacted ministers they tracked to offer ideas and perhaps co-operate. Few ministers paid them much heed, though there were rare exceptions, and as time wore on, there wasn't collaboration on much. In Martin's words, on a flight to Asia to view devastation after 2004's Boxing Day tsunami, when Layton asked what was up, "You're two votes short." That summed up how most of the year following the election unfolded: Co-operation in Ottawa was a fantasy. It was the Liberal way, or no way at all, as things began to unfold.

As September rolled around, the much-anticipated First Ministers' meeting on health care was set to find a fix for a generation, as it was once called, before it atrophied down to a deal for a decade. Somewhere, Martin and the premiers haggled over the details, but not much is known. The meeting he so breathlessly promised would be live in front of the cameras dragged on in secret until the wee hours of the morning. Martin was out to save medicare, as his "transformational change" sought to take flight.

Layton asked for opposition leaders to be invited, and for input into the federal offer. Given Martin's crusade to eliminate democratic deficits and 63 per cent of citizens voting for someone else, the NDP saw compromise and multi-party input as a natural outcome of the election. The opposition leaders were not invited.

When the health plan finally emerged, it was decent but hardly groundbreaking. Over 10 years, $41 billion would be invested, there were voluntary standards for wait times so residents of each province could see how theirs fared, and Quebec received a kind of side deal to show that federal asymmetry could work. This was important to Quebec Premier Jean Charest, who called opposition leaders to gauge their reaction. None objected, but Charest consulted more with federal leaders in a minority than Martin did during the health talks.

The agreement itself had failings. Despite an ageing population, there was once more no real progress on homecare or the cost of pharmaceuticals getting more out of reach. They were both key issues that Liberal Red Books had long pledged to fix. And surprisingly, given all the rhetoric, there wasn't a word about protecting public health care from a more profit-taking system. After an election where Martin picked the ritual fight over Alberta Premier Ralph Klein's for-profit plans, Klein ironically walked away with his share of billions without any new conditions on how it could be spent. This, on what mere months before was the fight of Martin's life.

The NDP and some valiant health care groups tried to point out how the agreement was less than true to Douglas's vision for health care, which created North America's first universal health system in Saskatchewan. Up against decades of Liberal branding as the federal good guys on health care, it didn't get far. Health care matters to the progressive rut we're in, however, because Canadians don't believe only in a mainly public system. We are also moved by the kind of progressive value it represents: class.

After Canadian Auto Workers President Buzz Hargrove's expulsion from the Ontario NDP[1] for campaigning for Liberals in 2006, the

---

1. Membership in the NDP is provincially based outside Quebec, unlike the Conservative and Liberal Parties, which both have separate memberships for federal and—where applicable—provincial wings.

Globe and Mail editorialized that it was a positive development since class didn't matter to contemporary politics. The sense of the *Globe*'s editorial was that it's passé and best left in the Depression when it had a place—not now, despite developed countries' manufacturing bases chasing often abused workers abroad in the wrong kind of globalization. On the same day, author and CAW economist Jim Stanford used his *Globe* column to explain why the NDP-CAW rift was a step forward for working people.

Both take a doggedly literal approach to politics' class component, and issues like health care are class-based, too. Douglas's progressive faith—he was, like Martin Luther King, a preacher—was powered by class to build a health system where no money didn't mean no care. It is his proudest achievement and one of Canada's defining traits, due entirely to the contrast with the United States, as every other developed democracy ensures each citizen is covered. In measuring ourselves almost exclusively against the U.S., it's easy to think that Canada's at the front of many packs, when we're often not. New Zealand won universal health care 30 years before Canada, and Britain beat us by 20.

Like how Liberals compare themselves with Conservatives, doing better than the Americans is often seen as good enough. It's quite Canadian to be cool with doing middlingly well, but the contrast between Canada and the United States on health care that we like to admire so much is neat for what else it says. Our devotion to public health care also makes class awareness a Canadian foundation, in spite of the kvetching that often results when the word itself is used. If class offends, how about What Would Jesus Do? if that's more palatable, and which Douglas was also good at answering.

History and its icons count today, and heroes matter to both Liberals and New Democrats. Pierre Trudeau's proudest legacy is encountered soon, as progressive icons start to shape the young Parliament.

But in September 2004, quibbling about the health plan was to no avail despite anglophones' devotion to Douglas being so great that they made him Greatest Canadian in a popular CBC competition. Ottawa was heading towards the throne speech to formally open the

House in October 2004, as the first and silliest of the three confidence tests to hit the minority began.

In late summer, opposition leaders met at a Montreal hotel. It was an informal affair arranged by Duceppe to chat before the first minority in 25 years, to see if there were areas of common co-operation. It turned out there were, and when the list was finalized it was mainly procedural. The package was presented as a joint amendment to the throne speech, whose approval is a confidence test. It was eventually added, but not before the minority's first mini-crisis.

Unforeseeable then, the silly throne speech spat helped shape the road ahead. In the immediate term, it earned Martin few points among the NDP and crystallized its budget approach, while in the long, sowed the seeds of distrust among opposition parties that burst into full bloom in the budget vote in May 2005. As Parliament entered palliative care a year later, the accumulated distrust let the NDP shape how Liberals fell—with all the ensuing progressive dismay.

The spat boiled down to the opposition thinking a minority House should compromise, and it argued that MPs' agenda in the throne speech should reflect more than the largest party's. It wouldn't be the only time the Parliament horrified constitutional experts. And as the game of chicken escalated between government and opposition, and the possibility of Governor General Adrienne Clarkson being asked to pick Harper as PM came up, Layton had second thoughts. The NDP staked out its own path, saying Martin should accept the changes but with nothing at stake other than a routinely ignored speech, there was no need for brinksmanship.

Harper and Duceppe continued their push, and a showdown loomed that evening. Lawrence O'Brien, a Liberal MP gravely ill with cancer that would soon claim him, flew in from Labrador for it. But with under an hour to go before the vote, Martin met with two opposition leaders and struck a deal. For the first time, a throne speech was amended by the opposition. There would be no confidence crisis that night.

This was welcome news to the NDP, but learning of the deal on television wasn't. Martin had not told Layton of the meeting and they spoke only afterwards. New Democrats were incensed that doing their part to mitigate a spectacle resulted in marginalization, while bellicose Tory and Bloc behaviour earned reward. It helped cement the NDP's budget approach, but positive reaction after refusing to play along also reminded it that House games often weren't all they were cracked up to be.

In the meantime, the NDP caucus had the fall of 2004 to encounter, and set out to create some fuss around key issues. But without much legislation to sink teeth into and little tangible occurring, slogging was tough as the party had difficulty creating any conflict. MPs knew they must stake out some issues on which they could fight should opportunity arise to make change, but circumstances were hardly ideal to gain much traction. There was little on the agenda and the few initiatives that were in the works, such as child care, were being developed well away from meddling Members.

The NDP struggled to remain visible. The government was adrift, there was not much to do, let alone change, and the lamentable Parliament plodded on. When *The Economist* decided Martin resembled Mr. Dithers, the moniker's adhesive—bordering on permanently attached—quality summed up the emerging view of his government.

Part of Martin's problem was missile defence, a controversial American idea originally dreamed up by President Ronald Reagan in the 1980s and referred to as Star Wars. It had been revived by Bush, who threw out an arms control treaty for a sci-fi system able to shoot down incoming missiles, though $80 billion hadn't produced a successful test yet. When complete, it would put weapons in space and had already sparked new arms development in Russia.

All the same, after Canada said no to Iraq, Martin supported signing on while running for the Liberal leadership. He has good Liberal company in dallying with American weapons expansion: Pearson supported controversial Beaumark missiles on Canadian soil in the 1950s, and Trudeau allowed cruise missile tests over Canada in the early 1980s. Party of peace, indeed. Jean Chrétien was undecided about Iraq War One—in opposition, as he prepared for the big job itself, instead of about to leave it.

Progressives opposed all the weapons and wars, and Layton seized upon Star Wars while running for NDP leader. It was a key focus for the Bloc as well, both facing a right-leaning Liberal avalanche until scandal hit. Before it did, real lefties in the Bloc and NDP effectively traded ways to whittle Martin down to size.

The NDP copied the Bloc's missile defence approach, while the Bloc adopted the NDP's critique of Martin's past as a shipping tycoon who avoided Canadian taxes, labour laws and green rules by flying foreign flags on his ships. Once, he dodged taxes in Liberia, then the haunt of the murderous Charles Taylor, and progressive parties were relentless and often merciless in attacks. They weren't alone. Author Murray Dobbin published the critical *Paul Martin: CEO for Canada?* as Martin's juggernaut couldn't be stopped, and appeared set for a majority of record size. The road proved rocky. It turned out the juggernaut could be stopped.

And was, in the spring 2004 election that cost Liberals their majority, which put Martin in a pickle by autumn. Canadians feared Bush, and joining his weapons program was unpopular. No longer just able to do as he pleased, he needed help but his natural allies were Tories. They were happy to sit and watch after Martin vilified their warmongering around Iraq, which he had somehow dodged having a position on. So he dithered.

By the time a freshly re-elected Bush came for a brief visit in November, almost two years had passed since Martin's first Star Wars musings and still no decision was in sight. Bush decided he'd had enough, and twice broached the controversy during his visit. Missile defence dominated coverage, and Martin's wincing when it came up made him look like a T-ball hitter at a major league plate.

Thanks to a minority House, he eventually said no in February, after appointing two defence ministers who were Star Wars boosters in Bill Graham and David Pratt. In 2006, the Liberal platform promised a global ban on space weapons, as Martin again took both sides of something he said showed his world view. As Ottawa discussed the dithers in the fall of 2004, missile defence was Exhibit A.

As January 2005 arrived, the NDP held its caucus retreat at the magnificent log creation in Montebello, Quebec. As the small party is prone to be thankful for, it was afloat although its visibility was sinking in the mire of a frustrating Parliament. It also wasn't exactly on fire, and like the Tories and Bloc, had mounting frustrations with Liberals habitually telling a Parliament they didn't control that it didn't matter. Old habits of hegemony were proving hard to break.

In spite of Martin's dramatic promises to democratize it and banish the democratic deficit to history, things weren't going well. There was no consultation on what few real bills there were, apart from in committees that were routinely ignored. It was hit-and-miss whether a vote meant anything. The MPs' agenda was regularly so empty, they usually bided time on the opposition's own, non-binding motions.

Come February, all three opposition parties defeated a government bill to split the departments of foreign affairs and international trade. Liberals went ahead anyway, saying as only Martin could that because the Tory trade critic first supported the bill but then changed her mind, how MPs actually voted didn't matter. (Let's just imagine lefty reaction if Harper tried that trick in his own minority.) Fortunately, these great champions in consistency were eventually united when the Tory critic, Belinda Stronach, joined the Liberal Cabinet soon afterwards.

Frustrated and unable to move anything through Parliament, New Democrats left Montebello determined to create some conflict. With a key confidence test coming in the budget, the NDP stepped up efforts to get ideas into the public domain to try and gain enough leverage to change policy. Progressives remember history well at times, and the rare chance of a minority Liberal Parliament was slipping through

NDP fingers. As a party that craves federal minorities to show why it deserves to grow, time was ticking to get something done. The clock's hands would soon begin to whirl.

In early 2005, big things approached, among them the Kyoto Protocol on global warming coming into legal effect. The Liberals' plan to cut emissions was expected soon—only 12 years after one was promised—and in the weeks following Montebello, the NDP released its own. It wanted to create a comparison to force the Liberals' plan, expected to fall short, to improve. The NDP also placed a priority on MP Pat Martin's bill to protect pensions, likely to be voted on shortly.

New Democrat MPs knew a budget was coming, and hoped to create contrast around it. Their goal was to continue what they began in the fall and set policy bars high in anticipation of Liberal failings to come. If conflict emerged on a policy test for Martin and pressure mounted, Layton believed he would change course, and that something better could be done. Minority Parliaments, after all, are not times for policies to pass unchanged. It's why they've proven such a jackpot for progressives.

If Newfoundland and Labrador Premier Danny Williams could dig his heels in and successfully force concessions from Martin, as he had earlier done on offshore oil revenue, the NDP figured it could, too. As Williams showed, when desperate to please, Martin would do almost anything. It would prove correct. But not yet, on Budget Day itself.

When Layton and finance critic Judy Wasylycia-Leis left the dingy room in the West Block after reading the 2005 budget, they had a spring in their step. The budget contained a promising gift in $4.6 billion in corporate tax cuts strangely absent from the last Liberal platform. It was just what Layton was looking for: a source of funds few progressive people would miss, in a budget with glaring weaknesses those funds could nicely fill. They left the room kicking up as much fuss as possible about corporate tax cuts, for which Liberals had no mandate.

Suddenly, the path from Montebello looked more navigable. Layton and Wasylycia-Leis began their post-budget interviews determined to avoid saying anything definitive about how they would vote. The NDP wanted to remain a free agent on the budget's future long enough to try and change it, and for about 10 minutes it seemed viable.

"The Budget's Priorities are Conservative Ones"

2

CHAPTER

O N BUDGET DAY, Jack Layton wasn't the only leader in the West Block's dingy room. Stephen Harper was there as well. By the time he'd made the short walk to the Commons foyer, which throngs of reporters and anchor tables transform into a floodlit circus on big dates on the Parliamentary calendar, he had something to say.

"The budget's priorities are conservative ones," he declared, pointing to its massive increases in military spending and corporate tax cuts. Within minutes of Finance Minister Ralph Goodale starting to speak, Harper announced Tories wouldn't defeat his budget. With one sentence, the opposition leader evaporated Layton's hopes for progressive leverage because, with Tories onside for passage, how the Bloc and NDP voted didn't matter. Its budget approach redundant, NDP ambiguity morphed into opposition and hopes for change were dashed. There would be no new budget yet.

As media interviews dragged on, NDP MPs became angrier. The 2004 election saw Paul Martin transform himself from a consensus pick as the Liberals' most rightward leader ever to a crusading lefty, who urged New Democrats to abandon their first choice and Vote

Liberal to Stop Harper. Now it seemed like another fraud, less emotional than Liberal David Emerson taking NDP votes in 2006 to enter Harper's Cabinet weeks later, but untrue to progressive progress even so. After seeking votes for progressive purpose, Liberals unveiled a budget Harper could support. And did.

It had surprise corporate tax cuts, but nothing for education, aside from a new plan to let dead students' estates write off their loans. Housing construction received zero, and foreign aid levels fell well short of Canada's long-broken promises. Employment Insurance rules were left unchanged, and pensions were ignored. Subsidies for the oil patch remained. But some areas fared better: cities got a share of the gas tax, and child care funding finally came. Neither was perfect, but after years of disappointment in Liberal majorities, Martin had come a fair way.

There's a bit of a carnival atmosphere around budgets, and parties aren't the only ones to take it in. Civil society comes out in force as well and the growing clout of many non-partisan players is, with the Liberals' seven-election-long losing streak in Quebec, the second key to politics' new rules.

In a separate room from the opposition, organizations of all stripes also get a preview. There, everyone from the oil lobby to environmentalists and unions to bankers pores over details before rushing to declare victory or defeat. For hours, the halls of Parliament swim with every interest imaginable, jockeying to frame the budget's offerings. It adds to the jostle on Ottawa's big days, which for better or worse are part of Canadian politics in action.

Before the budget, NDP MPs tried to convince broader progressive circles to restrain unjustified glee, for lefty framing is a team effort. The NDP hoped many would be moderate in reaction, not effusive, to help point out holes in the budget that needed filling. But it couldn't be done by the NDP alone. If parties criticize a government, it's often written off as partisanship. If independent, non-partisan groups join in, the PM likely has some explaining to do, especially if outrage is sustained after a one-day pique of anger.

As the dangerous decade going backwards on global warming shows, Liberals can weather a short policy storm, with Ottawa's resident lefty elite stuck in the Rideau's whirlpool of hegemony, often afraid to tell it like it is to Liberals, because they're destined to govern again and are known to be mean. But what if they won't? Or shouldn't? A party on the way out can't punish people with 40 or 50 seats, in the same way the NDP can't offer much to keep folks onside. The curse of the hegemony mirage often stops us from using possibility—by daring to bite the rarely generous Liberal hand that feeds when it's in the mood.

George Lakoff, author of *Don't Think of an Elephant*, is right. It is all about the frame, and being able to shape the ground on which political debate happens matters. Liberals know this, too, and they and the NDP battled for how the budget was seen—with Liberals enjoying infinitely more resources. They usually win. And along the way help us relate to our politics, which, conveniently, involves Liberals riding to rescue us from the fearsome huns in blue. It's often not so clear-cut. But with smaller progressive parties trying to eke out some turf, the dominant, Liberal frame of how politics works tends to stick, as we squabble over how the huns came to run the show again. Debate lurches right with each new cycle.

Authors Jim Laxer and Jim Stanford, frequent observers of progressive politics, sometimes accuse the NDP of being out of step with what's often termed "the movement." They aren't always wrong, but are often overly simplistic, as not having a common frame means both Parliamentary and non-Parliamentary players sometimes use different tactics.

That NDP tactics occasionally differ from some other progressives doesn't make it always wrong. It is sometimes wrong to be sure, but if the big progressive rethink ends at advising the NDP on where it erred, we're in for more disappointment ahead. A rethink is needed, and we should do it right—collectively examining our collective failure to let our majority get to work (covered in Part Two). But the different ways that progressives see electoral politics can't continue if we want to spend less time beating up on each other, and more on the neo-cons. We need to trust each other more, but also learn from cousins worldwide that victories are built. Mainly, by desire.

If we don't want to do well, we probably won't. But choosing a partisan path—or whether to take one at all—separates us, and stops setting sights higher than trying to make Liberals less odious. Indeed, that we debate *whether winning is the point* is a troubling point of departure, but the fact is we can win. So buckle in for a bit, because the first part of the minority Parliament lived up to its billing. It was a good ol' lefty time—both in the partisan sphere and not, as the movement won big time before summer. But you wouldn't have known it in February.

In the NDP's mind, whatever came down the pike in a minority was a first offering, not the final deal. That it was as far as Liberals wanted to go was nice, but they lacked control. If Martin wouldn't accept changes before policy was unveiled, well, a minority could always force it upon him afterwards and he could lump it then. But many progressives weren't convinced. After suffering so long under Liberal failure, any movement was often seen as better than none—and as good as it could get—which makes our cycle worse. And understandable.

If what's offered is seen as good enough, it's hard to improve it; belated progress can also happen, because enough harm has been done over a long wait to make it needed. They are two legitimate views, and also symbiotic, as getting more change sooner needs to be won, partly through partisanship. It's a bog, and we're stuck in it—disliking Liberals but believing they're the only option big enough to Stop Harper. Large parts of the movement—and millions of voters—keep trying to get out of it, and think elections should be about winning something, not stopping it. They mostly vote NDP, which as a smaller party that is growing, needs people to vote for something; but as a larger party shrinking, the Liberals need votes to stop it.

Hope versus fear—it gets us every time, and on the first real test of the minority Parliament in February 2005, the movement passed judgment on the budget. What a bog it is.

Cities were ecstatic with a budget that went a long way to meeting their needs. Their umbrella organization, the Federation of Canadian Municipalities, gushed, and its sentiments were echoed by progressive mayors who came to town to celebrate. Student and education groups such as the Canadian Federation of Students were withering in contempt. The Canadian Labour Congress was mostly negative, pointing to corporate tax cuts coming ahead of pension and EI reform. Housing groups were enraged, while the Canadian Child Care Federation was delighted with new funding and hopeful about the shape of the as-yet-unannounced plan.

CAW President Buzz Hargrove wasn't there to condemn Liberals ignoring the struggling automotive sector. Noted activist Maude Barlow was absent, too.

The NDP was also keeping a keen eye on the environmental movement's response. With the Kyoto plan due shortly, creating some room for a green fight was a priority and if the plan was seen as good enough, it would be almost impossible to improve. In NDP backrooms, the budget was a bit of a test run for Kyoto, and it didn't auger well in a movement with many voices but not many in Ottawa to challenge the Liberals.

The biggest Ottawa group, the Sierra Club led by new Green Party leader Elizabeth May, was thrilled, while most enviros were lukewarm or thumbs-down. Substantively, there wasn't that much new, and actually less funding in the short term as spending was stacked into later years—as things environmental are—but in the public sphere, was seen as quite green. Or in other words, more oil burned in the meantime as global warming menaces more, year after year.

Together, Barlow, Hargrove and May form the principals of the Think Twice coalition, which sprouted in the dying weeks of the 2006 election to press for Harper's defeat at Liberal hands. Their tactics differ starkly from the NDP's and bad blood sometimes erupts among them; the same is true with the Jims—Laxer and Stanford—who appear to enjoy it the most. If we're going to do better, we'll have to see politics more alike to let us push together, as our American cousins do in battering Bush.

Here, an explanation for the rest of Part One is needed, for it shows how commonly we see things—the spring—but also how different—the fall and subsequent election—with all the lefty acrimony that follows. For simplicity's sake, there are four broad labels. Two are partisan, Liberal and NDP, as combatants for the dominant progressive party. More accurately, perhaps parties, plural, with the addition of the third progressive component of Quebec. Lastly, there is Think Twice, which together with New Democrats and progressive Liberals makes up the shorthand of "progressive people."

We fight because, like American Democrats, we're stuck in a frame. South of the border it's a Republican one that often keeps the good guys down, which Lakoff urges progressives change so they can win more often. The 2006 mid-term elections were fun in both the U.S. and Canada, and the future might look brighter with larger, more progressive parties—north of the border, at least.

In Canada, the frame is complicated by multi-party democracy and its deep roots in history and region. We don't have one frame to fix. We have three parties that each has regional areas of strength, the Québécois nation and the unavoidable resulting confusion. To enjoy common tactics against common enemies, this needs fixing and quickly. Fortunately, the fastest way is also the easiest, but it's not pretty, and involves kicking the Liberal Party—frequently and hard—while it's down, and takes us back to how Liberals ended up on the floor during a time when more dependable minority governments make possibility possible.

All in all, Budget Day was a bad day for New Democrats. As the Conservatives and Bloc spent the next day's Question Period on scandal, the NDP's game efforts to engage in issues fell short. For each criticism of the budget, a glowing quote from someone in the progressive community was hurled back. Nothing stops debate faster than external praise for a government, and within 48 hours the Hill barely mentioned the budget. New Democrats were a frustrated bunch.

In the minority Parliaments that came before, they had enough MPs to do good things, but no longer. Without the numbers or conditions to win change, prospects appeared bleak as the Bloc and NDP voted against the budget on first reading. With Conservatives abstaining, Liberals could pass it by themselves. NDP MPs looked on with regret at how the minority was working. A $180-billion budget sailed through without a penny changed, and long-standing Liberal promises left undone.

The NDP's meagre numbers weren't the only key difference in this minority. 2005 brought with it a second year of headline coverage into the sponsorship scandal. In February 2004, Auditor-General Sheila Fraser was scathing about the Liberal program. She detailed flagrant abuses of the public purse in a curt, uncompromising way that made her a national hero to many.

Created after the 1995 Quebec referendum, won by federalists in a squeaker, the program tried to bolster federalism in Quebec through federal government sponsorship of events. From agricultural fairs to sporting events to bingo halls, Ottawa paid big bucks to put up a "Canada" sign to keep the country together. It turned out to be a kickback scheme for the Liberal Party. The capital was hooked.

Ottawa scandals are usually tawdry affairs that suck up news oxygen like a newfangled bomb. Lefties think pollution and poverty are scandals, too, and are often frustrated when other kinds dominate. And as Fraser released her findings, New Democrats were as angered as everyone else, but in the lead-up to the 2004 election didn't focus on it with exclusivity and avoided much of the scandal-mongering. Even so, after the NDP mentioned Liberal ethical failings in the 2006 election, Laxer—ironically, author of *In Search of a New Left*—accused it of helping the Conservatives because New Democrats dared agree that Liberal scandal was an issue. Only in Canada, eh? We decry what Liberals do and then often flail around trying to keep the party big, in a cycle that needs to end.

All scandals affect politics to a degree, and to a degree Laxer is right to bemoan that. There are more worrying things than what's often presented as essential, but the sponsorship scandal wasn't among them. It was different from run-of-the-mill troughing, with special resonance in Quebec and, less so, in the long-Liberal-hating West.

And so the first frame is encountered in Ontario. Its progressive citizens are the most likely to be conflicted about partisan politics, thanks to living in the only place west of the Maritimes that's yet to dump Liberals as its main progressive player. A Laxer-type response to the NDP trying to win—wanting NDP growth, but not at the expense of Liberals—isn't restricted to Ontario, but is common in it. Regional frames for federal politics are tough to discard in our progressive morass, but need to be challenged if we're going to join the global norm. By losing our dominant party of the meaningless middle.

As progressives rethink where we're at, the scandal's pile is too big to ignore. It creates possibility, keeping in mind that Ontario, Quebec and the West are all regions with real clout. Quebec also affects whether Canada has a progressive majority at all in the long run, or if we'll have a federal government with the power to put it to work. It's both key to why the hegemony mirage is still around, and also the true danger of Harper. If we fear him dismantling Canada's ability to work together, we can't overlook that the big question in Quebec isn't always the same, or that Liberals haven't won there in more than 25 years.

Scandal Costs Us the Bloc   3

WHEN GILLES DUCEPPE sat down for his year-end interviews at Christmas 2003, surprising things came from the
Bloc Québécois leader's lips. He attacked the NDP. Now, undeniably,
Jack Layton is fond of Quebec after growing up in Hudson. To be attacked by the Bloc, winner of the last three elections in Quebec, was
high praise to be sure. But Duceppe's comments, unfortunately for the
NDP, spoke more loudly about his own party's dark horizon than they
did about New Democrats' chances.

Five Bloc MPs, more than a tenth of caucus, had left since the
last election. Most recently, two quit to run for the Parti Québécois,
and the Bloc lost both by-elections to Jean Chrétien's Liberals in June
2003. Paul Martin's arrival as leader caused one last unwitting fool
to jump ship, straight into the Liberal caucus in December 2003, in
what proved to be a career-limiting move. He was trounced the following June.

With the sponsorship scandal yet to hit, Christmas brought little reprieve for Duceppe as the Bloc's decade-long slide continued.
Gradually, its caucus shrank and with the last referendum over almost
a decade before and prospects for another falling, the usefulness of

the Bloc in Ottawa was questioned in Quebec. Unable to form government since it runs in only 75 seats and because sovereignty was declared dead by some, many Quebecers were wondering why they shouldn't vote Liberal—for the first time since 1980.

Montreal's Martin had courted sovereigntist votes for years, and Bloc founder Jean Lapierre was his Quebec lieutenant, in a logical fit. The separatist-fighter he played with such relish in the 2006 election emerged only as Quebec slipped through Liberal hands. Upon becoming prime minister, he dumped Clarity Act[2] author Stéphane Dion from Cabinet. A natural progression after years of his campaign attacking Chrétien's unity approach, which in true form, he eventually championed.

It seems surreal now, but Martin was originally predicted to win the biggest majority in history. Strong in Atlantic Canada, enjoying a divided right in Ontario and poised to do well in Quebec, he also held apparent appeal in Alberta. No wonder Kyoto was missing from his leadership campaign. Just like his national unity approach, the Martin who later emerged on the environment and other Think Twice issues bore scant resemblance to the guy who got thumbs up from a North Korean-style 96 per cent in the 2003 Liberal leadership.

After decrying Brian Mulroney's inaction on climate change and then writing an ambitiously green 1993 Red Book, Martin managed to forget it in both his rambling convention speech and his leadership platform. He also didn't profess his love for unions, as done at a CAW convention in the 2006 election, or echo Maude Barlow's longstanding critiques of the wrong kind of globalization. The first PM of Century Twenty-One was so very silent on the crisis of our time, but suffered little public rebuke for ignoring global warming—transformational change if there ever was one. Elizabeth May was privately furious.

As journalist Susan Delacourt outlines, Martin's *Juggernaut* was poised for a sweep, and as also described, perhaps not a lasting one. The

2. The law was passed in the aftermath of the 1995 Quebec referendum and required Quebec to have a clear question in any future referendum on separation. In strict legal terms, it's usurped by both the Supreme Court and international law, and both say clarity's needed on questions of self-determination.

juggernaut didn't need progressive votes and showed it, gloating about right-leaning Liberals bleeding votes to the NDP. With Quebec and the West appearing to open up, lefty votes were expendable, what with predictions of a win in the 250-seat range being common. Ontario was safely red, due to the still-divided right and the rare conditions this created. It seemed Liberals were in for quite a bounty.

In following years as the electoral map became smaller, Liberals— politely put—began to clarify their progressive stands and we became much more precious. But in 2003, Martin needed to explain nothing and didn't, other than supporting Star Wars to apologize to Dubya after the whole Iraq thing. His chameleon-like ways aren't unique among Liberal leaders, which are a Pavlovian clique. But we don't have to bark on demand whenever Liberals say they are progressive again. We could try biting, if we've seen more than enough and think it's time to join almost every world democracy in ending the failed project of a dominant meaningless middle.

That said, the Liberal Party can seem just so big. It seems natural that they'd win. Then again, Canada sits in rare global territory in keeping the alleged centre dominant. In Europe, Liberal parties shrank in the early 20th century, as they did in Australia and New Zealand. Latin America and democracies in Africa or Asia rarely had dominant Liberals to begin with. Whether colonization was British, French, Portugese or Spanish, the New World has no dominant Liberals. Only in Canada—pity—and even then, not all of it, as western Liberal parties started to vanish in the 1940s.

Liberals undeniably have won a lot federally, mainly thanks to Quebec's dependable support for them. That support is now gone, and with it went Liberal hegemony. No longer a natural governing entity likely to be in office more often than not, it's on a slow, steady slide. It's on its way to joining its everything-to-everybody friends as democracy's first glitch. And bringing possibility for progressives.

Liberal shrinkage was on few lips as the juggernaut hurtled to an election. Its immediate victim was the Bloc. By the end of 2003, Duceppe was scrambling to protect whatever part of his base he could, even if it meant the humiliation of attacking New Democrats. He was grateful to be sure when everything changed on February 10, 2004. Sheila Fraser exposed a scandal and didn't hold back.

The Prime Minister's Office had had Fraser's report for some time, as she submitted it before Christmas, but couldn't release it while MPs weren't sitting. With the Liberal leadership convention in late November, the House had risen and due to Liberals also electing a new PM, wouldn't sit again until February. It became the scandal that hung over Martin's brief time at the top, and his long drive to get there didn't help.

When Chrétien announced his retirement, his departure dates were strangely tiered: He wanted to stop being Liberal leader in November and leave as PM in March. This was neither practical nor workable, and Martin made the dates coincide as only made sense. Had he not, the report would have landed in Chrétien's lap.

But did it ever land in Martin's. And did he ever make it worse. Despite knowing what was coming for months, he became ever-more angry about Fraser's findings until his no-doubt genuine rage echoed that of citizens. As Ottawa engulfed itself, Liberals eventually pledged an immediate Parliamentary inquiry and a public one soon. Martin also called in the RCMP and cancelled the program on his first day as prime minister.

These events don't only hang over federal politics. They permeate, shape and define debate in the near- and long-term. Progressive people may lament that they shape events and dislike the frame it creates, but whatever our feelings may be, we didn't create this report or the events it unleashed. Their outcomes can't be changed, but they can be shaped if we reframe, and join our cousins south of the border in taking on North America's neo-cons and their kind of globalization.

We like it when Americans fight back against Bush, because we hope that our best friend can play a better role in the world than it sometimes has. We want globalization to work, and hope for Al Gore-like allies on global warming instead of warmongers like Bush. We believe—inherently—that globalization should be a good word, but with that comes responsibility. To say what we're for, not only what we don't like.

Lopsided trade deals or Kyoto. The Iraq War or peacekeeping. Sweatshops or foreign aid. All six are globalization, but three are positive and help the world integrate in the right way. Europe is a good example of the right kind at work, where long and frequent wars were common until a better path was found through the European Union. We don't always have to be against something. Progress usually happens when we start to say yes.

The EU's environmental, social and foreign policies are very similar to what our majority would like Canada to do at home and in the world. European businesses make money and the EU's integration has helped them, but it isn't one-dimensional. It also includes tough rules on pollution and human rights, with both opposition and alternatives to go-it-alone Republican wars from Washington. Europe leads in rapid cuts to climate-changing pollution and enjoys many of the most successful social programs, for good reasons. It's the right kind of globalization, and there's no reason Canada can't push for more of it.

We like the idea, and examples like Tim Flannery's Kyoto epic *The Weather Makers*, or Mark Leonard's *Why Europe Will Run the 21st Century* are inspiring—as are the sage words of peace activist Helen Caldicott, African AIDS envoy Stephen Lewis or scientist David Suzuki. If we want to do more than listen to good ideas, and enact them instead, we'll need to strike when Liberals are weak if at last we've concluded they don't agree. Now's our time, and the scandal isn't only a Harper Helper. It can be ours, too, as Liberal scandal put the national question back on the agenda in Quebec and minority governments on the agenda everywhere.

Flowing from Martin's pledge after Fraser's report, the first by-product began in a House committee, which started hearings into the scandal. This is the first of the inquiries Martin promised. In his final recommendations, Justice John Gomery—asked by Martin to lead the second—urged that House committees get bigger staff and research budgets. There were good reasons why. The sponsorship scandal's first public airing was an unruly one that spun a horrid web of Liberal sin, but was hopelessly under-resourced to do its work.

Bedlam erupted as witnesses contradicted one another and incredible tales were told. It was a sham best shown by former Olympic gold medallist Myriam Bédard. In her testimony, she said her housekeeper kept Canada out of Iraq, and that race car driver Jacques Villeneuve took $12 million in secret sponsorship cash to wear a Canadian flag. In alleging she'd been forced from a job at Via Rail after fussing over strange sponsorship requests, the sexist response from Via Chair Jean Pelletier, Chrétien's longtime chief of staff, got him fired by Martin. A court later ruled Bédard wasn't fired by Pelletier. The Liberal civil war, and its scandal, was everywhere.

And it stayed there. Throughout the minority, politics groaned under a scandal that Liberals created and then publicized. Even when it seemed finally done, it emerged zombie-like again, as Bédard's deranged testimony was still news as Liberals fell. In November 2005, a court ruled Pelletier was wrongly fired, so he was fired again for something else. It's a fitting tale to show the impacts of a House committee being rushed into action without the tools to do its job. Which is worse is a toss-up: the committee's mission impossible or Liberals artificially ending it to let Martin say the facts were now out. There was an election to be had—the polls say tally ho!—and his timeline was etched rigidly in stone.

As former Government House Leader Don Boudria mused openly at the time, why all the rush, as a Liberal minority would likely result from a spring election in the Fraser report's wake. With that outcome likely and the average minority lasting only 18 months, he reasoned, why not have the Gomery Inquiry and then an election?

If done that way, the Liberal majority elected in 2000 could sit through November 2005—the five-year limit—and do a scandal probe correctly instead of the farce underway with Bédard. In hindsight, Boudria looks like a prophet. Key to our hopes is that even as he put the 2004 election in motion, Martin had options. He chose the Liberals' path with a majority's control, unencumbered by other parties' hands, and getting out of the progressive predicament is easier by looking at where events began. Liberals may gloss over how they sunk to a minority to begin with, but we don't have to lemming-like follow suit.

We now know this Liberal tactic was a dud. Their 2004 western breakthrough didn't happen, the united right showed strength in Ontario, the NDP doubled its vote but gained few MPs, and far from his dismal outlook at Christmas, Duceppe matched Lucien Bouchard's record with 54 Bloc MPs.

The scandal had transformed his landscape in months. Though overly simplistic to describe his campaign as little more than getting off a bus to remind people the Bloc didn't insult them and steal their money, it's not that far off. Under the slogan *"Un parti propre pour Québec"*[3] the Bloc cleverly invoked the corrupt angle, and exploited the scandal's insulting undertones that offended Quebecers.

So sweeping was the anger, almost generic Liberal birthrights were at risk. Pierre Pettigrew's seat in downtown Montreal was almost lost, along with the Ottawa suburb of Gatineau. Unbelievably, the federalist stronghold of Vaudreuil-Soulanges—the first Quebec riding that drivers from Ottawa and Toronto see en route to Montreal—was lost to the Bloc in 2004. In 2006, Liberals lost them all.

Many graft-weary people outside Quebec often see the sponsorship scandal as just more political corruption, and lefties typically dislike scandals to begin with. These factors coloured some views to the realities at hand in the Parliament. They're also central to why we can reframe politics to work better for us, since the new Quebec dynamic is what changes the rules. Our track record on issues such as Meech Lake isn't a promising preface to building common cause with Quebec, but our relationship with the Bloc and its voters is key to our majority getting to work. The scandal can't be overlooked lest we make the same mistake again.

In probing it, fairness requires noting that Gomery cleared Martin, who dodged some policy scandals but took this one squarely in the

---

3. The slogan had a double meaning, allowing it to read both as "A clean party for Quebec" and "Quebec's own party."

head. But beyond which Liberal is guilty, within Quebec it didn't matter. Liberals tried to buy fealty to Canada with trinkets of federalism, which turned out to be a kickback scheme. Effectively, a corrupt, sometimes criminal, veneer was applied onto federalism, which sovereigntists ruthlessly exploited. Overnight, the Bloc became rabidly more nationalist and ran in 2006 for an independent Quebec, which triggered light debate around a separate Olympic team.

The scandal had real impacts for progressive people, too. After Fraser's report, the Bloc was no longer a progressive party in Ottawa that would fight for sovereignty if it could get it. Now it was a sovereignty party that worked on lefty issues while biding time between opportunities. Accustomed to friendly relations with the Bloc through three Liberal majorities, many came to see it as a natural ally on our issues. Come 2004, faith that its prime goal was progressive, not sovereignty, was on shaky ground.

Its foundation used to hold more strength and following the Bloc's birth, it was often a dependable voice. In the 1993–1997 Parliament, when the NDP didn't have official status, the Bloc was regularly its loudest progressive voice. It laudably spoke often on issues that affected all Canadians, often working well with people outside Quebec. Those were majority Parliaments before the scandal. This was a minority afterwards. Tommy Douglas's and Lester Pearson's landmark minorities it wasn't, thanks to Fraser's impact in Quebec.

It's paradoxically our most progressive province, but also the one that keeps progressives divided. With the Bloc playing a large role in the minority Parliament, too, we can't figure out where to go next without some probing of where we've been. Liberals might use the NDP to explain their fate and try to stop progressive growth outside them. Their lustful gaze to lefties *outside* Quebec only underlines their weakness *inside* it, and belies how events really happened.

As the fall of 2004 progressed, MPs settled in. The government drifted still. The scandal came and went from the front pages. If testimony at the Gomery Inquiry, set up for its Ottawa phase of hearings, was juicy it would make news. But with a gripping American presidential race capturing attention and little happening on the Hill, Parliament was for the time being dragging sadly through the dithers. In any event, the big news from Gomery was coming in the New Year, when Chrétien would be summoned to the stand. Gripping though the intricacies of monogrammed golf balls were, other testimony would prove more eventful.

As 2005 arrived, a parallel universe of sorts unfolded in Montreal, which became an epicentre for federal politics. In March, Conservatives held their first policy convention there as a united party as Harper kept up outreach to Quebec on which any Tory majority depends. Of immediate impact was the second phase of the Gomery Inquiry, which had moved to Montreal to be closer to the scene of the crime.

It soon took over French television and delivered staggering ratings. During daytime, unedited testimony from the Gomery Inquiry sometimes drew 180,000 people. In relative terms, francophone Quebec had roughly equivalent viewers of testimony in the middle of the day to Peter Mansbridge's audience at 10 p.m. The ad executives and political operatives on the stand became cult figures and Gomery nothing less than a star. And through it all, support for sovereignty grew as the Liberal brand in Quebec began to infect federalism itself.

The fever reached its zenith in late March, when ad executive Jean Brault testified. Due to criminal proceedings, a publication ban was placed on testimony to seal it from public eyes. Little could stop scandal-addicted fans in Montreal. No longer able to watch on TV, they overwhelmed public galleries in a frenzy to hear the juicy details first-hand. It was so crowded, a theatre was opened with closed-circuit coverage to accommodate Quebecers who couldn't get enough. They turned out to have a front-row seat to a show that people everywhere else would only see in time.

Brault unleashed a political storm that nearly blew Martin down. But in the events his testimony triggered, a budget was delivered to Layton, a red sign to Belinda Stronach and a grateful nation's thanks to the late Chuck Cadman instead.

Omigod!

4
CHAPTER

HELL REALLY DOESN'T have fury like a Parliamentary Press Gallery on the hunt. Though plentiful, they can also be single-minded and the gift of a head start from the publication ban had every journalist in Ottawa thinking one thing: Omigod!

Due to the ban at the Gomery Inquiry in Montreal, the publication of Jean Brault's testimony was delayed. Television stations and front-page editors now had a bonus: days of extra time to work on coverage before anyone saw, and journalists preparing to explain the testimony had the rare commodity of time to prepare. Slowly and carefully, they graphically and vividly recreated what Brault had said. The evening the publication ban was lifted, CTV ran a mockumentary of cash being pushed across the table of a Montreal restaurant to a Liberal bagman.

Collectively, universally and with healthy lead time to plan, the media delivered Brault's words with a splash. In between the testimony and its publication, word quickly spread about the detailed descriptions of how Liberals recuperated funds from friendly ad companies drowning in government cash. The sponsorship scandal was long believed to be a kickback scheme. Brault's testimony confirmed it.

Back in Montreal, people in the inquiry's theatre weren't the only ones who could watch. Journalists could listen to their heart's content and each of the parties, except the NDP,[4] also had lawyers at the inquiry and numerous other hangers-on had access as well. It all combined to give almost everyone on the Hill an abundance of sources.

Word naturally sloshed about and Ottawa's groupthink began to define the revelations as more of a smoking Kalashnikov for Liberals than a smoking gun. As gossip and speculation spread, the six square blocks south of Parliament Hill that help shape how people see politics—and is in turn shaped by Think Twice—decided this was huge. The media presented the six square blocks' conclusions and framed coverage apocalyptically for Liberals.

It was April 8, 2005. The budget had passed only first reading. Scandal dominated the front page of all the newspapers and was the lead item on every newscast. In most cases, pretty much the newscast itself. Liberal fortunes plunged overnight. Within a week, Liberal MP David Kilgour quit the caucus and polls showed Liberals in freefall. A poll for CBC, *The Toronto Star* and *La Presse* forecast a Conservative minority; the *Globe* had the Liberals down to 28 per cent, just six points ahead of a soaring NDP.

An election was suddenly in the air as Parliament disintegrated at breakneck speed. Still salivating over the boost the scandal gave to sovereignty, the Bloc wanted an election. Now. As polls continued to show Liberals plummeting, Harper sensed opportunity too, but was cautious.

The NDP looked around and shook its head. It was a maelstrom, but New Democrats could only watch, without other parties' numbers or laser-like focus on the scandal. It didn't want an election, but wasn't thrilled with the Liberals, either, and still fumed over what it saw as budget fraud. Martin's appeal to lefty voters cost them the balance of power—why they could only watch—but the budget earned Harper's

---

4. Three of the four political parties had lawyers at the Gomery Inquiry, whose services were paid for on a shared basis by the parties and government. The NDP decided the cost didn't warrant one of its own.

support, not theirs. Attempts to make Parliament work better were ignored, as with each passing day Liberals became more toxic.

Among progressive people, panic hit. Our high hopes for the first real minority in more than 30 years were evaporating as the House teetered. Mayors, child care advocates, environmentalists and union leaders said Omigod!, too, and implored MPs to stop an election. Particularly worried were child care advocates and cities, which both waited years for a budget like the one they got. Equal marriage groups fretted as well, with the Supreme Court ruling four months before starting the debate on lesbian and gay marriage. Progressive pressure rained down onto Parliament as after years of not much good coming from Ottawa, something was going on. It was in danger, all thanks to a scandal from a prime minister who was not even in office.

Grumpy after the budget affair and increasingly rebuffed on policy, Layton was marginal. A 20-year veteran of city politics in Toronto, he hoped this experience would help get results in a minority House. But as time wore on one seat down, Liberals weren't interested in letting the NDP change policy before it came out and it didn't have the clout to do it afterwards. Its lot seemed set, and wasn't that different from Liberal majorities before.

This isn't rare for a party that usually elects more than 25 MPs, and it makes the tangible benefits of even two or three Green MPs— official status takes 12—unclear. Perhaps the solution to getting more done isn't more smaller lefty parties, but one larger one, for at least the time being. Certainly, if the NDP's greatest sin is being able to stop Parliamentary collapse only once, as Elizabeth May said while explaining her decision to run for Green leader.

Before Brault's testimony came out, the Liberals, 12 years late, unveiled a plan to cut climate-changing pollution. It came in airtight fashion with no tinkering allowed. Most MPs supported Kyoto, with Bloc and NDP support stronger than Liberals', but only Liberals had say. In the NDP's mind, this was unproductive for a minority, and they thought the leverage that the Bloc and it enjoyed should allow larger cuts to pollution. It didn't happen, and though 11 environmental groups formed a common front of concern, there was a twelfth lonely voice in May, in almost total praise. In fact, Liberals again dallied on what they now bleat is the crisis of our time and fell well short of the emission cuts they—and Canada—have long promised.

There was also a related squabble over a backdoor change to an environment law that Liberals tried to tack onto the budget, which had passed first reading without it. For a while, it appeared serious. Harper, who opposed the change, said Tories would withdraw their support for the budget if Liberals clung to this new addition. In response, the NDP offered to support the budget in return for changes to corporate tax cuts, should Tories move offside.

Layton repeated the offer in April, just before the Brault testimony came out, saying he would like to invest in education, and suggesting corporate tax cuts pay for it. By now, changing the budget was a long-lost hope, and Layton used tax cuts to show that Martin's progresssive words on the hustings were less than heart-felt. There was little else to do but talk.

Both speeches were given before Brault's testimony hit, and from the throne speech spat on, the NDP saw itself as trying to make Parliament work and improve policy. As New Democrats said often, they were giving away ideas such as pension protection, pollution cuts and democratic reform. The NDP was as frustrated with Martin's dithering as many media and senior civil servants.

As the Parliamentary crisis deepened, Layton had publicly made the offer that would resolve the situation twice. Two votes short, though, Liberals did not call on the NDP to help, and besides, Harper was supporting the budget so why bother asking? There was no confidence motion before the House, but it was an angry place.

The Conservatives, Bloc and NDP fumed at Brault's revelations, which were staggering and—it turned out—essentially true. The sponsorship program kicked government cash into Liberal coffers, tens of millions of dollars were missing and federalism dealt a severe blow, so there was much to fume about. The Bloc didn't seem that troubled by the federalism part.

The Tories and Bloc particularly focused on it and as the House grew angrier, it began to boil over. For their part, Liberals said the testimony was only unproven words on the stand and stressed Martin himself had called the inquiry. Give Justice Gomery time to finish his job, they urged, while making sweeping accusations about an overly partisan opposition, which few observers would apply to the NDP so far. Maybe George W. Bush had left some remnants of how he framed politics, as Ottawa now defined everyone as being for or against the Liberals. There New Democrats sat, big enough to talk, but too small to be heard as chaos reigned.

Harper and Layton spoke in the opposition leader's offices in Centre Block on Monday, April 18. The NDP had a wait-and-see attitude to confidence, saying it wanted to hear more from people before it decided if an election was needed. Over the last 10 days, public anger continued to sink Liberal numbers, but with the Easter recess one week away giving time to see if feelings had gelled, there was no rush. The House was rising on Friday and wouldn't return until May 2, allowing time to see if this would boil over into the unstoppable or turn into a blip.

Conventional wisdom said if the polls held over Easter an election was imminent. Parties rushed to prepare. With the Tories and NDP now saying the same thing—similar in essence, but different in tone—the opposition had a new common front; the Bloc would have had an election yesterday. To keep an election option open after the Easter break, the three parties agreed on a Conservative motion to re-order the calendar of opposition days.

Unless some rules are changed, opposition parties present motions in rotation based on the number of MPs they have. Changing these rules can't alter when the days occur, which the government decides, but can change which party moves them. In most Parliaments, this is pleasant trivia since opposition motions aren't binding and in a majority can be defeated anyway. But in both crises of the 38th Parliament, a cottage industry of procedural experts grew around opposition days, for each could be a potentially fatal confidence test, which was quite binding indeed.

The opposition's plan sadly looked a lot like a gun, and the schedule needed to be changed to load it. There were too many Bloc days directly after Easter and too many Conservative days in late spring, which couldn't be used without bringing on a summer-long election. If a non-confidence motion were to be moved, neither the Tories nor NDP could support one from the sovereigntists, and this new twist to minorities meant a new schedule was needed. Useful bullets—Tory opposition days—had to be moved earlier to give opportunities for an election if need be, while blank bullets—Bloc days—were placed in later slots that weren't much use.

The Tory motion to make it happen was to be presented that Monday evening. Tuesdays are regular opposition days and to debate a motion, the House needs to receive it by 6 p.m. the day before. It never did. Liberals were convinced that a non-confidence motion itself was about to be introduced, and Liberal House Leader Tony Valeri raced into the Commons at 5:10 p.m. There will be no more opposition days, he decreed, unveiling a schedule that moved them all to the end of June. He had just changed the course of the budget, as the Hill shook.

Opposition parties denounced it as a violation of Parliament's rights. Cancelling votes because of a potentially unwelcome outcome abuses core democratic principles, they argued, as anger ran over. Long-frustrated by Liberals' disdain for votes they didn't like—two months after seeing a bill's defeat written off—this was the last straw for an opposition with a majority of MPs. Procedural anger fused with Brault's testimony. The House ceased to function.

Tuesday's Question Period was vicious. Aptly, Martin was absent the day after his government stripped away a possible opportunity for MPs to judge it. The opposition howled. The chasm in Parliament widened. The House was disintegrating, and nixing opposition days changed a probability into a certainty. An election was coming.

Harper responded to Valeri's move simply and unequivocally, saying it was war. In retaliation, he withdrew Conservative support for the budget. For the life of them, New Democrats couldn't turn their seats into leverage. Now here it was, landing on their lap. Layton got out his speeches of late.

With no hope remaining for order, on Wednesday Martin announced he'd speak to the nation on television the next night. It was unusual. The most recent TV address was Jean Chrétien speaking the night of the 1995 Quebec referendum.

Under the Broadcast Act, a prime minister can command air time, but if it's used, the opposition gets to respond. To avoid such inconveniences, the democratic deficit fighter asked, rather than obliged, networks for airtime at 7:50 p.m. Having sidestepped the law that lets the opposition reply, Martin then helpfully offered to let networks begin regular prime time broadcasts at eight, which—wouldn't you know it?—was when his 10-minute talk would end. It was too much. Thanks to the networks, all four leaders spoke and the broadcast lasted for 30 minutes. It was half an hour that began the 2006 election, and as leader of the smallest party, Layton got four minutes.

It's fitting that a minority Parliament only worked like one on TV, not in a dysfunctional House. And it's sad that the only law changed was done live in front of the cameras. It was a minority in name only until the lights came on, Martin went first and said it all had to end.

He spoke to the nation on tape. Unlike other leaders, who spoke live from a podium, the PM was pre-recorded. He mostly focused on the still-swirling fallout from Brault's testimony and steps taken to address the scandal, which included calling the inquiry from which the damning testimony flowed. Martin also chided opposition MPs for the chaos in the House and spoke about important things to be done, ironically, after one of the barest legislative agendas in memory.

As Canadians watched from their sofas, the election began with a promise to call one 30 days after Gomery's second and final report on December 1. It was an historic first for any Parliament, to say nothing of a minority, that an election was called this far ahead. But with Martin's words, Liberals in the midst of a crisis that just worsened and from which they saw no escape set in motion their unpleasant autumn. They just couldn't imagine they had that long.

Harper and Duceppe spoke next, each focusing on the scandal. Layton came last, and touched on it, while mainly talking about issues on which MPs should get cracking. He again offered NDP support for the budget in exchange for corporate tax cuts coming out. "We're in no rush to judge on the scandal," he said in a continuation of the NDP's tone for weeks, "but we are in a rush to get something done."

It was 7:30 p.m. on Thursday. Omigod! was right.

Tom d'Aquino Asks for His Money Back

5

CHAPTER

V OTES AREN'T PERMITTED on Fridays, and so even dis-integrating, the House became eerily still before a week-long Easter break. Stephen Harper prepared for tour to listen to Canadians about where to go next, while Jack Layton flew out to do much the same. And then the Prime Minister's Office called the NDP on Friday, as its big orange neon sign saying "We want to work with you" finally proved too large to miss.

Layton's address the night before had generated more attention than the NDP was used to. In the midst of a scandal to which it couldn't add anything that others couldn't do so more loudly, and in a crisis it didn't have the votes to stop, being noticed was rare. But reporters began calling the PMO, asking if the tone was of interest to Paul Martin, who was saying he wanted to make things work. Consistency necessitated a call to the NDP to see what it was all about and media interest bubbled. By day's end, the PMO and NDP confirmed that Martin and Layton would meet that weekend, where and when undisclosed.

On Saturday morning, Martin suffered more bad news. Bono, lead singer for the Irish band U2 and a regular crusader for foreign aid, had been a high-profile supporter of his for some time. When the Liberal priority was foreign aid, Bono famously spoke at its leadership convention the night that Martin became leader, but had since soured on hollow words. On CBC Radio's *The House*, he lashed out at broken promises and it became a big weekend story to underline how bad things were for Martin. (Foreign aid, as it turned out, gets a $500-million boost shortly, as publicly trashing Liberals didn't do much harm at all.)

The parties' public comments through Friday and Saturday were an uncertain dance, but in the mushrooming thud of Brault's testimony Liberals were radioactive. Shellshocked MPs spoke about a wave of anger on the ground. Polls pointed steeply down. Aware of the dangers it faced cavorting with folks being compared to mobsters, the NDP went out of its way to say the meeting was not at all about propping Martin up. It cared about the budget alone and wanted to save it. If Liberals could be rescued, well, that wasn't the NDP's problem.

Like the NDP, the PMO was curious about what a meeting could do. On television, Martin said he wanted Parliament to work, and the PMO stuck to those words all weekend as the parties fumbled their way along. Neither knew what to make of all this, and both knew they could be facing each other at the polls in literally weeks.

Martin and Layton met on Sunday evening, in the prime minister's room at the Royal York Hotel in downtown Toronto. Coincidentally, Martin was in town anyway, as was Harper, and the three leaders were at the same Sikh festival that afternoon. With leaders' itineraries public, the media narrowed the window for a meeting to either Sunday night or Monday morning, when Martin's itinerary said he was leaving, and a frantic effort was underway to find out where. Reporters camped out at hotels all over town.

Martin may have had RCMP security to provide decent cover, but Layton had the subway, a friendly union local and an elevator in the back. He entered the meeting with a one-page sheet with the NDP's budget requests, which was ambitious. It wanted $4.6-billion in corporate tax cuts cancelled and invested the NDP's way. The tax cuts took effect in 2008, but Layton wanted the funds they represented spent right away, which meant re-ordering the budget.

The Liberals' contingency funds to allegedly prevent deficits—fiction, really, with Ottawa awash in surplus—were moved from the budget's early years to later ones. There, they filled the hole created by the corporate tax cuts which were moved from the budget's late stages to its early ones and, the NDP hoped, spent its way. Nineteen MPs tried to rewrite a budget that had already passed first reading. Many saw it as a pipedream, if not galling.

After the meeting, there was no agreement. Layton was not surprised and resigned himself to at least trying, and who knew, didn't get no for an answer. But how could it work anyway? The venom back in Ottawa was one thing, but pesky Parliamentary math also loomed large. If all Conservative and Bloc MPs were present and two of three Independents[5] voted with them, Martin would fall whether the NDP liked it or not. Liberal election tactics had cost a progressive balance of power, and this sweet justice nearly came home to roost.

There was nothing about the meeting in the morning news. They'd agreed that nobody would comment on Sunday unless a deal proved impossible. But Layton had once before thought of how a small party could get things done on a budget, as he left the West Block's dingy room. Without clout in Parliament, the NDP hoped to mount some outside of it, why it first hoped to remain vague on Budget Day.

Layton kept media interviews on Monday morning and called a press conference for midday, but never imagined he'd be trying to change a budget like this. The House was collapsing, Liberals could be contagious and were hardly welcome bedfellows, and the NDP feared Martin would drag things out. It needed to know where it stood before the House next week, and in Layton's riding office on Danforth Avenue, plywood tables heaped against a wall to let in a forest of cameras, he reiterated the terms: If Martin wanted to work with the NDP, they would need a deal by Wednesday. This was no time for the dithers.

---

5. The three Independent MPs were Chuck Cadman, elected as one, and two recent departures from the Liberal caucus—a resignation in Edmonton MP David Kilgour, and an eviction in Mississauga, Ont. MP Carolyn Parrish.

Talks began later that day. Libby Davies, the NDP's House leader, and Tony Valeri were each side's lead negotiators. They had been with their leaders on Sunday night, and brokered the agreement.

At the core of their deal was a trade, which gave the NDP budget changes, and Liberals perhaps blessed time to stave off their imminent and likely inevitable demise. This tricky question of time put the House leaders in the hotseat, since the budget would take at least a few weeks to pass, during which Liberals would almost certainly face confidence tests. If the NDP wanted a budget, it would have to take supporting Liberals as part of the trade, and negotiating these delicate details fell to the House leaders.

The NDP couldn't express long-term support for Liberals who were repellent to voters—and who just called an election for December—but figured it could justify wanting a more progressive budget. This balance was a knife's edge, and the angry reaction to the scandal was growing across all party lines. It also was a serious thing, with real implications for federalism, and counts for more than being dismissed as an irrelevant Harper Helper by Jim Laxer's crowd. But for the time being, it all rolled up into a delicate ball for Davies and Valeri.

Eventually, they agreed on fast-tracking the budget as quickly as possible. The deal was riskier by far for the NDP than for the Liberals, though Martin was harshly criticized in the near-term for it, by many who thought he smacked of an unseemly desperation.

For the NDP, the less time it was in Liberals' arms the better—generally a truism now underlined by an election seven months away—and fast-tracking the budget was a must. In return, the NDP agreed to support Liberals on any and all confidence tests until the budget received Royal Assent. With Liberal control of the Senate, the NDP had effectively signed on until summer. The Gomery Inquiry was still underway in Montreal and nobody knew what was next, as the party jumped for a budget without a parachute.

Details proved thorny and Layton met with labour leaders on Monday, and consulted others in the party and beyond by phone. Pension protection proved particularly tough, with the NDP only able to push Liberals as far as wage protection after weeks of public haggling. Due to this delay, the wage protection part of the NDP budget became a separate bill. This stranded orphan from the budget would, with Martin's early election pledge, determine how the government fell in a final, desperate autumnal lunge to shape politics' new rules pouring down the waterslide chute.

As Wednesday approached, so did the NDP's deadline. Over Tuesday, Davies and Valeri went back and forth with drafts, negotiating schedules and wording, to and fro, inching closer to a deal. On Wednesday morning, Layton called a press conference for 5:30 p.m. One way or the other, he'd have something to say and so strapped in for quite a day. The deadline was real and the NDP's budget pretty much a take-it-or-leave-it choice.

Hour by hour as the day wore on, Davies and Valeri narrowed the few differences that remained while Layton prepared his remarks in his office in Centre Block. By 4 p.m. a deal seemed almost certain, and by 4:30 was down to formalities. Come 5:10 it was sealed, and shortly Layton began to walk down Parliament Hill and across Wellington Street to the national press theatre. Danny Williams was smiling somewhere. He had company, as a radiant Layton announced a new, more progressive budget was on the way.

The party that wrote it unveiled it: $1.6 billion for affordable housing, free from mandatory provincial matching funds that made construction too-often impossible. $1.5 billion for the first increase to education transfers in a decade, earmarked to cut costs for students and improve training—like housing, with dedicated Aboriginal funding. There was $800 million for public transit, and $500 million to help Canada keep our promise to give more in foreign aid, and aim for Lester Pearson's target of 0.7% of GDP.[6] Lastly, $100 million created

---

6. For all our rhetoric, Canada is far from meeting our promise of 0.7% for foreign aid originally suggested by Lester Pearson before becoming PM, and recommitted by Liberal governments since. In fact, Canada's percentage fell from Mulroney's level during the dozen years of Liberal rule to about 0.4%. Since 1998, Ottawa has been in surplus. Only Scandinavian countries and the Netherlands are keeping their promise to help the world's most desperately poor.

an energy efficiency program for low-income homeowners to help save on energy bills and reduce pollution; and a $100 million fund to protect workers' wages in cases of employer bankruptcy.

It was a lefty win paid for by the Liberals' $4.6 billion corporate tax cuts forgotten from their platform. Layton's delight soared through his press conference and swamped progressive people. In sync with allies and delivering for them, New Democrats and progressives everywhere—including some in Quebec—fought together for our budget. Bay Street champions such as Tom d'Aquino, chairman of the Council of Chief Executives, asked for their money back as Tories wailed in dismay. What was good about the budget was protected, and improvements reframed it. Our budget was more progressive now and it felt great. Each new item was class-based, in the proudest tradition of Tommy Douglas.

With his core benefit being time, Martin set about using it to shape how the spring was seen. The spiralling effects of the Brault testimony notwithstanding, the deal briefly sidelined Harper from public debate, in much the same way the scandal marginalized Layton. Unusually, the NDP replaced Tories as the big opposition player in the premiere tangle with the government, and Ottawa's conversation changed from scandal to issues, which immeasurably helped Liberals.

When the budget replaced Brault's testimony on the front pages, it released the pressure the scandal had built up. This newly altered frame became Martin's starting blocks for the spring. From it he pushed off, gained power through a defection and picked up speed, ruthlessly branding Stephen Harper as a power-hungry opportunist who didn't care about important things. By the end of it, he headed off for a summer repair job to his image, instead of the election that had just seemed so certain.

As the conversation changed and the NDP moved onto the budget's side, Martin could also define the opposition exclusively as Harper and the separatists in league together. This remained central to Liberal tactics until they fell, but when that would be was the question. In the midst of his Easter tour, Harper said the time was now. The opposition leader said he wanted an election.

The Pantomime Victory 6

IN MONTREAL OR TORONTO, if you know the right street, you can have a good time. Ottawa's still the kind of place where you have to know the right address, but the capital let down its hair in style in spring 2005 in a raucous, bawdy spectacle it won't soon see again. Parliament Hill twirled through the emotions as disgrace and heroism, betrayal and humanity, love, secretiveness, insult, decency, contempt, drama, victory rolled into a romping affair. Canadians were hooked, and often ashamed.

With heroes to cheer for and villains to boo, the budget faced a Parliament in pantomime where progressive people outside Quebec cheered for the same side. It's an example of what things could feel like if we reframe, and imagine the difference having a majority of Quebec MPs onside would make, or how much bigger our victories could be. And also a reminder that a progressive party did more in Parliament than allegedly end it—no matter what Liberals say.

Ottawa was a-titter about the NDP budget deal when the House returned on May 2. The drama it contained deliciously increased the chance of some wild times to come, as without opposition days, the Conservatives and Bloc would likely devour the budget to get to the Liberals. Fangs bared and eyes narrowed, Stephen Harper and Gilles Duceppe were back from the break, sharpening their knives ready for a budget kill.

Paul Martin and Jack Layton would fend off their assault and guard the budget bravely, protecting its valued contents. Like Little Red Riding Hood at the mercy of the wolf, danger lurked everywhere for the budget. It was in peril, as Conservatives struck.

A Tory torpedo had launched a non-confidence motion headed towards the Liberals via a House committee on the first day back. It was the first of many novel procedures used by both sides in the Parliamentary war to come. With opposition days out of reach, the Conservatives and Bloc tried to use votes on committee reports to fell the government—launching stealth non-confidence motions.

It all began in a committee on which NDP MP David Christopherson had the balance of power. Bringing down the government was hand-to-hand combat now, as Christopherson voted for the budget by voting down the torpedo. In the first test of the deal's strength, it held. Nobody even saw the motion coming.

In the next short while, the Liberals and NDP scrambled to get legislation for their deal. Liberals, bowing to Bay Street pressure, said they would reintroduce the corporate tax cuts shortly, which created a sense the deal was shaky. And where *did* that $4.6 billion come from, found just like that, but so strangely unavailable in the budget presented only three months before? Not for nothing had Liberals been off on budget forecasts by $80 billion during their governments—none of which went to the lefty priorities in the Liberal Red Book of 1993. And 1997. Or 2000. As the cycle, when started, just keeps going until Tories win again.

The dog-to-bone fixation of Liberals to their tax cuts said more about them than Layton, particularly given voters never approved. Let's have a good debate about when they're a good idea, sure, but at least let voters know what's in the platform—especially with all those lefty promises undone from the long years before. Nevertheless, the new tax cuts wouldn't be in the budget, which was all the NDP cared about. It said it would vote against them when the time came, but the sense that either Layton had been had or that the deal was falling apart lingered, complicating an already dicey spot.

It was a dangerous time for the budget. Harper's and Duceppe's troops kept piling over the wall. The procedural arsenal was firing on all cylinders now as Libby Davies and Tony Valeri toiled away. While the Tories and Bloc worked to forge ammunition, the Liberals and NDP gathered the treasure at which they would shoot. A showdown was coming. Sides dug in.

The budget sat in two pieces, which soon became three. Bill C-43 was the original Liberal budget unchanged. Bill C-48 was the NDP budget that formalized the Layton–Martin deal's changes. A third, Bill C-55, which created the fund to protect workers' wages, was still in negotiation over the pensions issue and would be introduced separately, giving it its own day in the spotlight come November.

On May 10, the House voted 153 to 150 for the government to resign. Harper and Duceppe howled their outrage at Liberals' refusal to quit, and instead say it was all procedure and send the motion back to the committee from which it came. Tory and Bloc MPs vented plasma at another example of prime ministerial disdain for Parliamentary will. The NDP cited precedence that left determining confidence up to the government, which it was not, and clung tight to the budget as Martin glowed like a third rail.

Parliament appeared doomed as its pesky math didn't work. The budget needed every Independent MP to support it to get through, which seemed unlikely when one of them, David Kilgour, said he expected the government to fall. The Tories and Bloc continued their unrelenting attack, and then the pantomime whirled again.

On May 17, two days before the vote, Martin introduced a new heroine to a show with a budget in distress and billionaire Belinda Stronach strode in to rescue it, saying she no longer supported the Tories' alliance with the Bloc. Many of Ottawa's biggest events are carefully leaked well before, but nobody had written this new twist, as the one-time Conservative leadership candidate took her seat next to the prime minister in a press conference that stunned the country.

She was the new human resources minister. The capital stopped, gawped, and instantly froze at this thunderclap of a defection. Martin had re-jigged the Parliamentary math and a monumental vote loomed. The budget was not dead, after all, and had a fighting chance of making it through the woods alive.

And what's a pantomime without heartbreak, as Stronach became heroine and villain in the same dramatic stride. Her boyfriend was the Conservatives' deputy leader and he mourned from his pumpkin patch in rural Nova Scotia at his hurt. Peter MacKay lost a girlfriend and his heart ached on TV, and with political chaos around it, Ottawa gawped again. Across the country, millions took sides as Canada took in our Camilla moment and wondered what on earth the pantomime could produce next.

In time, it shone its stage light onto the Grewals, Parliament's first husband-and-wife team, with a tape recording they alleged—wrongly —to prove that goodies were offered for them to join Stronach and cross the floor. Gurmant Grewal, a Conservative MP from Vancouver, had recorded his chats with the Liberals. And so it was that spring.

For the time being, it was combat as heroes and villains dug into the trenches and fired volley after volley of procedural attack. Everywhere was a battleground, and the House rule book of Monpetit & Monfort fired off strategies like a Gatling gun. Parliament was at war. It was unkind.

The House math was indescribably tight. It appeared that two former Liberal MPs who were now Independents would cancel each other's votes out. Independent—and former Tory, speculation noted— Chuck Cadman's views were a mystery. Attendance for the showdown vote now became crucial. This in a Parliamentary session where an Asian-Canadian MP's gene pool was questioned, other MPs were compared to the Klan and Canadians witnessed the disgrace of leaders squabbling in the Dutch cemetery they visited to honour the 60th anniversary of V-E Day. Parliament sunk even farther.

Many MPs were gravely ill on both sides of the House, most with cancer, which became an issue that cut through the events spiralling wildly around. Even Ottawa in the midst of something as surreal as May had some decency left: In a move that infused humanity into the often appalling Parliament, Ed Broadbent said he would respect the time-honoured tradition of pairing. If a cancer-stricken Conservative MP couldn't vote, Broadbent would abstain. It was poignant with his own recent surprise retirement to care for his beloved wife Lucille, ill with cancer, and earned him person of the year honours from the *Globe and Mail*. The show, meanwhile, swirled around everything as the budget prepared for a pantomime finale.

In the House, heroes and villains faced off each afternoon in Question Period. For all anyone knew, this could be the eve of an election and the Commons was a poisonous, partisan stew. The Conservatives and Bloc were merciless, unleashing a torrent of contempt every day. They were the same entity as far as Liberals were concerned, who fused Harper and separatist together as rhetoric erupted. The NDP was not a major combatant. It helped produce this show, and its on-stage role was largely limited to that of opening act.

But Layton was also excoriated each time he spoke in Parliament, as the Tories and Bloc now had a special loathing for the NDP's choice that may have scuppered their election. (This would prove critical in the months ahead.) Ironically, the NDP could only act after Harper withdrew his own support for the budget. So now here it was, after being abandoned by Tories, the NDP improved it and carried it a long way that Stronach's defection advanced further. Despite all of that, still nobody knew whether it would claim the pantomime's heart.

Hundreds of people trying to get inside snaked around the Peace Tower's base, watched by a row of satellite trucks. After the vote, crowds waited outside to see the combatants emerge. When Stronach left to enter her limousine, the partisans gathered for possibly the first election rally either showered her with delight or pounded her with scorn, depending on whether they wanted an election less than a year after the last.

After its long winding journey from the dingy room, the budget was now ready for a vote[7] on which Parliament's life depended. Every MP was there—the vacant riding of Labrador's by-election was five days away—and it was May 19. Progressives had our sides chosen, and began to watch as the heroes and villains faced off.

> Liberal heroes voted first. Yay!
> 132 to zero for the budget.

> The NDP next. Yay!
> 151 to zero for.

> The Conservatives. Boo!
> 151 to 98 for.

> The Bloc. Boo!
> 152 to 151 against.

Then the heroes and villains intermingled.

> David Kilgour. Boo!
> 153 to 151 against.

> Carolyn Parrish. Yay!
> 153 to 152 against.

The House became quiet. Chuck Cadman, dying of cancer, savoured it.

The quiet, unassuming man who came to Parliament in his jeans and sneakers to fight for stronger crime laws after his son was killed

---

7. The vote on C-43, the original budget, occurred first but didn't mean much. Conservatives announced in advance they would vote for the Liberal budget, which they never opposed, and vote against the NDP budget in C-48, making it the big vote. The Bloc voted against Bill C-43 as it originally did, while the NDP altered its vote on C-43 and supported it, in keeping with its budget deal.

sat. Then he slowly rose to the deafening roar of Liberal and New Democrat MPs, and made it 153 to 153.

Peter Milliken fittingly ended it all as he'd never imagined in grade school, when he first dreamed about becoming Speaker of the House. He closed the curtain by passing the NDP budget. There would be no election this spring, as progressive people smiled and Canadians wondered what had seeped into Ottawa's groundwater.

Pressure from Montreal's Gay Village

7

CHAPTER

A DMITTEDLY, WITH the Grewal tapes playing in the background, Ottawa became instantly nicer, which helped as the budget faced still one more vote before Royal Assent. Spring was here, the air was warm and the sun seemed to borrow some of the joy of progressive people, after we sent Stephen Harper packing. As if to say that winning could happen in the capital, too, an historic vote on equality for lesbian and gay people loomed. A progressive summer was bursting to begin. Together, lefties thumped Harper, and winning feels pretty good.

Even the Bloc Québécois, so recently so spiteful, shared in the spirit, and transformed itself back into the co-operative lefty party often seen before scandal hit. Gilles Duceppe's metamorphosis resembled the chances provided after referendums in a sense, and once the push for an election was lost, the Bloc—incredibly, given the recent mutual venom—schemed with Liberals to get the budget through the House. Together, they manoeuvred in the middle of the night, fittingly, on Quebec's Fête Nationale on June 24, and much to Harper's surprise. The budget received Royal Assent in July, and with passage came the end of the Liberal–NDP deal.

The Bloc also tellingly gave support for the House extending its schedule and sitting until the vote on equal marriage. After years of debate and a clearly precarious House, it was time to move on and, in return for a written guarantee, Duceppe gave the Bloc's assurance it would keep Parliament going until then. It was thanks to pressure from the queer movement. They found common cause in Quebec, and as luck would have it, Duceppe's own riding is home to Montreal's populous gay village.

Queers began to apply pressure to the Bloc, as nationalist Quebecers provided the political heat for a swift vote on something progressive Canadians cherish. Joint efforts also proved potent on the Iraq War and first steps on child care. They should make common project with Quebec within Canada more lusted after. It feels good to win, and we should do it more often—charting our own course, not hitching a ride on the S.S. *Liberal* entering a perfect political storm.

The queer movement's going after allies such as Duceppe helped it go for the loaf, but also differentiates its tactics from the Think Twice coalition. Where queers delivered praise only in return for MPs providing loaves and ensured they did, Think Twice delivered praise in return for crumbs without the threat of punishment for not doing more. When the governing option is seen as so permanent that no matter how large its failings, pissing it off isn't allowed, we get hegemony. Then all the Liberal arrogance that comes next.

But queers often angered Liberals and won anyway, and the looming progressive summer may not have felt so warm if lesbian and gay people were only allowed to date. It's roughly the kind of crumb that Liberal climate change, trade or worker policies delivered in a decade of majorities. So why did Think Twice shy away from the same kind of pressure?

One possibility is that only queers[8] or massive opposition to the Iraq War can win the loaf in federal politics. The other is that they

---

8. Municipalities also fared well in the minority Parliament but aren't really part of the broader progressive community. Many mayors and councils are deeply conservative. The queer movement is alone in earning a progressive loaf from 1993 to 2006.

were alone in demanding one and threatening pain at the polls if not, which is closer to the truth. Neither a new budget nor equal marriage came from a stroll on the Liberals' preferred path, and progressives were happier for it. Queers did what activists worldwide do. They tried to win, and showed true non-partisanship along the way, even if it did make the odd Liberal miserable. In fact, Alex Munter's tactics were quite ruthless and effective, which propelled Duceppe to act and soon cost Paul Martin a treasured vote in the House.

Martin saw nothing wrong with this Bloc love-in of June, which was only weeks before so treasonous when done by Harper. In the 2006 election, he accused the Bloc of only being interested in showing that Parliament couldn't work, which its 15-year-long record shows to be a flat lie. Stephen Harper eventually said the equal marriage vote wasn't legitimate because most federalist MPs opposed it. In joining Martin in hypocrisy, he helped underline that Quebec is needed for our progressive majority to work, just as equal marriage shows us what's possible when we work with progressive Quebecers within Canada. Winning. We should do it more often.

As the weather warmed and tempers cooled, Parliament went through the looking glass in contrast to the rowdy spring. Everyone knew the election was six months off after Justice John Gomery's final report on December 1, followed by an early election call by Martin within a month. This certainty of fate gave the Hill serenity and co-operation it hadn't enjoyed before. During the dithers, serenity was around, and the budget showed co-operation could happen, too, but the two didn't co-exist until now. In June's warmth, almost a year after the 2004 election, finally Canada had a progressive majority of MPs.

This period was fondly remembered before the lefty fissure spread, as Liberals fell and Harper won. It also saw the most impressive progressive win in 15 years in equal marriage, which rivalled the landmark court ruling of 1988, which protected women's reproductive choice. The win added to the jubilation of the pantomime victory, and feelings fermented during a very progressive summer. As the winter guillotine—yet to be encountered—began to slide towards Martin and begin the election, the contrast with spring's warm glow was jarring. It helps reinforce the Liberal line on how Parliament ended, which we're sussing the truth of.

But on June 29, history's vote on equal marriage was at hand, which also protected religious freedom to perform them or not. It was moving. The galleries above the Commons floor were jammed with people, many recently married, to witness something few thought they would see in their lifetime. Others had come, too, smaller in number but horrified by what they thought they'd never see, either. The vote was expected to be close, but pass. If it did, Canada would join Belgium and the Netherlands as the world's only countries to acknowledge this right.[9]

After years of often-bitter struggle led by brave people, queers emerged from a past marred with violence and an epidemic. Progressives watched as we contemplated the sea change in a brief time. Canada was about to provide lesbians and gay men with human rights equality, a victory made more vivid by the fundamentalism surging in the United States. It felt good to be Canadian, and terrific to be a progressive one. We were on a roll: Iraq, Kyoto, a progressive budget, now this. It was going to be quite the progressive summer once equal marriage passed, as it did.

Parliament voted 158 to 133 on a divisive, two-sided issue and the progressive majority smiled to ourselves again. The last two months were rip-roaring fun. Harper looked weak, irrelevant and wrong.

The vote came about after the bevy of brilliant queer lawyers began firing torpedoes of their own years before.[10] Bit by bit, legal and

9. Spain legalized equal marriage shortly after the Canadian vote, followed by South Africa. Many northern European countries, including the u.k., and New Zealand also provide legal recognition of lesbian and gay relationships though stop short of marriage itself. Vermont was the first u.s. state to recognize civil unions and other American jurisdictions have followed.

10. The push for lesbian and gay equality had many allies, notably the labour movement, which funded some successful court challenges. Many unions made benefits such as pensions for partners of lesbian and gay workers priorities in collective bargaining. Similarly, many employers—including large banks—voluntarily extended benefits, in some cases in the early 1990s. In contrast, the Liberal government was fighting lesbian and gay pension benefits in court into 2005.

political victories mounted and the scope of lesbian and gay equality grew. It continued the swift politicization of a minority group that kicked off with a riot at the Stonewall bar in New York City in 1969, started by drag queens bitchy at police harassment. The demand for equality quickly spread and pressured politicians, first at city halls over the police and recognition of Pride Days, then provincial and territorial legislatures, finally Ottawa. The gay AIDS epidemic in the 1980s powered activism as inequality led to dramatically reduced life expectancies. This was a movement on the move.

The legal battle was a final chapter, enabled by Pierre Trudeau's Charter of Rights that was added to the Constitution when he returned with it from London. It was his second bequest to queers after voluntarily decriminalizing homosexuality, along with relaxing heterosexual divorce laws, in the late 1960s as a young justice minister.

Despite failing to include sexual orientation, by 2003 the Charter was proving strategic. After Ontario's landmark court decision cleared the way for equal marriage, BC and Quebec followed, then others. Soon after, Jean Chrétien asked the Supreme Court if Ottawa had to change the marriage law, recognizing that six provinces plus the Yukon were practising court-ordered equal marriages. Only courts in Alberta, New Brunswick, Newfoundland and Labrador, and PEI were still offside, making the vote on marriage an equality victory, not a Liberal one. Parliament provided crucial symbolism, but didn't win the fight. Ninety per-cent of Canadians had access to equal marriage by the time the vote allowing it passed.

MPs had once before voted on marriage, in 1999, on an opposition motion put forward by the Canadian Alliance to restrict it to a man and a woman. A Liberal majority House voted for it, with most Liberals, Chrétien and Martin included, voting with the Alliance. The Bloc and NDP, including both party leaders, opposed the motion but neither was unanimous. And so before another vote, Chrétien wanted a Court opinion behind him to push reluctant Liberal MPs into supporting equality, with the Court providing cover for irate constituents. It was smart.

One of the first things Martin did as prime minister, in a majority, was to ask the Court a fourth question as it pondered Chrétien's three. In the 2006 election, he shamelessly pledged to end federal use of the notwithstanding clause—ostensibly to save queers from Harper—but human rights champion he wasn't. Not one year before the marriage vote. To say nothing of two.

During his run for Liberal leader, Martin supported using the notwithstanding clause if the Court said equal marriage threatened religious freedom. He also floated what he called options. They're better known as civil unions, and provide the legal rights of marriage without the name in a kind of back-of-the-bus equality. Martin managed to avoid having an actual position until after the Court ruled, which he delayed by asking it a question so pointless, it refused to answer. Liberals also appealed a Charter ruling on pension benefits for lesbian and gay couples, incredibly, in the din of telling Harper how vital the Charter was.

Once more, Liberals' fundamental values on the verge of a romp were quite different than those displayed on the way out the door. When he didn't need our votes, Martin ignored us and pursued at best a moderate centre-right path, as Liberals went for a sweeping victory—not a progressive one—as he, literally, seized the reins. Nonetheless, in the weeks following his defeat, Jim Laxer wrote an opinion piece for *The Toronto Star* that saluted Martin's innovative progressive career, as lefty guilt about Liberals losing got stuck in its 1988 view. You'd think Gandhi had lost.

Ironically, one of the main reasons why Martin refused to change his timeline for the 2004 election in spite of Sheila Fraser's damnation was having one without the bother of defending equal marriage. The dithering seen on every issue he claimed so dear—the Iraq War and missile defence, or ratifying Kyoto—also plagued marriage and overturned the underside of the party that Think Twice advised progressive people see as allies in the election.

Following the Court's ruling in late 2004, the equal marriage bill was introduced and Martin told members of Cabinet to support it. It's unlikely this ensured passage, but several Cabinet ministers were opposed and one resigned in protest. The rest of the Liberal caucus, which contained MPs as bad as and, in some isolated cases, worse than Tories' most egregious social conservatives, could vote as they liked. And when it came, no party had unanimity though similarities ended there.

Thirty-two Liberal MPs, five Bloc MPs and one NDP MP opposed the bill, and three Tories were in favour. In the election rhetoric to come, you'd never know that if only Liberal and Conservative MPs voted on marriage, equality would have lost. It passed thanks to the Bloc, with the NDP padding the margin. True, if only Liberals had voted the bill would have passed. But despite Liberals' fondness for pointing to how many voted for equality, at issue is their blasé acceptance of opposition to a fundamental Charter right. Two, actually, with a woman's right to choose also flowing from a court ruling almost 20 years earlier.

All parties held free votes on equal marriage—those where MPs can vote how they would like—except the NDP, which deemed it a human rights issue. Martin and Justice Minister Irwin Cotler criticized New Democrats for it, which did not prevent Martin at least from defining it precisely thus in the 2006 campaign. This isn't a trivial detail. It helps separate the Charter from the Liberal Party to reunite Pierre Trudeau with original kin in the NDP, his first partisan home.

Trudeau and the Troglodytes

8

CHAPTER

S HOULD HISTORY MOCK Pierre Trudeau by anointing Paul Martin hero of equal marriage, the drag queens of Stonewall should let its writers have it. Trudeau's impact shapes life long after he left office and fuels wins today. He was imperfect, but also stands alone among Liberal prime ministers in voluntarily bringing progressive triumph. His lefty victories are few, but large in the Constitution and Charter, and also reforms as justice minister in the 1960s and bilingualism, as a first step to reconciliation with Quebec.

Many may argue that Lester Pearson deserves similar standing, but sadly it's not the case. Pearson was an admirable diplomat and his invention of U.N. peacekeeping during the Suez Canal crisis earned him a Nobel Peace Prize. But as a prime minister—except the new, Union Jack-free flag and another key step towards nationhood—his largest wins came from Tommy Douglas, who forced change upon Pearson's minorities. Only if the NDP's budget is seen as Martin's choice can the medicare, welfare and pension wins—all class-based—of the 1960s be Pearson's legacy, not Douglas's. Or shared.

Perhaps the best contrasts with the Pearson whom Liberals romanticize are found in foreign aid and U.N. peacekeeping, where

Canada is now a humiliating 33rd in providing personnel to the system we invented. Liberal PMs may have governed competently here and there, but can lay claim to few key blocks of nation-building. Victories were often Conservative, not Liberal.

John A. Macdonald brought Confederation and the railway; Robert Borden ushered in true nationhood in the First World War; Richard Bennett built the CBC; John Diefenbaker created the first Bill of Rights; and Brian Mulroney forged ahead on Aboriginal issues by creating the Inuit territory of Nunavut.

It's a mirage that Liberal Party values are interchangeable with Canada's. In truth, the party descends from American integrationist Wilfrid Laurier, leader as the 20th century began; and Mackenzie King, who helped quash workers in the Depression through a disastrous Liberal–Labour coalition exactly as the CCF—forerunner of the NDP—was building a class-based party. Even the anglo establishment's *Globe and Mail* saw a need for class awareness then, but King and union acolytes didn't and the results were, shall we say, unhelpful for workers.

Trudeau was not so helpful to workers, either, but he also defined our Canada, as the geyser of grief at his death in 2000 shows. It differed by region and generation, but as roses sprouted on lapels, people waited around the clock to pay their respects in Ottawa and thousands lined the train's procession on the brilliant autumn day that carried his coffin to a state funeral in Montreal, it's impossible to deny his legacy. Canadians remembered what dreaming together was like, and whether Trudeau's prescription was right or not, almost everyone agreed a giant had passed.

He was not always a gentle giant, though, and the War Measures Act remains a blight on his crusade for individual freedom. Nor was his legendary lust for a stronger Ottawa always so apparent. The slow federal withdrawal from a health care partnership with provinces began under Trudeau in the 1970s, and his disdain for victims of the 1980s recession earned him plenty of one-finger salutes in return. Though often dreary, arrogant affairs, on one glorious day in 1982 a Trudeau majority brought one big win at last. His Charter stands aside Tommy Douglas's medicare as a progressive triumph.

Long driven by quashing Quebec separatism, the Charter took some time in coming, but after Trudeau's second chance and the 1980 referendum, he set out to bring the Constitution home from London. Its Charter shaped equal marriage, just as it had in 1988 when Mulroney refused to write a new abortion law after courts struck the old one down. Canada doesn't have an abortion law to this day, and thanks to the void, women have the right to choose. In Liberal lore, these are their values, and flow interchangeably among the party, the country, and the man himself.

This could be hokum, and perhaps it's time to ask if Trudeau does represent the Liberal Party, or if his victories were due to him— not it. Abraham Lincoln freed the slaves, but few today think his Republican Party is a staunch ally of African-Americans, and as we consider the progressive mess we're in, we may want to ask if Trudeau wasn't a one-off. And if today's Liberals, by their own choices, haven't shown it.

In his two elections as leader, Martin used the Charter rights of equal marriage and choice as key reasons why Harper should not be PM. The gall of him daring to champion queers has been covered— and will be some more—but his support for choice is also blurry. He's actually the only leader to support restricting women's rights, when he blurted out support for parental notification in the 2004 campaign. This is a growing concern in the U.S., and effectively means a young woman raped, even by a family member, needs family approval before being granted choice. Martin unequivocally supported this restriction before Liberals tried to muddy the waters, yell boo, and make Harper out as the one trying to roll back choice.[11]

---

11. In truth, Harper had a stronger position than Martin. While Martin catered to social conservatives running—almost unopposed—for Liberal leader, Harper took on the fundamentalists within the newly reunited Conservative Party, making it clear that rolling back choice wasn't on. At the first Tory policy convention, he succeeded in passing a policy supporting choice.

Rolling it back is a big deal. So big, it's worth asking why so many Liberal MPs are fundamentalists, if the Charter rights they oppose underpin Liberal values. The common excuse is that equal marriage and abortion are moral issues, best left to individual consciences. If true, Liberals had no business attacking anyone for opposing them. But it's untrue, and if church and state are separated, should someone find either equal marriage or abortion taboo, they're entitled not to have one. Indeed, if equal marriage became illegal, religions like the United Church would be denied the freedom to perform ceremonies their faith allows.

How Martin defined both equal marriage and choice in the 2006 election was bang-on. They were Charter rights and, if one believes in the Charter as Trudeau did, supreme. But Trudeau had long left the Liberal Party, though his legacy's frame shapes politics into today.

Until this midway point in the minority Parliament, progressives mainly saw events and desired paths in common. We didn't want an election, or a halt to progress on any recent steps ahead, and no matter whether we were partisan, or if we were Liberal or NDP, how New Democrats dealt with events was seen as pretty good. This is not true in Quebec, but fairly sums up the progressive mood elsewhere as summer looms.

But as an election gets closer with each day, progressive paths begin to diverge and we fight. Friction is produced when frames collide, as best seen first among Liberals themselves. During elections, they like to say they are true to Trudeau's values on issues such as equal marriage and choice. If this Trudeau Liberal frame were honestly applied, candidates and MPs who oppose the Charter would have a harder time than they do. Instead, consecutive Liberal leaders—Martin, Chrétien and John Turner—preferred the Liberal to the Trudeau, allowing us to separate the Charter from the party he happened to belong to when he wrote it. Today, you can be as anti-Charter as you like, as long as you're a Liberal.

The Trudeau fumes on which the party's run for years are dissipating. In his place are troglodytes, who inundated the party after its 1984 wipeout. Particularly in Toronto, fundamentalists overran Liberal riding associations, and stacked nominations to elect thug-like opponents to a woman's right to choose and equality for lesbian and gay people. To this day, calls to Vote Liberal in the GTA elect some of Parliament's retrogrades. Good ol' Liberal Toronto had more MPs vote against equality than any other city.

Many, such as Tom Wappel, first won in 1988 and have been re-elected to defend the values they entered Parliament to oppose up to five times. Wappel's "God Squad", as it's known, fought abortion rights and those for gay and lesbian people more visually than the worst of the original Reform caucus that the 1993 election dragged in. Liberals like to portray them as harmless, clout-free flotsam, but this isn't the case. Once, they managed to sow doubt over a Liberal majority passing its own bill on new reproductive technology, which right-wingers opposed, along with the Bloc, as it dealt with an area in provincial turf. No gender parity on the oversight board put the NDP offside, too.

Courtesy of the God Squad, Liberals couldn't guarantee passage, although the bill did end up passing after the NDP used its leverage to win gender parity. Relations with many women's groups were tense at the time as the Liberals' best offer was seen as better than nothing, and mounted progressive pressure in the faceless backroom—though not in public, where it does the most damage. And achieves the most change, for Liberals are always most useful when weak.

On rights for lesbian and gay people, anti-Charter Liberals' opposition was universal and began on issues such as including sexual orientation in hate crime laws or adding it to the human rights code, which stops someone being evicted or fired due to race or gender. PC MPs, though mainly opposed to equal marriage, supported these steps forward, as did marriage dissenters in the Bloc and NDP. Anti-Charter Liberals showed no such moderation. They cut their teeth digging in against basic human rights for lesbian and gay people. Chrétien allowed their assault.

As victories on basic human rights were won and larger ones such as marriage sought, anti-Charter Liberals became more aggressive. Together with Conservatives, they delayed and fought equality at each step with nary a word from Martin, whose leadership campaign reached out to many of them. Often, a juicy bone was tossed their way, such as supporting using the notwithstanding clause to protect religion. In due course, long habit of reversal won out and in the 2006 election he tried to remove any control on the courts, by trying to axe the notwithstanding clause entirely.

In explaining why, Martin said that he was wrong to want to protect religious freedom in the first place as he tried to find anything for a wedge with Harper, no matter how dangerous or absurd. And echoing the frenzy was Think Twice, urging people to Vote Liberal to protect human rights in 2006, as if the two are one and the same. Sadly, they are not.

After the budget's pantomime victory, queers set about obtaining as swift a vote as possible on equal marriage. They pressured the Bloc from Quebec, but put pressure on Liberals as well. After more than three years of debate, Martin was happy to keep on talking, hoping to find someone, somewhere who hadn't made their mind up if two men or two women marrying was all right. Polls showed 4 per cent of Canadians were so torn, but this didn't stop Martin giving the nod to anti-Charter Liberals that still more study was in store. For as long as it took, until the last 4 per cent were found.

This was the last straw for queers. They told Martin the time for debate was over, and expected a vote—now—given the House's precarious state. Most MPs were firmly on the record in support, nine courts had ruled and citizens couldn't be accused of failing to debate the issue with vigour, queers pointed out. Martin was forced to agree, which triggered the resignation from the Liberal caucus of London MP Pat O'Brien, a nasty fundamentalist. His exit will change the pesky House math in ways Liberals won't like, but nobody's yet blamed queers for triggering an early election, though Jim Stanford's *Globe* column ripped the NDP over it. Pesky House math be damned.

O'Brien is the sole MP gone from the Liberals for viciously opposing Trudeau's Charter, and left because he wanted to. None of his counterparts was spanked—both a pleasant and repulsive thought—by any of the three Liberal leaders who faced their intolerance, even as Reform/Alliance punished MPs for woeful comments about African-Canadians, gay men and Aboriginal people.

Without Trudeau at the helm, Liberal leaders ogled the Liberal in the Trudeau Liberal frame, and saw a few more Liberal MPs as more important than the Charter they devoted their MP lives to undermining. Pity poor former Liberal MP Carolyn Parrish, booted for stomping on a Bush doll on a TV comedy show—a fate that Wappel, on his 17-year-long crusade against choice and equality, never worried about once.

This wasn't on for queers, who were quite Trudeauesque in dividing friend from enemy, and saw no difference in party. For equal-marriage advocates, an MP who supported marriage was an ally and an opponent of it was not, without exception or blurring what was okay based on an MP being Liberal or Conservative. They were out for a loaf, which made their tactics jive with those of Douglas before, who didn't stop pushing for public health care until he won it.

Here, they enjoyed an ironic similarity with Trudeau himself, who before wandering the Middle East and founding the magazine *Cité Libre*, had his first partisan dalliance with the CCF. Trudeau was drawn to the truly progressive party, not the drifting, smug Liberal Party of the 1930s, 1940s and 1950s. King and successor Louis St.-Laurent ran machine-style governments that resembled Chicago of old, though admittedly without the shootings.

Never from Liberal circles, Trudeau spent his time travelling, writing and occasionally doing legal work for unions, including a particularly nasty asbestos workers' strike in Quebec. But there weren't many CCF circles to enter. Aside from future Senator Thérèse Casgrain and McGill professor Charles Taylor, the CCF was a low-profile, hardy bunch in Quebec with few visible members and was solidifying in the West, with isolated pockets in Ontario.

Like Quebec, Canada was stuck in a backwards, 19th-century way that exploded into oblivion with our centenary in 1967 and the Montreal World Exposition. It helped spark Trudeaumania as the young Montrealer became Liberal leader in 1968. He won the first Liberal majority since 1953 shortly afterwards.

That Trudeau entered politics in the Sixties as a Liberal is coincidental, not defining, as he picked the most viable vehicle he saw, which at the time in Quebec was the Liberals. He's not alone in being drawn to a more viable path by Liberal electability, but this also means he and the Liberal Party are not inseparable. They can be split for the same electoral conveniences that first drew him to them. And what could be more Liberal than that, with the incentive that we could then strive for the loaf our numbers allow.

For better or worse, this is a partisan route for now, as Douglas always believed. Clearly motivated by class, the other ingredient to his brilliance was seeing the ballot box and—like the queer movement— Parliament as key tools of change. He didn't form a loose alliance of people concerned about medicare to achieve the goal. He built a political party and removed from office medicare opponents, in his case, the governing Liberals of Saskatchewan. Though he never became PM, he tried to when he harmed Liberals in elections, while forcing change upon them in between.

All progressive people celebrate Douglas's pioneering ways of medicare but not all—chiefly Liberals, but also Think Twice—agree with his certainty that the Liberal Party is an enemy, not a friend. This difference ended the good progressive times from spring, turned the fall unpleasant and magnified our division—all because the meaningless middle keeps the left divided in elections. We all like the idea of a just society, but despite Trudeau's long shadow it's also possible that New Democrats have always called it, well, just Canada.

John A. Macdonald, René Lévesque and the Race

9

CHAPTER

WHEN THE HOUSE rose for summer the day following the equal marriage win, federal politics went into a kind of hibernation. The previous three months were among the most intense on the Hill in memory, and the fall session seen as little more than a prelude to an election. Only 10 weeks of sitting time remained before the campaign, kicked off by the second of Justice John Gomery's reports into the scandal. The rough certainty of when the next election would be was almost without precedent in a majority. It was unheard of in a minority, and parties prepared for the early election that Paul Martin called on TV in April.

The looming fall's events prove troubling for most progressives, but navigating them is both a partisan and non-partisan task for the time being, if we're going to create the conditions to win. If governing is the goal, it's time to get serious about building a party that can form it. We've put that off for too long, leaving us stuck in the purgatory of not wanting either Liberal majorities or building an alternative that can win its own. As long as the meaningless middle is in the way, we won't be able to replicate what progressives worldwide have managed to do and win by enjoying more common tactics in elections.

The other loop that hurts progressive hopes is what goes on in Quebec, where Tories find favour every now and then in a dance that is as old as Canada itself. The Tories and Quebec regularly enjoy their cycles, but there's little reason lefties can't become an option, too, as the Quebec–Tory romance perhaps begins once more.

Tommy Douglas and Pierre Trudeau help shape progressive frames and enjoy iconic status within the NDP and Liberals, respectively. But they're not the only icons, and John A. Macdonald enjoys similar status in the Conservatives, for his cunning alliance with Quebec that made him the first prime minister. A fourth, following John Diefenbaker's and Brian Mulroney's, Tory flirtation with Quebec now looms, and if conjugated will leave us with a desperately weakened federal government designed in part by neo-conservatives.

Most profoundly, it's here that Stephen Harper can change our country in ways we don't want, through his 2006 election campaign approach that invoked the name of sovereigntist icon René Lévesque, the Parti Québécois's founding leader.

There are many bogeymen about Harper, and some are bang on. He is a Republican warmonger. Other charges hold less water, and he is not a Christian moralist, but something more dangerous: a libertarian who loathes government, the military not included.

Nobody would mistake us for Amsterdam, but Harper's Canada would happily take married queers if it means less meddling in other areas—like oil drilling or a race to the tax bottom that leaves governments too weak to do much. Quebec, too, is leery of federal intrusion, and their interests mesh in wanting a federal government too weak for our majority to work together—and provinces too small to deal with key challenges ahead. Global warming. War. Trade. Poverty. They're all security issues, and the problems aren't provincial.

The Bloc Québécois could well be endangered, now starved of its rejuvenation fuel in the high-octane Liberal scandal that enraged and insulted Quebecers. Or Gilles Duceppe could appeal to the very Canadian values that lefties elsewhere do, point to the Bush-like clone in office, and ask why Quebec can't be more progressive by itself. Either way, our progressive majority loses, but there's no obvious reason why Liberals are the answer.

Their scandal also fuelled Harper and led to his Conservatives now being the dominant federalist party in Quebec, with only one majority path leading straight through the Bloc. His goal should spook us: a repeat of the Mulroney coalition, now laced with a neo-conservatism, bordering on Republicanism. If he pulls it off, Ottawa will become too weak to let us work together. Our majority will be squandered on regional bickering that can't deal with the big challenges to come. The climate is changing. The economy is globalizing. Our capacity to shape this matters.

We're in a race, and the first one to find common cause with Lévesque's followers wins. If it's Harper or Duceppe, we will see decentralization of federal power almost overnight, and with it, our majority's clout. If we can win, we could try to use Ottawa to progressive advantage, by keeping national fingers—and Quebec's thumbs—on economic, environmental and social levers. How to beat him is the question, and Canada's rare, archaic partisan structure holds us back. In a period of changing politics, it's a problem to fix.

With region, history and parties each factoring into where we're at, it's odd but helpful to imagine it as a horserace. There are three riders: Douglas, Macdonald and Trudeau but only one horse can reach Lévesque first. With the race so regular, it could be time to rethink which horses can race and which should be closer to glue. Liberals believe their hegemony makes the choice clear, and argue that Douglas's NDP can't be trusted given its habit of letting Tories up the middle. But the stakes are too high to jump on the wrong one, and before accepting a Liberal steed for eternity, we need to probe the 1988 and 2006 elections to see how Tories did well, and why Liberals lost. And in a way, why icons matter.

As we do well, though, we make our predicament more painful by disagreeing on who's to blame for Harper winning. Usually, Liberals aren't one of the accused and as we attack each other, they happily prepare to return to office and off we go again. But our progressive frames leave us with many explanations. Douglas types hold Liberals responsible for Liberal failure, and note another option was available in the NDP. Liberals hold the NDP responsible for joining with Harper and triggering the election he won. If reframing politics so it's easier for progressives to work together in elections is worthwhile, we need to see which paints the truer picture.

Harper's choice to recognize the Québécois as a nation only underlines the real question at play. He is trying to appeal to decentralism to form the fourth alliance between Conservatives and Quebec. With politics in flux, the uncertain federal scene of late is likely to continue for a while. Minority Parliaments are more likely than not, making the tedious race for biggest slice in a pizza Parliament less relevant than ever. Even with the biggest slice, Harper wouldn't automatically win. But we could, by producing productive, stable minority Parliaments where progressive parties could grow thanks to merit. Not history, which isn't always how Liberals tell it.

Regions make our mess worse. Neither the North nor Atlantic Canada has enough people to determine a path, but this is not to suggest either can't help push. But currently, each of the three largest regions has different main progressive parties: the West has the NDP; Ontario the Liberals and Quebec the Bloc. If we're open to rethinking electoral tactics, we need to remember the dominant progressive party in our own region doesn't dominate either of the other largest regions. If we want to work with cousins across Canada, we're going to have to catch our partisan regionalism come election time because we don't vote the same way country-wide.

Of the three largest regions only Ontario, as the most populous and home to most national institutions, sees itself as a mirror image of the nation, not a component part. Ontario is also the last province west of the Maritimes with its dominant progressive party being Liberal, backed up by years of tradition. Tragically, its regional frame is entwined with a Liberal one, allowing Liberal versions of the 1988 and 2006 elections to gel in circles beyond the party itself, such as Think Twice.

Its three principals all live in Ontario, but they're not driven by the same kind of issues. Like Douglas, Buzz Hargrove is motivated by class, but not so much by the NDP. Both Douglas and Hargrove are socialists, but the division is on the partisan not ideological side. When they collide, it's often highly divisive as Hargrove can attest following his regretfully forced exit. But that's what happens when we keep trying to stuff two-sided arguments into multi-party holes, and eventually you're either a New Democrat or not, leaving socialists like Hargrove nowhere partisan to go.

His counterparts in Think Twice have long been there. Maude Barlow left partisan politics two decades ago, while Elizabeth May is now entering it after decades of snuggling with Liberal and Tory governments alike. Barlow and May are also motivated less by class, and more by other, Trudeau-like, concepts of democracy and sustainability. They're united with Hargrove in a common hatred of Conservative governments—or *this* Tory government, in May's case—and their seeing Liberals as the only viable option to Stop Harper. In a sense, because Liberals dominate their part of Canada, they are the only left-leaning governing option. Viable, Liberals often were. Progressive, not so much, and if we don't try to keep them down now, they'll get up eventually.

Europe has long known what happens when Liberals fall, and powers ahead on many green, social and foreign policy questions quite nicely. Western Canada knows what happens, too, and keeps electing some of North America's most progressive governments in the NDP; it's often true in New Zealand as well. Everywhere else never had them to begin with. Liberals are the norm only for 32 million Canadians, on a planet of six billion. With whom we rarely share the dirty little secret that we are one of its biggest polluters.

We rarely boast, too, about a society that prides fairness slipping ever-deeper into stratification, which we see all around us and getting worse. If Liberals keep being re-elected, we know what we get. Around the world, though, citizens often receive better with fewer Liberals. But it's the question of what happens next that stalls us, and whether there really are more options than Conservative or Liberal majorities in Ottawa.

Nowhere is more bogged down than Ontario, the last populous province in the world's last outpost of Liberalism that thinks the habit is normal. Ontario can't see something else happening in Ottawa other than Tories doing well should Liberals fall, and often tries to keep them up. It's the cyclical loop that we can't break until seeing Liberal defeats as cyclical, too, and feeling good that they're down when they are.

But fear, not opportunity, often guides us when Liberals lose, particularly in Ontario, where decades of branding make federal Liberals seem invincible. They're just supposed to govern, which makes a split progressive vote—not their record, ethics, tactics or fed up voters—such a convenient explanation for how they came to lose. And if all that counts is not being Conservative, a Liberal vote and an NDP one do the same thing, which is exactly as Liberals need to stop the NDP rising. Until Liberal decline is seen as a good thing, this cycle won't end. Quebec is at the heart of why Liberal decline is not only positive, but likely.

When Liberals head for oblivion in Quebec, like 1988 or 2006, there's a momentary fusion of purpose with progressive people in Ontario. Along with Atlantic Canada, it is where Liberal electoral bacon is saved as Quebec goes elsewhere, which is now a 25-year-long trend. With populated Ontario also being the last remaining Liberal bastion, the rhetorical levels over progressive votes are most desperate within its borders as Liberals can't win seats elsewhere. And when natural governing entities are on the way out, they squeal—loudly.

As the only region they dominate, Liberals feel pain from both left and right in Ontario on the way down, with 1988 and 2006 being prime examples. The assault against them in Quebec is different almost by definition, and they've not yet built a dominant base in the West to attack. This makes Ontario the region with the most pronounced progressive division, and also where Liberal stakes are highest. And buttresses Liberal rhetoric that defeat was caused by a rising NDP and its rampant partisanship—not, heaven forbid, anything Liberals could have done that did them in.

Minority Parliaments only complicate things. They are popular among progressive people federally, and are also usually Ontario's most progressive experiences, period. A good reason to shrink the Liberals a bit, perhaps, but it tends to end up as delight in productive minority Parliaments, which in Ontario typically see a larger Liberal Party propped up by the NDP in return for lefty progress. It has happened federally four times since the 1960s, and as home to national institutions, the centre of the universe pays more attention to federal politics than elsewhere.

It also happened once provincially in the mid-1980s, while other provincial minority experiences—in Manitoba, Nova Scotia and Saskatchewan—almost always had either the Conservatives or NDP as the governing party. A Liberal minority government is most common in Ontario, both on Parliament Hill and at Queen's Park.

No surprise, Ontario often sees Liberals and New Democrats as natural allies after this co-operation, with its predictable progressive wins. In this Liberal frame, the NDP's highest ambition is to steer Liberals leftward in a minority as opposed to governing itself. But this isn't how Douglas progressives see things, and they're mainly from the West where his ballot box path shrunk Liberals long ago, and won through the NDP alone. This partisan spat between Douglas and Liberals can't be reconciled, for its core scrap is the role of the NDP.

The West sees the party's role as governing, while Ontario sees it as a large conscience that's good to have around but isn't going to govern, and so should not try to win. Western progressives often see little reason to heed Ontario's advice and cede power to Liberals or Tories. And it's all complicated by minority situations, partly because the NDP chooses to work with Liberals—when they are weak.

Coming from the region where progressives won first, western Douglas types like to win. To them, minority governments are not stepping stones to future growth but second best, since the NDP failed to govern itself. Minorities also have a raw underside for the NDP, which rarely gets credit and instead habitually sees its policies morphed into Liberal progressive branding when in truth, NDP work in minorities provides the bulk of what Liberals claim to hold so dearly. Without this progressive injection, the Liberals' majority record is often quite conservative.

The explanation is Liberals almost never reach out to New Democrats when the NDP is weak. Apparently it's natural for the NDP to co-operate with its weakened prime rival, but not for natural governing entities to sully themselves with non-partisanship unless they need to. Nothing forced Douglas or David Lewis to work with Liberals in minorities. In the current minority, despite many good faith efforts beforehand, the storm unleashed by Jean Brault's testimony forced Martin to enact the NDP's changes, but it took the fear of God first. Jack Layton wasn't forced to offer, however, and had he capitalized on soaring polling numbers in the spring, an election—not a progressive budget—would have come.

Nonetheless, in a 2006 election column, Jim Stanford accused the NDP of ignoring how important minority Parliaments were, and being driven by self-interest in wanting some space between it and Liberals. Partisanship, Liberals spit. Those New Democrats, they'll do anything partisan for a few more seats, even if it means Harper winning. Evidently such partisan drive is nowhere to be found in the ruthless backrooms of one of the world's most meaningless yet previously electable entities. Us? Partisan? Never, Liberals claim, in the fetching delusion that their party does something other than be elected.

But despite a budget being rewritten only seven months before the election, Stanford began repeating the line that all New Democrats were concerned with was partisan gain. This is dangerous, not only for allowing one of the world's most partisan things to appear saintly, but also for historical wrongness. If the NDP's judged on its most recent things, such as allegedly triggering an early election, while decades of Liberal choices are forgotten as we rush to put Humpty Dumpty back together again, we'll have dominant Liberals forever. Good for Prozac sales, but not for progressive progress.

And yet progress is why many progressives oppose the NDP trying to do well. How the 2004–2006 minority ends allegedly made Elizabeth May run for Green leader, and Stanford's beef with the NDP is similar. Both think that because the minority Parliament contained 208 progressive MPs—Liberal, Bloc and NDP—anything that ended it was irresponsible, given its rarity. But if Parliament with a progressive majority were all that counted, the previous three should have been lefty nirvanas, too: 240 progressive MPs were elected in 1993, 220 in 1997 and 223 in 2000. The difference among the four Parliaments wasn't that the minority had more progressive MPs, but fewer Liberal ones, so why not create conditions that elect many fewer Liberals? Permanently.

Outside of Quebec, we don't have a consensus and troublingly drift towards something like a dimmer switch for a light, which can be finely adjusted until just the right amount of Liberals win. That's essentially Think Twice's position, which wants a Liberal government not because it's good, but because it is better than the only viable alternative. Despite urging people to Vote Liberal, Think Twice doesn't see stopping Tories as a partisan affair, but instead a multi-party effort in which Liberals are happily participating, but harmed by self-interested attacks from the NDP.

This opens New Democrats to charges of partisanship—valuing more NDP MPs over fewer Tory ones—and helps set the stage for the post-Liberal-loss playbook. It shifts blame for why Liberals lost onto an alleged split vote, a charge most vigorously levelled by Liberals, but with an echo in Think Twice-type lefties who overwhelmingly call Ontario home. We need to rethink if it's right.

Politics' new rules make minority governments more likely, and they're worth a decent look as we figure a path ahead. With how the current one ends feeding much of the analysis over how Liberals lost to Harper, the Liberal line on things is worth even greater scrutiny. And a brief history of minorities shows that times when Liberals didn't write the rules ironically provide the bulk of the party's progressive credentials. It also shows which party troubles itself with getting things done, and which would make even Machiavelli often blush.

The Liberal Party is not a benevolent entity untroubled with winning elections. Stanford's advice for the NDP to snuggle closely with it—no matter what—doesn't stand history's test.

For more than our first 50 years as a country, minority Parliaments had yet to arrive. Our politics were like Britain's at the time and America's now, with two parties in the Conservatives and Liberals, the rabble-rousers of the 1860s. Conservatives were the more successful and formed the first government, thanks to Macdonald's wily alliance with Quebec's George-Etienne Cartier.

Wilfrid Laurier became the first francophone leader in 1887, when he won the Liberal leadership. He ended Quebec's Tory bias and it became more reliably Liberal until Canada, and with it the Liberal Party, was torn apart by the conscription crisis of the First World War. By the time it began in 1914, almost half the Liberal caucus was from Quebec and deeply opposed to mandatory military service, in its eyes, for the British King. The Liberal Party split in two over Laurier's anti-conscription stand, and for a period its future was in doubt.

Conservative Robert Borden won in 1911, and in the war-delayed election of 1917, ran as a Unionist to continue the governing coalition of Tories and pro-conscription Liberals. The post-war demise of this Unionist government triggered the Conservatives' first splintering, giving birth to the original third party, the Progressives, who came second to Mackenzie King in 1921. These fractured politics created minorities throughout the 1920s until the Progressives faded away, electing their last MP in 1930, en route to reunification with the newly named Progressive Conservative Party.

As politics sorted itself out after the war, Liberals won minority mandates in 1921 and 1925, the latter ending in the infamous

King–Byng affair, when the governor general refused to honour King's request for an election. Instead, he installed Tory Arthur Meighen as PM, who was immediately defeated by the House with King winning the election that followed.

The 1957 election ended 22 years of Liberal majority rule under King and Louis St.-Laurent, the longest uninterrupted one-party government so far, and Conservative John Diefenbaker won a minority mandate. It was helped along by the growth of two western populist parties born in the Depression: the CCF on the left and Social Credit on the right, which won 25 and 19 seats, respectively. On unfamiliar opposition benches, Liberals soon elected Lester Pearson leader.

The Diefenbaker minority was progressive and much more useful than the politics of entitlement St.-Laurent practised, which led to his stunned bewilderment that voters dared say enough. His comments in defeat at the time resemble today's Liberal explanations—at least in public—for how a party entitled to govern forever could have been so meanly cheated, but progressive people in the 1950s didn't mind much.

The first Diefenbaker government saw our first woman Cabinet minister in Ellen Fairclough and introduced advances like Unemployment Insurance. But it ended abruptly as Pearson, bizarrely, tried to replicate the King–Byng crisis and asked the governor general to make him PM instead. Diefenbaker seized on the stumble, called an election and won it in 1958 with a then-record 208 MPs. For the first time since 1887, Conservatives won Quebec, and went from nine to 50 MPs. Elsewhere, Diefenbaker all but wiped out the CCF, which limped out of the election with only eight seats and its worst finish ever—but what would be seen as a Green breakthrough.

The disastrous 1958 result ended the CCF's name and brought an alliance with organized labour to broaden its western base, vulnerable to Tory attack, into Ontario's industrial centres. A New Party was born in 1961, and fresh from a bitter doctors' strike and the big win of medicare, Tommy Douglas became the first leader of the soon-renamed New Democratic Party.

Come 1962, Diefenbaker was less popular and won only a minority. His government had difficulty functioning and a non-confidence motion passed in 1963 to trigger an election, which Pearson won with his own minority. The Douglas–Pearson minority was legendary, and its medicare and pension policies are cornerstone social policy to this day. It was such good stuff that Pearson called a snap election in 1965 to end the progress, capitalize on it and try to wipe the young NDP out. Voters demurred and returned a second minority instead, which lasted three years before Trudeaumania in 1968, and another early election call to end a minority.

Unpopular in the West, Trudeau never won consecutive majorities, and after 1972 was left with a minority with David Lewis holding the feeding tube. He set a high price for support, and the NDP won a new national affordable housing program, the foreign investment review agency and Petro-Canada, to provide some domestic ballast against the oil crisis. By 1974, Trudeau was rehabilitated in the polls and introduced a budget designed for the NDP to oppose, and he won a majority. The NDP lost half its seats, and won only 16 in an election dominated by inflation and the Tory proposal of wage-and-price controls to curb it. Liberals opposed them, which, with a majority once more they naturally introduced.

In 1979, Trudeau retired for the first time following Conservative Joe Clark's win, who said he'd govern as if he had a majority. He did not. Six months later, Trudeau had un-retired as the government fell on a budget opposed by Liberals, New Democrats and Creditistes. A Christmas election returned Trudeau with a majority in 1980, with 74 of 75 seats in Quebec. Politics' rules, however, were soon to change and the 1980 election is the last time that Liberals won Quebec.

Of the three populist parties—the CCF/NDP, Reform/Alliance and Social Credit—the NDP is the most enduring and consequential on a policy front. But only Social Credit branched into Quebec through an aligned cousin, which did better than the western Socreds, who petered out in the mid-Sixties. The Creditistes won 26 Quebec seats in 1962, a major reason why Diefenbaker was reduced to a minority as the Quiet Revolution began. They resurfaced after a hiatus as the Parti Québécois grew en route to its historic 1976 provincial election win.

The last six Creditiste seats were lost in 1980. The party's demise matters to our path ahead, and as Quebec shed its parochial past, Pearson's Liberals kept pace by recruiting figures like Trudeau. This stemmed the growth of the nationalist Creditistes. To Stop Harper winning his majority and keep ours intact, Quebec's required, and if Pearson could attract its most exciting people in the 1960s, we could always give it a shot. But not before determining how Liberals really lost, and using the possibility we now have.

Fast-forward 25 years from the last minority Parliament, and the most striking difference in how the 2006 election began is that the Liberal Party did not agree. This is rare, particularly after the Second World War, and 2006 was only the fourth in 20 post-war elections fought on a timeline Liberals didn't like, with the other three following Tory majority governments. But as the winter guillotine approaches, they'd set in motion 16 of 19 post-war elections including those following six minorities which all ended when Liberals wanted.[12]

Habit was cemented by Liberals choosing when each of the three elections prior to 2006 occurred, which were all called when Liberals sniffed a win in the air. In 1997, the election was called three and a half years into a majority during a major flood in Manitoba, and the election in 2000 began with the year's second budget. In 2004, scandal or no, the long-desired Martin timeline remained intact.

None of the three Liberal majorities elected since 1993 passed the four-year mark and each, despite large surpluses from the late 1990s on, left key components—pollution cuts, child care and prescription

---

12. The 1945, 1949, 1953, 1957, 1972, 1979, 1984, 1997, 2000 and 2004 elections all followed Liberal majorities when they decided the date, just as 1962, 1988 and 1993 followed Tory majority Parliaments. The 1963 and 1980 elections flowed from non-confidence motions supported by the Liberals; 1965 and 1968 were called by Liberals in a minority situation. This leaves 1974, begun as Liberals wanted via a budget designed to elicit NDP opposition, and 1958 when Pearson inexplicably tried to be appointed PM. It's debatable whether Liberals wanted the election, but that they tried to change government isn't.

drugs—of their alleged agenda undone. It is pure piffle that an alleged early election in 2006 stopped progress, which lagged as Liberals wanted for more than a decade. If one so-so year out of 12 isn't the best we think we can do, we need to get over how the most recent election began, and focus on how to win future ones.

It's not easy, though, and losing an apparent right to decide when voters may judge Liberals caused many who use its frame to lose perspective over what's to come. For so long, Liberals were used to politics following the path most convenient to their needs and, at the end of the second-longest stretch of the same party governing in history, couldn't imagine this changing. In reality, the events of the fall were less monumental than Liberals portray.

How we see what follows depends on the partisan frame we use. Was it shameless partisanship to cash in on Liberal distress and bring a productive minority House down? Or a shot at the most orderly end to a minority in history on a timeline first outlined by the prime minister, which allowed progressive progress to happen before the House fell?

Events in a
Progressive Summer

A S MPs PREPARED to return to Ottawa in fall 2005, its landscape had changed from the one they left to begin the recess. Events in the summer of celebration for progressive people had altered things come fall. What was true in May wasn't by November, though Liberals kept this gem well under wraps. When MPs left a warm, lush Parliament Hill in June, the next election was set to begin in January based on Paul Martin's televised promise to call one 30 days after the second report from Justice John Gomery, then scheduled to arrive on December 1.

But as parties returned to the capital after the progressive summer, events changed things and left May and June as the two lonely months when what could have been a progressive House actually was. The biggest was a switch to Gomery's schedule, which would now present a second report on February 1, 2006. No longer would findings into Liberal scandal come in quick succession with the first outlining what went wrong, and the second, steps to clean up the mess.

There was now a three-month lag between them, with a period over Christmas and into January, when the House wouldn't even sit. In February, Liberals could present their platform as a budget, receive the second Gomery report long after the damning first, and then kindly permit voters to judge them on a good news budget in the election called in March. Those weren't the terms that Paul Martin suggested in the spring, and trying to apply a fly-by-night promise then to a calendar newly beneficial for Liberals now—well, it proved presumptive. A majority would have fixed all that, of course, but sadly, voters didn't want another Liberal majority because they were mighty fed up with them.

Even without the change in Gomery's date, Parliament entered autumn in a sorry state thanks to Martin, who when facing a crisis that seemed unstoppable in April, called an election eight months away. This added to the already strange factors at play, and created something similar to the long pre-election periods that fixed election dates have brought to BC and Ontario.

But an apparently revised election timetable wasn't the only change that autumn delivered. The always-pesky House math also changed and brought with it new hurdles. Chuck Cadman had sadly passed away in July, and the vote on the budget was his last in Parliament. The queer movement's pressure on Martin for an early vote on equal marriage also drove Pat O'Brien from the Liberal caucus, and Manitoba MP Bev Desjarlais left the NDP in October after losing the party's nomination in her riding.

The one bit of good news for Liberals was that they won a by-election in Labrador, but the net change to the budget team's votes from spring was minus two. As the pantomime underlined, there was no margin for error, and any Tories looking to join Belinda Stronach on the Liberal benches almost certainly would have bolted by now.

This created a conundrum for the NDP. Unlike previous minorities, it was without a balance of power, but not having it didn't allow it to duck the question of confidence, which that pesky math said was symbolic. In a House with a Liberal speaker, 154 opposition MPs win a vote and the new House math had Conservatives with 98, the Bloc with 54 and two Independent MPs who had left the Liberals in disgust. If they all voted no-confidence, it didn't matter where the NDP went.

As politics' new rules continued to flow from Sheila Fraser's report, New Democrats had only enough numbers to control their own destiny, not Parliament's—much like a waterslide chute realizing gravity was stronger than its sides in holding back the tide. What could get done in the four Parliamentary weeks in February that led directly into an election call was also murky.

And then there was the immovable reality of pesky House math, which gave the NDP even less leverage than the spring. In sum, it was going to need convincing of the need to support Liberals for a few weeks. How credit was allocated for the NDP budget didn't provide much incentive, and as the progressive summer wore on, New Democrats were reminded how Lester Pearson, not their icon, was often seen to be behind Canada winning medicare.

Over the summer, Liberals announced the NDP budget with scant mention of how these good things came to be. Listening to Liberal ministers and watching their string of photo-ops of money they tried to spend on surprise corporate tax cuts, it was as if lefty priorities were theirs all along. Infrastructure Minister John Godfrey shared the credit when announcing new public transit initiatives—once, before being reined in—but New Democrats saw the underbelly to minorities they knew well unfolding. The NDP budget wasn't a Liberal creation, and Martin had as little business claiming credit for it as he did announcing that a new one was on the way.

In the lead-up to the First Ministers' meeting on Aboriginal issues, the NDP budget became particularly contentious and Liberals, New Democrats and Aboriginal groups fought in public over whether NDP funds added to, not subtracted from, what Liberals had already pledged. Everything was sorted in the end, but it served as a reminder of the danger of sidling up to Liberals mere months from contesting an election against them.

As you'd expect for the West's dominant progressive party, the NDP also began the fall under increasing attack from Conservatives, who used the budget deal as proof that New Democrats tolerated Liberal corruption. In BC and Saskatchewan in particular, Stephen

Harper portrayed his party as the dependable Ottawa scrubber-upper, and New Democrats faced a troubling future of watching anti-Liberal votes coalescing behind Tories. All in all, a difficult autumn seemed in store for the NDP after the recent good times.

For its part, the Bloc's mood hadn't changed much from the spring, saying Liberals had lost the moral authority to govern, but that it couldn't move on a non-confidence motion. Harper stopped recognizing Liberal legitimacy after they refused to resign as the House had voted in May. Lastly, Martin wanted to show he still had things to do, and pointed to an annual U.N. meeting on climate change upcoming in Montreal[13] and November's First Ministers' meeting on Aboriginal issues in Kelowna, BC as proof.

The Supreme Court again seemed set to top the agenda, following a potentially sweeping decision on June 9 about public health care. The Chaoulli decision, named for the Montreal doctor behind the case, ruled if the public health system could not provide timely service, citizens had the right to buy private health insurance for treatment outside it.

Its immediate impact was felt only in Quebec as the Court ruled its ban on private insurance contravened its provincial Charter of Rights. With other provincial bans unaffected by a ruling based on Quebec's Charter, the Chaoulli decision's national impact was only implied. Had Martin's 2006 election promise to eliminate the notwithstanding clause come true, Parliament wouldn't be able to do anything should a future Court ruling ever hurt health care across Canada.

The case became a magnet for health policy advocates on both sides of the non-profit debate as Chaoulli was overtly supported by

---

13. Of all the NDP's alleged sins, allegedly pushing for an early election during the Kyoto conference is the most spurious charge. This recklessness supposedly propelled Elizabeth May to seek the Green leadership, as if progress at a global meeting is hurt by a local election. Nor was this the Haley's comet of summits, but a yearly thing: in 2006 it was in Kenya, and in 2004 Argentina hosted it. After a dozen years of Liberal climate damage, it's myopic to think that one more meeting in Canada without an election underway would make them get serious. If May wants to get into an effectiveness battle, there's also the $900 million for efficiency and transit in the NDP budget. More could be wrung from Liberals, and was, which is strangely glossed over in May's revisionism—perhaps because she was happy with less.

some of Canada's most prominent advocates of a greater role for profit in health care, including Liberal Senator Michael Kirby. As fall arrived, many felt the Liberals had yet to provide a response to the Court decision as the impacts of it rolled up into a very Liberal ball.

For their part, Liberals pointed to the September 2004 health accord they said preemptively fixed everything through an agreement on wait times. The root of the Chaoulli ruling, they contended, was that unduly long wait times were prohibited, which put any benchmark on wait times, though voluntary, from the Liberals squarely at the fore.

Generously, it's circuitous logic. Cheerleaders for more profit in health care, such as Kirby, were also behind the Liberals' new fixation with wait times. This new approach could either be seen as prophetic brilliance in addressing wait times, or a self-fulfilling prophecy that profit would pour into the health system in the most direct threat to single-payer public health care since Douglas and Pearson took the system national.[14]

As the winter guillotine approaches, these events shaped how the last portion of the budget—the orphaned wage protection fund—came to pass the House after its long trek from the dingy room in West Block. The events of a progressive summer also ended up dividing us more, as Harper transformed himself from weak, irrelevant and wrong in the spring to prime minister by February with enough blame to go around, but often not directed at the party he defeated in many progressive eyes.

---

14. In one absurdity, Liberals ran a Tory MLA in Winnipeg against the federal Tory health critic. The federal Tory supported the Canada Health Act, while his Tory-cum-Liberal opponent was a firm opponent. We don't need to know who won to know that health care didn't, but such are the travesties of the meaningless middle. Former Alliance leadership candidate Keith Martin—now a Liberal MP—is also opposed to this supposed Liberal value. But hey, Vote Liberal, maybe we'll get an okay one.

Ghosts of Springs Past   11

A S FALL BEGAN in earnest, the spring's wild ride proved to have a hidden effect. For anyone under 50 the minority Parliament was the first real one of their life. Joe Clark's brief premiership showed how temperamental federal minorities could be, but not the co-operative element progressives fondly recall. The spring's budget deal had brought something Ottawa hadn't seen since David Lewis and Pierre Trudeau in the 1970s: a kind-of working minority government.

This long wait fed disappointment as the Parliament ended, and with it, the best chance to win short of shrinking the Liberal Party considerably. Thankfully, as politics' new rules keep flowing, that's easier than they let on with plenty of productive minorities as real progressive parties earn their stripes. Liberals are already out of power, and if their last dozen years isn't the best we think we can do—or the litany of majorities before that—could show some spine when the chips are down, and challenge the Liberal hegemony mirage so we can really challenge Harper. But the Parliament's not done yet. The most contentious part is ahead.

For the NDP, the novelty of a minority both hurt and helped. On the helpful front, it was now seen as a quasi-king maker with more attention than normal. Long-suffering for platforms, this was welcome for New Democrats, whose size makes most of their public image reactive. The party has enough MPs to be asked what it thinks but can rarely shape the agenda, which sometimes leaves the impression it focuses on issues it rather wouldn't. This helps make newer parties seem more appealing, but the same plague will get them, too, as the PC Party can attest during the right's division.

Within the NDP, purer policy is often seen as the big fix and after the 2006 election, Jim Laxer wrote an article in *The Walrus* magazine that questioned the party's ideological direction. The debate about leftish or lefter is popular but ignores that until politics is reframed, it's likely self-defeating. Without being able to focus debate on issues it picks as Liberals currently can, ideological purity might be secondary for the same reason the NDP often doesn't frame what elections are about: the party's not big enough.

Some of the frustration at how key issues are overlooked helps make having more debate popular, and occasionally morphs into believing we'd be breathing cleaner air if only seatless Greens were let into leaders' debates. But we've been debating climate change for almost 30 years now and it doesn't lack attention. That battle's won. With emissions soaring, it lacks action. Undeterred, we press on, but troublingly not to win power to do something about it. Instead, we often strive for more attention in the hope that someone in Ottawa will listen, or help Liberals come back to do it all over again. It hasn't worked often, and now's the time to set sights higher: aiming to solve problems, not speak about solutions.

Chances to draw debate to issues—better still, change policy— were rare and welcomed by New Democrats who spent the early fall outlining things they'd like to get done. But without a sensible framing of politics that lets the largest progressive side mean it, elections often see the loudest lefty argument being whatever Liberals prefer. It's usually seen on health care, but the issue is not alone. Often the problem isn't that Liberals don't deserve to be the lefty champion on whatever they like to bring up in elections. Sometimes, the problem is what's overlooked altogether.

Consider human rights. In recent elections, debate has focused on where parties stand on Court-demanded equality like equal marriage, without much focus on civil liberties concerns such as Maher Arar being deported to Syria for torture, or the related RCMP raid on *Ottawa Citizen* reporter Juliet O'Neill's home. (Also, a good example of what happens when the fourth estate doesn't probe The Establishment enough.) Though Alexa McDonough did bring the Arar case inside Parliament, the party couldn't broaden the story to cover its legislative—and Liberal—roots.

Paul Martin's first foreign trip as PM coincided with the raid on O'Neill's home. In Switzerland, at one of the world's more right-leaning forums, Martin was asked if he thought she was a criminal. Clearly not, he sputtered, after voting for the law used to criminalize her and appointing its author, former Justice Minister Anne McLellan, to oversee the RCMP and security service. Both the Bloc and NDP voted against the law in the midst of the rush to restrict civil liberties following the 9/11 terrorist attacks on the United States.

And let's not forget—Liberals initially blocked the Arar inquiry and had to be dragged kicking into it by McDonough, in her finest hour. After then overseeing the blacking-out of the inquiry they didn't want, they rushed to pronounce outrage as Justice Dennis O'Connor presented his findings. Eventually, we've got to stop letting Liberals pick up the narrative when it suits them, and judge things more holistically. If there's a party that frightens me on civil liberties, it's the Liberals, who believe in so little they'll do almost anything to keep up to enraged public opinion. Worse, turn around and present themselves as champions of liberty after helping erode it.

The NDP also opposed their War Measures Act of 1970, which brought in martial law to respond to isolated separatist violence in Quebec and shows history's power on the progressive mess we're in. For younger Canadians, Trudeau is a hero, and his legacy shapes us today; people born after the Charter in 1982 have voted in up to three elections and are entering their mid-twenties. But there were also the hunted, an older generation driven into hiding as civil liberties were suspended nation-wide. Winners get to write history, and the Liberal version tends to skip over quite a bit.

Like health care, it's tough for the NDP to mount pressure against Liberals on issues like civil liberties. It is also a joint effort, in a chicken-and-the-egg kind of thing, and the NDP needs external help to drive a progressive point home. Our rethink shouldn't gloss over this because small parties can't create political space alone, and it's a collective failing that we've yet to really bring debate onto our turf. But as fall progressed, the danger of the Chaoulli decision prompted the NDP to nonetheless try to show how Liberals were being less than true to Douglas's legacy. Who knew? Perhaps like the budget a progressive win was again possible, even as Parliament's life drew short.

The party's challenge was magnified by the Liberals' dominance, which lets them often appear to valiantly protect public health care from the profiteering marauders in the Conservatives. This frame doesn't fit facts such as Liberals explicitly allowing Alberta Premier Ralph Klein's first large experiment with profit. It also ignores that Liberals deleted part of the Canada Health Act to make privatizing easier, and after running three elections against more profit in health care, hadn't changed a thing to help halt its spread.

Indeed, that health debate all but ends at support for the Canada Health Act says it all, for the law was brought in to stop extra billing by doctors, not prevent massive privatization. Using it as a proxy for real health vision is like saying Star Wars is all right because it doesn't violate the landmines treaty. The question isn't do we want profit, but how much of it, as more meaningful debate slips by, thanks to two-sided debates where the bigger progressive side doesn't mean it.

Embarrassingly, it's as good as debate gets in a string of elections, but in truth the main difference between Liberal and Tory health policy is the rhetoric. They're substantially identical. In 2006, the biggest Conservative health plank was to guarantee the outcome of the Liberals' plan, whose platform again was silent on ways to keep more of health care non-profit. But with the Chaoulli decision so large, the NDP chose to use it to try and wring more change from Martin to protect public medicare better, while saying it would be happy to work on a real Kyoto plan, protecting pensions and voting reform, too. Trying to change something was the upside of newfound NDP clout.

It came with a downside, and after the budget pantomime, it was perceived as propping the Liberals up and enjoying a balance of power. Neither was technically true—the budget deal expired in July, and the NDP never had the balance of power—but both seemed close enough. This perception, which it couldn't fight and eventually decided to use, was fed by Harper continuing his mantra that the Dippers' tolerance for corruption would set when the election began. A last Tory laugh from the budget treachery of spring.

The situation was complicated by low legislative stakes, as even with the revised Gomery timeline, only 14 Commons' sitting weeks were left before an election. Yes, the great early election call of 2006 wiped out all of four weeks of MPs in Ottawa. All parties saw these additional weeks as nothing more than a pre-election bonus for Liberals, since with holidays tacked on, they represented two months of pre-electioneering that could only help them. A party with 36 per cent of the vote wanted 100 per cent control over when it would be judged. It held up a panicked TV promise from the PM as to why.

As the House resumed on September 26, Tony Valeri's office had yet to release the schedule of opposition days, which Gomery's change made newly important. A non-confidence motion moved on one of these days was now all that stood between an election roughly on the timeline Martin first wanted, or the new date well into March. On this later timetable, Liberals would have a two-month, multi-billion-dollar head-start on the 2006 election. The Conservatives, Bloc and disgusted former Liberal MPs had exactly enough votes to deny this dream re-election scenario.

September turned into October and Thanksgiving loomed as time ticked on, whittling away precious weeks and still the opposition day schedule was a well-guarded secret. It became a fixation, as Valeri's office kept delaying deadlines by which it had promised to release it. In the spring, the key question surrounding opposition days was which party would sponsor them, but the fall changed the focus to when they would happen.

Ottawa became obsessed with the opposition day schedule, for unless Liberals did the inexplicable and placed one on November 3, there were only two possibilities. Liberals could schedule the days before November 1 and dare the opposition to trigger an election before Gomery's report, or put them afterwards. Factoring in the Remembrance Day break, this put the earliest confidence opportunity on November 16 with six more opposition days after that before Christmas.

If Liberals waited until then to allow confidence to be tested, the only way to stop Gomery's eight-week gift from being opened would be for the opposition to call an election over Christmas and nix the upcoming First Ministers' meeting[15] along the way. Finally, the schedule was released, and put the first opposition day on November 16. Liberals unveiled it nervously, expecting a repeat of the anger that surrounded opposition days in the spring. They were surprised by how cavalierly the opposition took the news, but as things unfolded, the shock proved unfounded.

As his precision-like march through the first week of the election made clear, Harper was ready to go. If Liberals thought a holiday election would cause the Conservatives and Bloc to rethink the wisdom of allowing Martin a free pass until March, boy, were they wrong. This was Harper's last chance as leader, the Bloc's fortunes never looked better and neither supported Martin's preferred election timetable in the spring and weren't about to start now, particularly given the new House math. And it was highlighted by the opposition's pre-election campaigns.

The early fall saw Ottawa gearing up for an election coming sooner or later, and the three opposition parties unveiled their slogans. The

15. The meeting itself was scheduled two months late. At the September 2004 First
    Ministers' meeting on health care, a subsequent one on Aboriginal issues was pledged
    within the year.

Conservatives chose "Stand up for Canada," aimed squarely at scandal's impact in Quebec, where Harper had invested much time in the sure knowledge it held his majority key. Tories were trying to get going again in Quebec, en route to replacing Liberals as its dominant federalist party. Other key issues for Tories were lower taxes, a crackdown on crime and a wholesale cleansing of Ottawa after a dozen years of Liberals troughing it.

Scandal dominated the Bloc's slogan, too, and it unveiled a fall campaign of the greatest hits from the Gomery Inquiry to remind Quebecers of what they heard in the spring, sometimes clambering over each other in public galleries in Montreal. While their 2004 election slogan blurred corruption with separation, the Bloc's pre-election campaign tagline in fall 2005 was equally clever. "*Je me souviens*," or "I remember," it said, in the words René Lévesque had stamped on licence plates in the 1970s, as sovereigntists continued to profit from the sponsorship scandal's fallout.

Summer 2005 was busy for Gilles Duceppe, and as we ponder progressive tactics, we can't overlook why. With the Liberal scandal helping sovereignty to soar, the Bloc was on a roll. Its provincial cousin, the Parti Québécois, was also benefitting from the scandal's fallout but also from progressive anger over Jean Charest's conservative reforms. Less pronounced than elsewhere, they were Quebec's version of what Alberta and Ontario experienced in the 1990s; and in BC under Premier Gordon Campbell.

Small-l liberal sentiment and resentment at big-L Liberal corruption mixed together for an exciting summer for Duceppe. The Bloc was soaring, sovereignty was on the rise as P.Q. Leader Bernard Landry stepped down as the party, high in the polls, again devoured a leader. Immediately, Duceppe became the front-runner for the job, outpacing his rivals to such a scale that he would have none should he choose to go to Quebec City, instead of being lead negotiator in Ottawa as Quebec separated and prepared to elect a president.

He went for negotiator, and a messy brawl erupted for the P.Q. leadership. Among the eight candidates, two emerged as front-runners, including longtime Cabinet minister Pauline Marois, who demanded that Landry step down and said that she wanted his job. Her rival was the youthful, openly gay former Cabinet minister André Boisclair who hung out at Harvard. Marois was the old hardline separatist and Boisclair the new, as the sovereignty movement spread out and sought to take root in almost the first generation of global Quebec.

Like other cities, Montreal's diversity is growing, and it's a prime target of the new sovereignty movement. In the last four elections, the Bloc has elected MPs born in Cameroon, Chile and Haiti, in a rebuke of how sovereigntists are often perceived, and also of former P.Q. Leader Jacques Parizeau's hateful referendum night rant in 1995 that blamed the tight loss on money and the ethnic vote. As urban Quebec changes, the sovereignty movement changes with it.

Electorally, it's assaulting the Montreal area to try and hive off some of its plentiful federalist votes that are essential to a future referendum win. The breakthrough has yet to occur, but sovereignty is globalizing and Boisclair represents its new face. Cocaine scandal or not, he won the P.Q. leadership on the first ballot. Martin's choice of Haitian-born Michaëlle Jean as governor general was widely seen as smart in helping federalism respond to this new threat. For federalism it may have been, but for Liberals it was too late. Harper is now lead negotiator with Quebec. It's a big nut, and to win we have to crack it.

Boisclair and Duceppe marched towards the 2006 election on a wave of apparent invincibility. The Bloc's platform was a blueprint for Quebec assuming federal powers and come the election, the Bloc's confidence spoke for itself. *"Heuresement, ici c'est le Bloc"* the signs and ads all read: Fortunately, the Bloc is here. So deep was the anger towards Liberal scandal in Quebec, nothing more needed to be said.

The NDP harkened back to the spring like the Bloc, but with a different take. At an October conference, it unveiled "Getting results for people" and tried to remind voters of the tangible impacts of voting NDP they had just seen in a rewritten budget.

At the conference, Layton set out the party's path for the fall. "If these Liberals want to get to work on issues like those I've mentioned, we'll be there in the weeks to come," he said. "If not, Mr. Martin should understand he better not count on the NDP's support in those weeks to come." In blunt terms, Layton repeated what he said in the spring: Implement NDP items or don't count on us to keep Liberals away from voters. With it, New Democrats embarked on a path with two possible answers to the question the autumn wouldn't ignore: Do you have confidence in the Liberals?

The NDP's fall couldn't please everyone and some of the resulting anger made the election more challenging. The genuine hope of a progressive minority Parliament turned into frustration at the prospect of its demise, and Buzz Hargrove best exemplifies what fuelled anger at the time and the Think Twice coalition itself.

As Parliament's life grew short, Hargrove urged the NDP, Bloc and progressive Liberals to work together to keep the minority situation going for years. How this could work wasn't outlined, for even if Martin wanted to cleave his own party—or cleave it some more— he'd also long promised an election and Duceppe long demanded one. Wanting a world where everything was defined by progressive issues, Hargrove refused to see corruption, separation or the NDP's size combining to make this Parliament's life short-lived. Or any constellation of failings that made Liberals undeserving of more time in office.

This Think Twice view harmed the NDP in the election, but Hargrove came to be bothered by it as well, specifically CAW's endorsement of the Bloc.[16] As the 21st century began, many anglo progressives saw the Bloc as primarily an ally, not folks out to break up the federation, and essentially contracted out federal politics to Duceppe in Quebec. In critiquing NDP tactics, lefties like Jim Laxer and Jim Stanford leave the Bloc's role in triggering an election aside, despite it having three times the clout of New Democrats. But what might work

16. In December 2005, the CAW explicitly endorsed the Bloc's 75 candidates in Quebec. Hargrove's comments at the Liberal rally flowed from this endorsement and were not off-the-cuff.

in abstract is often harder to do for real, as Hargrove discovered in the 2006 election, when he suggested that Quebecers Vote Bloc to Stop Harper. At a Liberal rally.

As Martin distanced himself and the imbroglio led the news, Hargrove altered his long-held views. Instead of respecting Quebec's right to choose its own progressive vehicle in the Bloc, he now began advising Quebecers to Vote Liberal to defeat Conservatives. At the time, so dim were his hopes, Martin wasn't campaigning in Quebec, giving Hargrove's invitation all the appeal of a last fling on the *Hindenburg*. It's an alarm sounding on the urgency for a progressive, federalist alternative that we have the opportunity to build.

When theory collided with the complex dynamics we face, Hargrove met the harsh realities that, comfortable or not, exist. Harper's win didn't come about when or how Liberals say, however, and neither did their demise. It did not begin in the fall, but in the two preceding springs—Sheila Fraser's report and Jean Brault's testimony—and politics' new rules haven't stopped since. As ghosts of springs past came to haunt our hopes, Layton faced a choice on a vote that neither he, nor Hargrove, could control.

In the end, NDP MPs made their choice based on issues, as they had in the spring, and demanded the biggest thing that could be passed by a vote that wouldn't test confidence. With no budget options before it, the NDP decided its support for Liberals would depend on their willingness to rewrite the rules of medicare in response to June's Chaoulli decision. It was Douglas's program and his descendents decided it needed a bit of an update.

Unless Liberals would attach new conditions to health care transfers to stop funds from going to for-profit care, the NDP wouldn't vote confidence. If New Democrats were going to endorse Liberals' preferred election timing and get tagged with their scandal, sweeping new health rules were required. Martin had once called this the fight of his life, and if Liberals refused to protect public medicare, New Democrats would not help elect Liberals. That was the job of the Liberal leader. The NDP's Douglas frame clearly saw progress in defeating Liberal candidates, as their icon did well in 1944 when he first removed them from office in Saskatchewan.

After some public haranguing made worse by the pre-election mood, Layton and Martin met at 24 Sussex Drive on October 22. The NDP had four ways it wanted provincial transfers for health care changed, which are Ottawa's only enforcement tool on health policy. If the NDP's new federal conditions on health funding were implemented, they would be the first since the Canada Health Act was passed in 1984, thanks in part to pressure from Bill Blaikie, then the NDP's health critic. It now tried again.

The meeting at 24 Sussex resolved nothing, but the tone was open enough to arrange a second meeting between NDP health critic Jean Crowder and Health Minister Ujjal Dosanjh. Crowder left the NDP's written objectives with Dosanjh, awaiting a response. The deadline was November 3, two days after Gomery's first report, partly to provide the cooler conditions of a House break should crisis erupt upon arrival. New Democrats had seen Parliamentary collapse once before and wanted to control as many variables as their small numbers could.

On November 1, Gomery released his first report. Like Fraser before, he didn't mince words in describing a kickback scheme that funnelled government funds into Liberal coffers. A culture of entitlement existed, he said, and Jean Brault's searing testimony from April was substantially true. The Liberal Party repaid more than $1 million in ill-gotten funds and suspended 10 members for life, but the report again ignited a political firestorm.

The opposition howled as accusations formerly dismissed as wonky words on the stand were now judge-stamped facts. It was a kickback scheme, and national unity was threatened thanks to it. Tories focused on the tens of millions of dollars still missing, the Bloc was out for names of Quebec Liberal MPs who accepted graft for their campaigns, and together they hurled abuse at Liberals. Martin and Public Works Minister Scott Brison pointed to the repaid funds, and some reforms made after the program was cancelled. Martin also reminded that he called the Gomery inquiry itself, shortly before the

2004 election that he also called—in the midst of a Bloc revival. The latter fact was somehow forgotten.

The NDP frothed as well and before the report came out, released its own ethics plan, written by "Honest Ed" Broadbent. It called for toughened conflict-of-interest rules around corporate lobbyists, proportional representation to make entitlement mentality rarer, and a ban on MPs joining other parties without a by-election. The Tories released their ethics plan soon afterwards, with many similar goals, though different approaches to democratic reform.

Party caucuses meet on Wednesdays, and, one day after Gomery's report, election fever was about. Duceppe said the Bloc would vote non-confidence as soon as it could, while Harper said Liberals lacked MPs' confidence and were afraid to test it. He lashed out at the NDP, too.

In one angry outburst telling of how the West was shaping up, Harper dared Layton to demand that Liberals test confidence, or risk displaying contempt for British Columbians. Polls showed an emerging race between the two in BC, although conventional wisdom said a Liberal minority was likely given polling numbers weren't in spring-like freefall. The sense that another Liberal minority was probable held until the campaign's third week, and as the government fell, Liberals enjoyed a rough five-point lead on Tories in media polls; the NDP was flat as the Bloc inched up.

The House had yet to pass Bill C-55, the orphaned legislation to protect workers' wages included in the NDP budget. Nor was the Bloc the only party that had reverted to old ways. Liberal dithers were also back, and Parliament soon became inactive. In addition to failing to pass wage protection quickly, long-delayed Chrétien laws such as decriminalizing pot possession for adults also languished. And why not? Martin had no incentive to be busy. The more left undone, the more that would be lost if the government fell, which would make campaigning a breeze, chalking up any damage to the opposition. Perish the thought that Liberals would ever stoop to consider partisan gain, of course.

In addition to Bill C-55, rising oil prices worldwide highlighted Bill C-66, a something-for-everyone law that provided rebates to low-income people to help with heating bills in winter, partly through energy efficiency.

MPs were also tepidly dealing with changes to the voting system, and Broadbent, working with Democratic Reform Minister Mauril Bélanger, won unanimous support from a House committee for the first federal study on changing how elections work. As if to underline that little had changed, Martin killed it and refused to act, infuriating MPs from all sides. In vintage form, he ran for Liberal leader on a pledge of more democracy, but blocked an all-party step forward on the aspect of it that involves voters. It added to the volatile mix at play, as Liberals denied Parliament's wishes while demanding it respect their choice for an election.

Nineteen months after Fraser first decried the sponsorship scandal, Gomery's report tightened the grip of politics' new rules on the minority Parliament. Ghosts of springs past had arrived and sat ready to pounce, facing a party in office for a dozen years that did not control the House, and habitually ignored its advice. A winter guillotine loomed. It was Martin's last choice as prime minister.

A Clumsy Dance 12

JUSTICE JOHN GOMERY released his report on Tuesday, just be-fore Thursday's deadline on health talks, and the NDP was under concerted pressure to demand an election. With votes not allowed on Fridays, the only way for an election to be over before Christmas was to call one this week, as anything afterwards would put one into January. This displeased Stephen Harper and Gilles Duceppe, who demanded a confidence test for a government they said lacked moral authority, which all put New Democrats back in the cross-hairs anew.

If the House collapsed, Bills C-55 and C-66 and the First Ministers' meeting on Aboriginal people would go with it. Cognizant of this, like Paul Martin in the spring, Jack Layton asked for time. In the days following the Gomery report, the NDP stuck tight to its health talks, saying it decided confidence based on issues and that if progress could be made then it would help. Layton refused to attend a joint press conference with Harper and Duceppe to demand the Liberals test the House's confidence.

Late on Thursday, the Bloc seized the Commons agenda in a rare and airtight filibuster that gave it control over what the House did, which it decided would be talk about the scandal. Duceppe alone now controlled whether bills could be introduced or voted upon, and his control lasted as long as he liked.[17]

The Liberals' health offer was given to the NDP very late on Thursday night, but it brought little reprieve as there were still 11 days before the first Conservative motion on November 16. This gave Harper plenty of time to sit, say he was ready to go when the NDP was, and allow Layton to choose his poison. Eventually, he was going to have to say where New Democrats stood on confidence and with it become instigator of an election or collaborator in corruption, without enough votes to mean much to Parliament's palliative state.

Layton took the weekend to review the counterproposal and ponder the situation Parliament was now in. Time was not the NDP's friend. In a speech on Monday, he delivered his response to the Liberal health proposals—such as waiting a decade for new conditions on transfers—saying they were plainly insufficient to respond to the Chaoulli ruling and so weak they couldn't be made better. The NDP's proposal was an all-or-nothing suggestion, and Liberals had said no. The party stepped up preparations for the election, which was already coming soon, and was now certain to arrive.

If it was unfair for Martin to wear a scandal in which he was exonerated but his party was condemned, New Democrats felt it was a bigger injustice for them. Liberals created the scandal, and it was their job to elect Liberal candidates in its wake, or that of any other failings. The NDP spent no time fretting if they could and, indeed, hoped to defeat many Liberals itself as Douglas first did.

Nothing could get done legislatively in the New Year, both due to time and inevitable pre-electioneering, and with confidence tests coming before then, the New Democratic Party saw itself as independent from the Liberal Party. Not an appendage. Layton said he couldn't express confidence, though did not call for an election. Nor would he

17. Only Liberals ending the Parliamentary session could end the Bloc filibuster. All legislation would have to be re-introduced before passing, and Parliament would have to re-open with a throne speech. The certainty of a throne speech defeat and constitutional crisis that ending a Parliamentary session without testing the confidence would bring caused Liberals to rule prorogation out in October.

reveal the subject of the NDP's own opposition day on November 24. The speech was widely seen as ending NDP support for the Liberals, though the budget deal that bound them together expired in July.

Afterwards, the opposition continued its clumsy dance towards an election that had begun in press conferences the week before. The NDP was less of a free agent now than it had been as the Gomery report was delivered, but the distrust first displayed during the throne speech spat and which magnified several-fold during the budget's pantomime now loomed large.

Duceppe's position was clear. The Bloc would vote non-confidence at the first opportunity, but needed another party to move the motion, as one from a party out to break up Canada couldn't pass. In control of the House, it was going to have a confidence vote or there would be no votes at all, putting either Harper or Layton in the glare of being the first to say they were moving a motion. The question of which federalist would go first became a hot potato, as they frantically tried to offload responsibility for a Christmas election onto each other. Sometimes, comparisons between the Hill and kindergarten are fair. The potato proved hot to be sure as it was tossed back and forth.

The clumsy dance continued through Monday and Tuesday as Harper tried to narrow Layton's options and obtain NDP support for a Conservative non-confidence motion. Layton's speech was passive, saying that New Democrats wouldn't express confidence if asked, but weren't going to actively pursue Parliament's end, either. Though clear on how the party would vote on a confidence test, the opposition's bad couple of first dates left Harper unwilling to call the NDP's bluff.

As he tried to pin the NDP down, Layton played for time to try and find a way out of the box he and the Parliament were now in. A decent analogy to the disintegrating House is the guns of August scenario that began the First World War, when a series of disconnected events fused and picked up steam, creating an unstoppable crisis. Politics' new rules kept snowballing. The situation was untenable, and Martin was a by-stander—without control of the House numerically and, thanks to the Bloc filibuster, procedurally, too.

All party leaders had planned pre-election tours in the Remembrance Day break, and by midweek Layton was in Vancouver. Unwilling to stand with Liberals and facing a possible non-confidence motion on Tuesday, the NDP decided to take Harper up on his months-long contention that it would determine when the government fell. If NDP numbers couldn't give it leverage, perhaps initiative could. For a second time, constitutional purists shuddered at what a strange Parliament contemplated next.

On Wednesday November 10, Layton became the first opposition leader to say his party was introducing a motion to end Parliament. The NDP would use its opposition day on November 24 to call on Martin to dissolve it in January for an election in February, he said, trying to wring every drop of leverage from his 18-member caucus. If they couldn't change whether an election was coming, perhaps they could shape how by being the first up to the plate.

Overjoyed with the spring's gambits, many progressives were dismayed. The NDP was now firmly opposed to Liberals being granted their preferred election timeline. This wasn't how a minority was supposed to work. The NDP should see its interests as communal: there to work for all until Liberals needed some seats or time, when it would be subsumed in the larger push to Stop Harper. Douglas progressives never concurred, and on this the frames can't agree, just as they differ on whether the Liberal Party is a good enough progressive vehicle.

Looked at through a Douglas frame, the opposition parties' eventual alliance was the surest bet for progressive accomplishment and prevented a one-sided pre-election period that would lead to fewer NDP MPs and possibly a Liberal majority, with the corresponding and ensuing disaster in Quebec all but certain. Looked at in a Liberal one, the alliance hurt hegemony and therefore was good for Harper as frames collided in November and bitter progressive division resulted.

To try and prevent Harper announcing his own motion of non-confidence and with the Pacific time zone working against it as the day unfolded further east, Layton's Vancouver statement was billed as containing clarity about what the NDP would do next. The Tories and Bloc were contacted as the day began in Ottawa, advising them to pay close attention, as all hopes lay on the proposal gaining traction. With no legal standing, if written off by Harper and Duceppe as a non-starter upon delivery, then Parliament would assuredly fall on Tuesday. There could be no turning back now. For a second time, New Democrats jumped without a parachute for what was left of their budget.

In an often crazy minority Parliament filled with firsts, the NDP tried to add one more. Without the constitutional authority to ask, but nothing stopping the prime minister from saying yes, it suggested that a Parliamentary vote set election timing; not a fly-by-night televised promise in the spring, which had no legal standing, either.

On the proposed timeline, Parliament would sit until the end of December to deal with legislation, and let the First Ministers' meeting on Aboriginal issues take place. Immediately following the Christmas break an election would be called for mid-February, allowing the second Gomery report to be heard before people voted, albeit not on the timeline Liberals preferred. The NDP reasoned it met the tests of a productive fall, avoided a Christmas election and gave a fairer opportunity for Liberals to be judged than the self-serving timeline they clung to in futility. True, the solutions part of the second Gomery report would land in mid-campaign, but the gap between the first report's damning revelations and election day was the same as Martin's promise from April.

The NDP called it a common-sense compromise. It protected things New Democrats and Liberals wanted to do. It also stopped the Liberal pre-election waltz that the Tories and Bloc would have had nothing of, and which didn't enthrall New Democrats, either. Whether a non-confidence motion would have come if the original Gomery timeline was unaltered is—as Donald Rumsfeld may say—an unknown unknown, but unlikely. Even had they wanted, the Tories and Bloc would have been hard-pressed to justify ending Parliament two weeks before the second report, and Liberals controlled the timing of opposition days in any event.

With the election timetable now changed, the NDP gamble rested on the Tories and Bloc being amenable to a productive fall if their key fear—the New Year's eight-week gift to Liberals—were prevented. As for Martin, the NDP reasoned, he would have a tough time explaining why anything was endangered when something could save them.

As he did in the spring, Layton sought the public sphere to raise pressure that the NDP's 18 MPs couldn't leverage alone, and he gambled on it. A progressive summer's events had changed how NDP influence could be applied. To protect its own budget, New Democrats needed new partners because Liberals weren't able to get laws through. The NDP doesn't hurt progressive interests solely because it doesn't do what Liberals want, and, indeed, another progressive party in the Bloc also helped get things done by compromising on election timing.

Their timeline would become the only way to protect things the NDP came under fire for trying to kill. And how lefties applied pressure shows the power of the Liberal frame. No longer in control of the House agenda and long since at the mercy of its votes, Liberals weren't in charge, but pressure was used as if they were, in a quasi one-party-state approach. Liberals had managed to convince many that because they once called the shots, they would forever. But this was true no longer and the Liberal Party did not control Parliament's fate, no matter how desperately it wished politics' new rules away.

In mulling over the race with Harper, how we choose the horse most likely to win matters. In deciding, a horse's dependability and efficacy likely count a lot, not whether it has won some earlier races. Few bettors at a racetrack get rich this way. Even Secretariat had to win a race once without winning one before.

As the winter guillotine approached, historical habit, not future possibilities, guided many progressive choices. Too often, only the Liberals' path was seen as workable, which in a multi-party democracy is limiting at best, and counter-productive at worst. Things had also changed since the spring, chiefly the irrelevance of Liberals to what is about to transpire, but also the question that Parliament had to answer. In the spring, MPs were asked if an election should come, but now were asked when it would happen. This made the NDP's small leverage work only on election timing, not prevention. It also changed the Parliamentary target against which progressive pressure could be applied from Liberal to Conservative—and the extra-Parliamentary target from Conservative to Liberal.

If politics is a tactical alliance towards goals, like progressives in loose alliance with Democrats against George W. Bush, a goal-oriented look at the fall made the Douglas frame more reliable. The Liberal frame only looked backwards at what control used to exist, while Douglas's looked forward to what progress could be made—ironically, with Harper's blessing given to items in the same NDP budget he voted against. It seemed a good idea to only parts of the left.

To create a common frame to apply pressure, we need to throw out what used to be true, and focus on what can be made true. In weighing options, we should wonder what might have happened if progressive pressure were applied in November on Liberals to accept the NDP's election timeline, not the reverse. The NDP's proposal was called a compromise but was largely seen as an ultimatum and in wondering how politics could look, imagine an autumn in which Martin is seen as the source of diktats and Harper open to reasonable compromise.

This is the polemic's only hypothetical question, but its subject is most raw as Douglas and Liberal frames paint vastly different versions of what happened. Which frame is correct is for progressive people to decide, but whichever it is, the facts aren't up for debate: A Liberal scandal fuelled sovereignty in Quebec, and Martin faced a Parliament in which combined Liberal and NDP votes would not carry the day. There's also something admittedly more debatable: unprecedented progressive opportunity that is possible after the events and election that follow end.

Two choices face progressive people in the present, however, as we alone could frame the election and decide when it began. We could have an election commencing in November or one starting in January; and an election seen as hasty, partisan, greedy and reckless or a dignified, productive and orderly end to a Parliament long-destined to conclude. We now know which won out in this battle of frames, but also that Moses couldn't help Liberals get their way. As the NDP unveiled its proposal, it took a deep breath and awaited reaction from its opposition counterparts.

Duceppe came first, and was skeptical though welcoming of anything that may get the two federalist leaders moving. Harper's reaction came a few hours later and called the proposal novel, saying he looked forward to hearing more on how it may work. Liberals were unusually silent until late in the day, as Ottawa tried to decide what to make of it all. But the NDP's suggestion was not written off and led to media stories the next day that a February election was in the works. Progressive people looked on aghast, as a Liberal minority we'd waited a long time for began to count down the last days of its short life.

That afternoon, the opposition leaders spoke separately by phone.

The Winter Guillotine Falls

13

THE OPPOSITION LEADERS met on Sunday, November 14 in Stephen Harper's offices in Parliament's Centre Block. In the days after Jack Layton unveiled the NDP's election timing proposal, a meeting was arranged. For the first time in seven months, the opposition was speaking again.

Gossip again covered Ottawa like the miserable chill of pre-winter that set in on the weekend. Media shivered outside Harper's official residence through Sunday morning, believing the leaders to be meeting there, in an ominous forecast of the glaciated trek that politics was about to follow. Winter elections are rare with good reason, conventional wisdom soon decided, as one of the world's coldest capitals—second only to Mongolia's for frigidity—felt like it. This wasn't like the warm green Hill that ushered in a progressive summer.

On Saturday evening, CTV reported the Conservatives were planning to introduce a non-confidence motion on Tuesday as a blizzard of rumours flew, and few bode well for a compromise. Harper, Layton and Gilles Duceppe had met infrequently since the 2004 election, and lasting distrust over confidence crises past lingered. Ottawa was barren, grey and unforgiving. Politics' new rules were preparing to congeal. And freeze.

As the day progressed with leaders trying to agree on terms, it rapidly darkened outside with winter's near-arrival. This summed up much of the mood of many progressive people outside Quebec, as parties representing 172 of 308 MPs met to decide how and when Liberals would fall. That Parliament would end before Paul Martin wanted wasn't in doubt. A winter election was coming.

The long meeting ended in late afternoon and the opposition prepared to hold press conferences that evening, one leader after another in the space of an hour. They had a deal, which proved resilient despite pressure from prominent Tories and lefties alike. But no chance of a joint press conference, as Harper spoke first, followed by Layton then Duceppe as the opposition outlined Parliament's new rules, which, to underline the oddities at play, Liberals had to accept before they could oppose.

The Bloc's control of the House let the opposition extract guarantees from Liberals that its preferred schedule of votes would stick. And like the Bloc extending Parliament's sitting after pressure from Montreal's gay village, Duceppe wanted the things in writing before control would be relinquished now. In return, Martin committed to not repeating spring shenanigans of cancelling votes. Also like the spring, the slots for opposition days were re-ordered to suit the guillotine's design, which wasn't up for negotiation, as Liberals took marching orders from those now in charge.

The winter guillotine was simple and its blade sharp as it began an unrelenting fall. In Harper's words, only a solemn declaration from Martin that he would respect MPs' vote on election timing could stop it from falling. If not, the Liberal government will be summarily ended, as the timetable for Martin's dismissal as PM was outlined in stark, foreboding terms that gave choice only on the question of when, not if, decapitation would result.

The winter guillotine's first show of strength will occur on November 18 when the Bloc will give the NDP its opposition day, the opposition said, with which the NDP will move a motion calling on Martin to call an election in early January for mid-February.

This vote will pass, the opposition assured, and begin 10 days when Martin will choose between Parliament's wishes for an election in February, or one starting very soon—as the victim was shown the instruments well before they were used.

As the guillotine was explained further, if the Parliamentary vote is ignored then the NDP will give the Conservatives its opposition day on November 24, with which Harper will move a non-confidence motion seconded by Layton. This vote will pass, likely on Monday, November 28, following the First Ministers' meeting on Aboriginal issues that weekend.[18] One way or another, the opposition will determine how this Parliament ends, it said, and offered Martin a short stay of execution if he compromised. If he did, he could govern until December as he had asked on TV in April. If not, he would be on the hustings soon.

There, the opposition said, choose the winter campaign you prefer but do not doubt that the blade will fall as outlined, no other. New rules are at play in politics and the Liberal Party will obey instead of write them, the opposition essentially concluded.

But it wasn't all so unforgiving. Opposition parties gave unanimous and immediate support to pass four bills, including bills C-55 and C-66, which both included items from the NDP's budget. Also included were a Liberal bill dealing with natural resources, and a justice bill moved by a Conservative MP. Not all of the parties supported all the bills, but with Liberals' votes included, all would pass the House if introduced separately so the opposition proposed one vote on all four. With protection for the First Ministers' meeting, the legislation the opposition offered to pass represented the most orderly end to a minority yet, and more generous than its sweeping House majority allowed.

The NDP timeline now enjoyed the support of both larger opposition parties which, in return, had a united opposition front that could and—as it transpired—would win any vote it put its mind to. It also made Martin's task harder, since the rhetoric used to brand Harper as

18. With many MPs leaving Ottawa for their ridings votes are rare on Thursdays and not permitted on Fridays. Holding a debate on Thursday and a vote early the next week was common.

irrelevant, weak and wrong through the spring was only made possible by the NDP's budget choices. Progressive leverage was again used for a budget, but this time not how Liberals would have liked.

Liberal House Leader Tony Valeri turned down the compromise late Sunday, saying the opposition couldn't have "confidence light" and that if it wanted to fell the government, it would have to vote no-confidence. Liberals would govern, he said, until the second Gomery report. If the opposition didn't support it, then it should vote no-confidence, trigger a Christmas election and take the blame for anything ended along the way. The winter guillotine, evidently, would fall quickly. Progressive people howled.

On Monday morning, lefty pressure pounded Ottawa again, demanding the opposition abandon plans for an early election. Though neither in control of the House nor the votes to pass laws, progressive pressure mounted to allow Martin to govern until February, for no ostensible reason other than he wished to. Pressure on the NDP was intense as Aboriginal organizations, unions, cities and some environmentalists denounced the apparent early election, and the minority's imminent demise.

But all the progress that Martin claimed to want in the scant months left, even on his own timetable, was granted protection by the opposition. Liberals also lacked control of the House to pass anything, and the fate of the laws on the table lay in the opposition's goodwill. And as Liberals tried to wriggle out from underneath the guillotine's blade, the billions in off-book surpluses first seen in May were now dangled before every interest imaginable—often, directly asking for public criticism of the opposition's election compromise in return for booty.

To underline the Liberal zeal to govern, an orgy of announcements ensued over the next two weeks. No wonder the opposition fretted over two months of taxpayers—again—funding Liberal campaigning. In the week before the winter guillotine fell, some media counted more than $40 billion in spending and tax cuts. The floodgates had broken and every goodie planned for the pre-election binge flowed uncontrollably. On just one day, 30 separate announcements spilled from government coffers, as a three-month pre-election bribe-fest collapsed into 10 days. In the frenzy, Ralph Goodale announced changes to income trust taxation after months of dawdling, causing a suspicious spike in related trading before anything was made public. More on that to come.

Here, we have to go back a bit and recall the budget's original path from the dingy room, when the NDP tried to convince non-partisan allies to veer on the side of objectivity, not euphoria, in describing it. It was true in the spring and it's true in the fall: progressive analysis of politics, such as Jim Stanford's, too often sees tactics as being right because they're not partisan. This may not be so, and as non-partisan civil society assumes larger roles in electoral politics, their tactics need to be analyzed, too.

The winter guillotine's fall sparked panic in wider progressive circles, who naturally hoped to protect progress made. This distress feeds Stanford's analysis, which sees non-partisan groups to be more motivated by issues, not the grubby affair of parties or elections—in one of the laziest slights at the NDP, as if its partisans consciously choose a smaller party because they don't care about things. It's also not always right, as shown by the municipal, environmental and Aboriginal funds allegedly at risk now, and in large part put there by the NDP's own budget. The goal of electing more MPs to put more things in budgets can't always take a back seat to non-partisanship unless we really have decided that power is something for others to have.

There was little at risk as the House fell. But as frames collided, NDP tactics seemed to threaten instead of protect progress, with cities showing it best. As the budget first left the dingy room, municipalities were, with good reason, thrilled. But it was subsequently changed to provide a bonus, with $2.4 billion more in housing and transit funds. If Stanford's analysis held water, cities would have mounted pressure on Martin to accept the NDP's offer of more funding at the time but this was, largely, not publicly done in a city where lobbyists get rich trying to arrange a fraction as much.

Cities certainly delighted at perhaps more from the NDP budget, but in April, pressure was almost entirely applied to Liberals in private. But funds came to be seen as endangered if anyone tinkered with election timing, and in the fall cities publicly demanded the Liberal timeline for an election be honoured. With the opposition providing cover for these funds, it's difficult to see why, for the Liberal Party was the least effective friend around and not in control of much.

Without say over the calendar, and lacking enough MPs to win votes, Liberals' only refuge was in the same public sphere the NDP had long lusted after to bolster its case. That Liberals can find explicit external validation but the NDP can't reveals a selective non-partisanship on civil society's part. How we frame politics matters if we're going to Stop Harper, but to use our latent power, Liberals' most lethal weapon—their frame—needs disarming.

Consider the notion that the election was early, which is so common a phrase, we often don't question whether it's right. With the experiences of 2006 similar to those of 1988, we need to be certain the facts Liberals find useful to reinforce are true, or if they only seem true thanks partly to progressive back-up. If we'd like a government that reflects our values, we'll need to see beyond what the Liberal Party wants us to. And chart our own course, based on a progressive—not Liberal—map.

Pressure was sadly applied not only exactly as Liberals wanted but, worse, in return for nothing other than a remote hope that it would stop something worse. Without pushing for better, Ottawa will see more progressive losses than wins, keeping us stuck. But even organizations that traditionally stick tight to a Douglas Socialist frame such as the Canadian Labour Congress, a founding partner of the NDP, shied away from even mildly spanking Liberals as they fell. Fear of angering a party destined for hegemony caused the CLC and NDP to interpret politics' new rules differently, as the mirage keeps getting in the way of lefties punishing governments that don't do what we want.

Key labour leaders CLC President Ken Georgetti and Hargrove left the prime minister's residence as the House was about to fall, worrying publicly about Liberals' imminent demise. A rather long list of labour priorities, such as pension protection or E.I. changes, was also around, however, and ignored in Liberal majorities and minority alike. These failures were left aside, despite ample proof that Liberals do the most when endangered. There wasn't a public peep about *being ignored on every big union priority for more than a decade*. Liberals needed help, and lefties were too often eager to provide, so why would they do what we'd like, if unpunished for saying piss off.

This isn't the kind of activism queers used, or, before them, suffragettes or workers in pivotal strikes such as Winnipeg's in 1919. They went for a loaf. But here were leading labour leaders failing to make a government pay a price for, only months before, joining with most Tory MPs and killing a Bloc bill to ban replacement workers in strikes in federal jurisdiction, which is about as fundamental a value as unions hold. If only the NDP's tactics are fair game in a rethink, we can't ask why crumbs are all we sometimes think federal politics can deliver. Both partisan and non-partisan players count, and the progressive rethink should cover both, so we can win more often on the road ahead.

Part Two deals with getting out of the box we're in, but debate for the moment surrounded the box Martin was in as the winter guillotine sped downwards. The democratic reformer could listen to Parliament's advice because he'd like to, or ignore it because he could. He chose to govern until stopped and picked the shorter of the opposition's two timelines, but nonetheless authorized Valeri to enter into talks about how to pass the laws that the opposition supported before their guillotine arrived.

The Liberal case against accepting the opposition's offer was that it could not want both the benefits of a stable Parliament and an early election, or express confidence and non-confidence. In response, the opposition asked why. What's wrong with Parliament outlining things it wanted to get done before calling an election on a date a majority of MPs decide? To buttress its logic, it pointed to efforts to pass laws in spite of three opposition parties stamping a best-before date on the government. De facto confidence had already been lost, and at any time Liberals could have formalized it by testing the House's confidence.

They did not, and instead worked with the opposition. Why this could work for two weeks but not for two months who knows, but whether you could see it working at all depended on the frame. The Liberal one was hooey since if MPs could not set the date for its termination in advance, Martin should have called an election the instant the NDP motion passed Parliament—or received majority support outside it. He didn't, preferring to martyr himself at the altar of partisanship to start an election that could have resulted in 18 straight years of Liberal government.

All four bills passed before the government fell, as suggested by the opposition as it outlined its winter guillotine. With this productivity out of the way the Liberals settled in for symbolic martyrdom at the hands of the icy blade now inches away.

On the Thursday before the First Ministers' meeting, a Conservative non-confidence motion was introduced. Its outcome was never in doubt as the cold, pesky House math meant Liberal hopes didn't count for much. Parliament had seen its only pantomime of this session and an encore was not in store, only the preordained formality of beginning the 2006 campaign.

As televisions flashed countdown clocks and MPs filed in, a simple motion of non-confidence in the government was read. Moved by Harper, seconded by Layton, and expressing no sentiment or cause other than lack of confidence[19] in the government, MPs began to vote. Progressive people looked on in disdain as the Douglas and Liberal frames, so similar in spring, were now a gulf apart. All of the budget made it from the dingy room and narrowly escaped the guillotine, whose blade completed its methodical fall devoid of emotion.

19. Two versions of the motion were released. Initially, a motion outlining reasons why confidence was lost was released, but this lacked opposition consensus. The eventual motion was a simple, declarative statement of non-confidence.

Parliament simply rendered cold judgment on a government that chose its date. And braced for execution.

It was November 28 and Conservatives were the first to vote.[20] Non-confidence 96, confidence 0.

The Bloc next. Non-confidence 150, confidence 0.

The NDP. Non-confidence 168, confidence 0.

The Liberals. Non-confidence 168, confidence 132.

Bev Desjarlais, David Kilgour and Pat O'Brien.

Non-confidence 171, confidence 132.

Carolyn Parrish.

Non-confidence 171, confidence 133.

The 38th Parliament fell.

---

20. Two Conservative MPs stricken with cancer who voted in the spring did not in the fall. With the result obvious, the ugliness of the spring's cancer politics did not return.

Class War:
Tories versus Tommy

14

THE MORNING FOLLOWING the winter guillotine's last few inches of fall, Paul Martin visited Michaëlle Jean's official residence at Rideau Hall. Though certainty an election was coming was known for some time, speculation was rampant as to when precisely, and with federal votes on Mondays, guesses settled on January 9, 16 or 23. Liberals went for the longest of the options, and decided on January 23, making the 2006 campaign wearily longer than the typical 36-day affair, and also strangely severing it into two acts.

Act one took place before Christmas, with the second coming in the New Year with—it appeared at the starting gate—an uneventful intermission in between. Door-knocking with turkey leftovers strewn about loomed over the first winter, and first Christmas, election since the fall of Joe Clark's minority in 1979.

A lot has already been written on the 2006 election. *Maclean's* printed a complete edition recanting it shortly after January 23 and its main author, Paul Wells, expanded it into his book, *Right Side Up*. It's insightful for showing why multi-party democracy matters when facing two options that are broken. Breathe a sigh of relief that we don't have the American system, eh?

True four-party affairs make a minority all but assured, but if only the first-place race is dwelled upon, we will miss hidden possibility. Or, for that matter, the type of government that an election is likely to produce. Politics' new rules give us more options, though, and accordingly the 2006 election as presented here often ignores Liberals. This might seem odd and unfair given it is, so far, among the world's most victorious parties, but Liberal election tactics are covered elsewhere. Unabashedly, as fodder for the fire they have dodged for too long.

The core of anglo progressive angst is whether the NDP is viable enough to hope for better as Liberals slide, which makes probing the election worthwhile. And within it is hidden a battle best described, doubtless to the *Globe and Mail*'s chagrin, as a class war between the Conservatives and NDP. Indeed, the campaign mirrored each party's icons as Stephen Harper tried to replicate John A. Macdonald's alliance with Quebec, while Layton adopted a version of Tommy Douglas's striking class-based language, as a hidden battle evolved. Both Tories and Tommy were at war to speak for the working class.

In the introduction, I said I thought, as the 2006 election began, that the NDP may have cost the 1988 version, but that's simplistic. What I meant was that the Liberals' only issue was free trade, while the NDP focused on free trade, ordinary Canadians, Ed Broadbent's popularity and the environment, which, in the late 1980s, was the turf of Brian Mulroney, who that year hosted the first major global conference on climate change. For 17 years, I asked myself why the NDP didn't do as Liberals did, and turn the campaign into a referendum on free trade.

It seemed to work so well for Liberals in 1988, the Ontarian in me said, before being hit by a two-by-four in 2006. I soon realized my old thinking was dumb, and bogged in the quicksand that because Liberals see an issue as useful and try to frame an election about it, that it's smart to let them. Other frames are possible, and also why Liberals won't unite the left here for the same reason they haven't worldwide. Douglas Socialists won't ever accept the Liberal Party, thanks to its regular attacks on working people. Their strict adherence to the NDP is a minority domestically, but the class angle that glues them's the rule globally. They're the norm, not the exception, if we take a broader lefty look.

Canada's alone among developed democracies in class not being an inevitable large aspect of elections. Consider the 1992 and 2004 U.S. presidential elections, which both followed a Republican president named Bush invading Iraq. In the first, "it's the economy, stupid"[21] explained how Democrat Bill Clinton beat Bush the Elder, his apparent rout of Saddam Hussein aside. Democrat John Kerry tried something similar against W. in 2004, but failed—even in key rust belt states like Ohio, which bled manufacturing jobs—to move the election onto class-based terrain. Junior was sadly re-elected.

The terrorist attacks on the U.S. on September 11, 2001 obviously had a large role, but key is that our American counterparts have never lost the class component from their dominant party, the Democrats. Even millionaire Boston Brahmins such as Kerry or policy wonks like Al Gore use "working people" phrases often, though it's debatable whether this mantra-like chant is more effective than Republicans' wooing of workers as begun under Ronald Reagan.[22] And as Canadian elections and Kerry himself both show, class doesn't always win.

Progressive parties need many available arguments, but we suffer from an NDP that can only credibly use class, and a Liberal Party that sounds—aptly—like the big-monied front group Working Families for Wal-Mart when it does. So Liberals usually stick to the environment, equality, peace and sovereignty, but sadly rarely mean it, either, which only makes our progressive division worse as we rush to put bad back in office to get rid of worse.

Around the world, this isn't the case. Progressive parties use many arguments, and most get at class somehow, just as the NDP did in its new budget. In Europe, class plays a key role in campaigns and every dominant centre-left party has some arrangement with unions, but a broader focus, too. In most of mainland Europe, like the U.S., the

21. Democratic strategist James Carville.
22. *Politics Lost*, by Joe Klein.

labour alliance is loose while in the U.K., like the NDP, it's formal and the Labour Party still enjoys sometimes strong ties with Britain's unions. Australia's and New Zealand's Labour parties work similarly to developed Commonwealth cousins in Canada and the U.K.

We're the exception to many rules. Unlike all of Europe, the Americas and South Pacific, we've yet to build a dominant progressive party that includes class in its approach. Instead, we got lumped with the last of the world's Liberals, whose majorities are rarely kind to workers and the middle class. We're also alone in the developed Commonwealth in not having a Labour party, which given everything, makes now the time to do as Britain did in the 1930s, and shrink Liberals down until they can't win a majority again.

This gave poor Britons universal health care long before we covered all Canadians, and on global warming today, oil-producing Labour Britain is miles ahead of oil-producing Liberal Canada. Labour parties are more multi-dimensional than their name implies; New Zealand's has kept that country nuclear-free. This isn't to suggest Canada needs a Labour Party per se, but that we urgently need a multi-dimensional, dominant progressive party that appreciates economic injustice.

These rules are broken only in the West, where Liberals were long ago removed as dominant players in British Columbia, Manitoba and Saskatchewan. This may seem strange given that BC has a Liberal government currently, but the usually seatless BC Liberals fell victim to a neo-conservative coup as right-wingers sought something untarnished to replace their corrupted Social Credit Party. (It's contagious among western right-wingers, and Saskatchewan's Tories also had to be abandoned.) Much though it would help make a case to erode federal Liberals, Gordon Campbell's government is not a twin to federal Liberals, though the two enjoy some hanky-panky—rising at times to heavy petting.

Thanks to being alone in the developed democratic world in being stuck with a dominant meaningless middle, Canada's also alone in rarely seeing class as large issue in national elections. Take an issue like manufacturing job loss: Our manufacturing base is as exposed as that in the U.S. to the wrong kind of globalization, but Americans enjoy more debate on this threat than we do. Often, debate in the U.S. sees progressive people and conservative isolationists on the same page, with CNN knuckle-dragger Lou Dobbs's *Exporting America* providing a ringing call to protect working Americans. No similar right-wing analysis exists here, perhaps due to debate that's increasingly out of step with the world's.

Indeed, in looking at debate in the Americas, an impish argument could be made that the party most like Liberals is Mexico's PRI, which pillaged and bullied its way to one-party state status until voters tired of the contempt. The PRI, which ruled Mexico with apparent invincibility for 70 years, is now in third place. Hegemony's often not as permanent as it may seem. If Mexicans can end it, we can, too, by using current flux to our advantage.

So back to the campaign, which for the NDP began in Oshawa, a town troubled with recent bad news that a General Motors plant was going to close, despite having the highest GM worker efficiency ratings in North America. Oshawa's MP was a Conservative who pipped the NDP by fewer than 1,000 votes in 2004 and whose win was helped by people voting Liberal to stop him. Jack Layton went to announce his auto policy, which bore a stunning likeness to the CAW's. From Oshawa, he flew to Saskatchewan and BC in the first week to underline that voting NDP could Stop Harper, too.

At each stop, he also reminded workers the NDP had stopped the Liberals' multi-billion-dollar gift to their friends in surprise corporate tax cuts, and pledged that voting NDP would deliver priorities more in keeping with theirs. In essence, it asked people to choose between Bay Street and Main Street in the same way that Broadbent did in the 1980s, with compelling budget proof that Martin walked firmly down Bay. And decent evidence that more NDP MPs got things done, too.

While Layton was courting workers in Oshawa and reminding the West that its dominant progressive party was the NDP, Harper was busy, too. His campaign began with a blitz of promises that dominated week one. Two were big and aimed straight at working families, in a pledge to cut the GST and give families small cheques to help with child care. Certainly both were worse for working people than alternatives, but were simple prescriptions that put cash in the pockets of folks whose real incomes were down in a right-wing formula that works throughout the world. Tories made successive headlines throughout week one as the class war heated up.

One day after Layton's Oshawa visit, Paul Martin attended a CAW convention to profess his long love for unions, so often hidden from his corporate past in busing or shipping, or Liberal budgets, come to think of it. There, he obtained an essential endorsement from Buzz Hargrove. In the midst of a class war between Tories and Tommy, Canada's most prominent union leader was on stage with a Liberal. Their frame of how the winter guillotine fell proved powerful, but the CLC's Ken Georgetti stumped for the NDP in the end.

In other early developments, Martin equated the election to a referendum on Quebec sovereignty as the Bloc was above 50 per cent in polls, and accused Harper of actually wanting separation. For its part, the Bloc openly spoke about Liberals' looming extinction in Quebec as it continued to soar. Gilles Duceppe and André Boisclair were often inseparable at campaign events.

With the high-profile Hargrove–Martin event feeding the sense that the campaign was a two-way affair between Tories and Liberals outside of Quebec, week two became challenging for the NDP. It struggled to maintain relevance as both larger parties launched their ad campaigns. The Tories' specific policy proposals made it clear that Harper had been ready to go for some time and the hokey production values highlighted his ordinary folks target. The NDP's were light-humoured attack ads that rhymed off Liberal failures and urged voters, in the spirit of the season, to give them Santa's boot.

Unlike every lefty party in the world, the NDP is stopped from running directly against right-wingers more obviously at odds with progressive values thanks to Liberals' lingering dominance. This forces the party to often run two-pronged campaigns, while parts of its base sometimes long for a frontal assault on Conservatives alone, which all eventually boils over and makes the post-election cycle worse. But with minorities more likely, more interesting possibilities are available than the tired old system in an often one-party state.

As December progressed, the NDP's language became more representational, and the party's slogan as unveiled in October—"Getting results for people"—morphed. In response to Harper's overt appeals to working families, the word "working" was increasingly inserted as the class war intensified between left and right, with the middle often just getting in the way. In media interviews, Harper boasted about how workers were returning to Conservatives, as Tories borrowed from successful techniques used in the U.S. Polls during the campaign's first act mirror this battle, and the blue and orange lines moved in rough correlation. If Tories were up, the NDP was down as Liberals troublingly continued to encroach on NDP ground in the West.

Through act one, questions lingered about whether Liberals resolved the taxation of income trusts ethically. In the panicked spree before the winter guillotine fell, a policy was finally revealed and prior to it, there was a massive spike in trading, which forensic accountants publicly concluded wasn't coincidental. We now know there were several meetings with stakeholders before the tax change was made public, and not to forget Liberal Cabinet Minister Scott Brison popping emails to banker friends letting them know they'd soon be happy. The emails were sent before the tax change was made public, though he said he didn't know what it contained.

The NDP, not Tories, pursued this worrisome development with the most zeal. Both before the campaign and during it, the NDP's truer concern with the well-connected perhaps feathering each other's beds led it to sink its teeth into the possible scandal. In contrast, Tories fixated on former Liberal Cabinet minister David Dingwall's bloated expense accounts at the Mint, which included a high-profile claim for a pack of Dentyne chewing gum. For her part, Judy Wasylycia-Leis filed a request with securities commissions and the RCMP asking them to investigate possible insider trading.

Both the Tories and NDP also made forays into Quebec prior to the Christmas break. Harper chipped away at the Bloc's sizeable lead by pushing a third option for Quebecers beyond the current choice of "separation or corruption." Meanwhile, Layton went to Montreal's U.N. climate change conference to release part of the NDP's green plat-form and, the next day, call for reconciliation with Quebec, although without details. NDP leaders' Quebec trips are usually quagmires; Ed Broadbent, Alexa McDonough and Layton all braced themselves for election visits. The visit this time went fairly well though it resulted in stories about a reversal on the Clarity Act, which Layton formerly opposed.

Elsewhere, Liberals struggled for tangible news after having made most conceivable commitments in the two weeks between the winter guillotine's unveiling and final descent. Gradually, they slipped in the polls as Tories began to enjoy a slow but steady climb.

The campaign's unique structure also led to two sets of leaders' debates—each with debates in English and French on consecutive nights—which moved out of Ottawa for the first time. The first was in Vancouver, and each leader performed reasonably well, with Layton exceeding expectations and Harper perhaps not meeting them.

Allegedly the pivotal moment was a saccharine display from Martin informing Duceppe that the country was not for tearing up. This from the leader of a party that almost lost the 1995 referendum and whose scandal helped sovereignty soar, which was so troubling the 2004 election was called in the midst of it. The Vancouver debates marked the end of the campaign's first act, and most figured the real event would begin in January after a quiet Christmas break.

On Boxing Day, however, a fatal afternoon shooting took place in Toronto outside the city's busiest mall to end one of the most gun-filled years in Toronto's history. A teenaged girl tragically lost her life on a street teeming with shoppers, and it struck a national nerve; though residents of western cities with higher murder rates observed, a Toronto shooting assumed a magnitude that tragedies in Regina, Saskatoon or Winnipeg did not. Gun control had long been a key Liberal platform difference from Conservatives, and earlier in the campaign Martin pledged a ban on handguns with the full support of Toronto Mayor David Miller that added to the charged atmosphere surrounding the shooting.

The Liberal pledge amounted to confiscating gun collections. Next to nothing had been done to stop guns flooding across the U.S. border and, indeed, Canada has banned handguns since the 1940s. A dozen years into government, Liberals promised to boost border security with the U.S., but also left it up to provinces to implement a new ban or not. The Conservatives had long made rising crime a key issue, while the NDP—which released a relatively tough crime plank of its own—had focused mainly on the Liberals' appalling record of poverty creation, which included abolishing the affordable housing program.

But news that the RCMP was starting criminal investigations into the finance department over income trusts dominated much of the campaign's second act. The fax alerting Wasylycia-Leis arrived late on December 23 but was left unread in her office, which was closed for the holidays, until December 27. News that the police were probing possible insider trading in the finance ministry was, simply put, huge. It also came from an NDP torpedo launched before the election began that found its Liberal target in the midst of the campaign, though if MPs' vote on election timing were respected by Liberals, the campaign would have yet to begin. And the desperation to do everything in two weeks wouldn't have been there—both rarely mentioned by Liberals.

The Tories, Bloc and NDP demanded that Goodale step aside until the investigation was done, as is common practise. Martin decried their partisanship, after boasting for two years that he called in the cops to investigate Jean Chrétien's scandal. In any event, nothing obliged the RCMP to say yes. But details mattered little. A scandal-plagued party was under investigation by the police in mid-campaign, which ce-mented long-held suspicion that Liberals looked after their friends, not ordinary folks. On CBC Radio, Hargrove said it was much ado about nothing, as anything that threatened the Liberals was attacked to pre-vent Conservatives benefitting as a result.

The probe into income trusts dominated the opening of the election's act two, which began on January 2 as New Year's Day fell on Sunday. Harper and Layton both delivered speeches calling for change, while Martin held a scrum outside a bagel shop and saved his fire for the following day. Then, he dared invoke Douglas's name and compared the Tory day care proposal, which cancelled new child-care funding, with Douglas's and Lester Pearson's approach that created medicare.

As only he could, Martin tried to marginalize the NDP by crowing about how Douglas forced Liberals to do what Britain did long before. He failed to note that Liberals were in office from 1945 to 1957, when British Labour PM Clement Atlee voluntarily began the reforms that Douglas forced upon Liberals here. This was ridiculously presented as a good reason to reward the forced—not the force—which in the last year also rewrote a budget with 19 MPs.

For the rest of the campaign, the NDP was relentless and mer-ciless in its muscular abuse of Liberals while upping its class-based language to fight Conservatives. Knowing well what being marginal in campaigns is like, it was resolute that relevance wouldn't slip away this time and braced for the inevitable Liberal campaign-closing push to overlook failings and Vote Liberal to Stop Harper. This helped cre-ate the sense that both Tories and Tommy had similar tactics, since neither was pleasant towards Liberals. As the campaign wound down, only Martin decried the dangers of a Conservative win, which with the RCMP investigation and a Liberal campaign largely a carbon copy of the 2004 version seemed evermore likely.

With two weeks to go, the Think Twice coalition emerged and began to place ads, urging people to reconsider electing a neo-conser-vative PM. Liberal messaging began to include the words "think twice" often and Hargrove prepared for more campaigning with Martin, including the ill-fated third appearance where he urged people to support the Bloc. By now, Tories were ahead in the polls by a few points, the Liberals and Bloc continued to sink while the NDP remained in the high teens and stubbornly refused to be marginalized by the losing dominant party.

Within Quebec, Liberals plunged and the Bloc's attention swung towards the Conservatives as January progressed. Tories were inching up in Quebec, particularly outside Montreal, and were competing hard with the Bloc in most of the province. Without the scandal helping him along, Duceppe floundered before a decentralizing Harper who invoked René Lévesque's name at events. Politics' new rules brutalized Liberals, who could no longer use even holding Canada together to anchor a disintegrating campaign.

But the Bloc was not Harper's only new target, and with a possible majority in sight, Tories launched attack ads against the NDP in BC. Like Macdonald, John Diefenbaker and Brian Mulroney before, Harper was trying to rebuild the Tory coalition of the West and Quebec. In neither region could the Liberal Party do much about it.

Particularly in the Vancouver area, another exciting development was underway as Chinese-Canadians demanded that the Liberals' long-loathed immigration landing fee be scrapped. Brought in during in the mid-1990s to battle the deficit, it remained an irritant for ethnic communities and compounded anger on failures to recognize foreign credentials, which leads to doctors and engineers driving taxis. Ethnic communities are often dependable allies for Liberals, and pressure from them was a new hurdle. No longer could Liberals patronize newer Canadians by reminding them that Pierre Trudeau let them into the country, and as many of his and Lester Pearson's reforms came in minority situations, Liberals might not be alone in bringing them in.

But fewer people were willing to Vote Liberal on faith that Liberals believed something. Usually extracting some principle comes only after some public prodding, and true to form a switch only came following Chinese-Canadians brought pressure to bear.[23] This triggered another *volte-face* from Martin, who pledged in mid-campaign to abolish the tax he brought in and left in place for almost a decade. Both the Tories and NDP enjoy much support in ethnic communities in BC, as politics' new rules create danger for Liberals on many fronts. Harper in particular is helping to erode one of the large underpinnings of the hegemony mirage. As PM, he's already halved the unpopular landing fee.

As the second set of leaders' debates approached, the class war between Tories and Tommy was intense and greatly influenced each of the parties' platforms. With the exception of the Bloc, no party's platform was yet public as the terrain of a long election in two parts was unfamiliar. Parties were feeling their way along, which led to some progressive grumbling in the media, oddly, for if policy were all that mattered, history would make Liberals unpalatable long before their 2006 platform was read.

Unlike the previous debates in Vancouver, the Montreal debates turned out to matter a lot. In French, Harper and Duceppe engaged in more visceral combat than was seen previously in deference to the shifting situation underway in Quebec. Instead of the federalist champion he played in Vancouver, Martin was relegated to second-tier status. In English, Layton continued to attack Martin with the class-laced language on which the party relied to defeat Tories. Martin's focus was Harper, which descended to a new low in a mid-debate stunt, when he dared Harper to join him in doing away with the notwithstanding clause. It was a crusade so vital and thought through, that the prop didn't make the Liberal platform.

Also plaguing Liberal efforts at salvation were their own aggressive attack ads, which turned out to be the electoral equivalent of friendly

---

23. British Columbia has long been home to conflict involving Chinese-Canadians. In the 1930s, the Liberal Party also launched one of the most racist campaigns in Canadian history against the CCF for its support of giving Chinese-Canadians the right to vote. In uncompromising language, CCF Leader J.S. Woodsworth's support of voting rights was viciously attacked by the Liberals, who used it as a key wedge between a party attempting voluntary progressive progress and one that rarely does.

fire, with one alleging that Harper planned to invade cities with soldiers with guns. Its sombre ending assuring viewers that it wasn't made up resembled the stereotypical American tourist in Paris, desperately speaking louder in English in the hopes the French would understand. Such was the extent of Liberal panic as they encountered politics' immovable new rules and caused the rapidly escalating rhetoric about a Harper win, minority possibilities or not. The ad became a laughingstock.

The NDP picked the industrial city of Hamilton to fire the next volley in the class war, through the release of its platform. In clear, uncompromising terms, Layton made clear whose side he was on and, ironic for some, released the cheapest platform of any party with no tax hikes and a few low-income tax cuts. The Tory platform, mostly outlined in Harper's campaign-opening pledges that caught Liberals off guard, had little that was new.

The Liberals' platform contained little of anything other than the sterling promise to ban space weapons such as missile defence—yes, the same program Martin wanted to join—which Liberals helped along by shamelessly picking two fights with Bush's ambassador in the campaign. The Bloc's was a manifesto for independence, made tougher by the Tories' sneak attack in Quebec, which continued.

The Green Party was less of a factor in 2006 than in 2004, in spite of a million dollars in public financing. Outside of three seats in Alberta won by Tories in a landslide, Greens did not come third anywhere.[24] In its strongest riding from 2004, Saanich-Gulf Islands in BC, their vote count fell by 4,000. Its best riding in 2006 was Ottawa Centre, where it got fewer than 7,000 votes and came fourth. The Tories came third, but Elizabeth May urged the local Green to drop out of the race to Stop Harper. Months later she set out to lead the party, defeating David Chernushenko, the same popular candidate she urged bow out of the election.

24. The Greens came second in Wild Rose, with 6,000 votes to the winning Tory's 39,500. They also came third in two other Alberta ridings, beating a Liberal and a New Democrat. In 2004, they came third in more than 20 seats, mainly in Alberta and Quebec, with one in rural Ontario, placing ahead of both Tory and NDP candidates, but only in those parties' most abominable ridings.

Into the home stretch, the NDP was hell-bent to avoid a repeat of the Liberal assault in 2004 that cost lefties the balance of power. Pre-emptively, it urged Liberal voters dismayed by scandal, policy or the flailing Martin to lend the NDP their vote in 2006 as the attack continued, unrelenting. By the campaign's last weekend, open criticism of the NDP tactics grew in progressive circles with the Jims leading the charge, as the fever to Vote Liberal to Stop Harper sunk in.

Even the smart, Julie Mason, McDonough's chief of staff and columnist for the *Ottawa Citizen*, urged people to Vote Liberal on the final Sunday. It made for a rocky ride for the NDP, which ended the campaign under heavy progressive fire stoked by Liberals, and the resulting fusing into 1988's experience. The Liberals weren't asked to change tactics once in the panic, as New Democrats stood firm for working families. The benefits of big progressive caucuses in minorities, only recently so crucial, counted for nought.

Harper's class language continued to strengthen, too, although he made odd attacks on judges at the campaign's end that heightened fears about what he really was like. In Quebec, Duceppe fought for seats as the Tories' rise ate into the Bloc base, while the Liberals predictably—and given the polls, manipulatively—urged progressive unity in the desperate push to Stop Harper.

On election night, Conservatives won 36 per cent of the vote and elected 124 MPs. They gained seats in every province west of the Maritimes except British Columbia and Saskatchewan, including a clean sweep of Alberta. In Quebec, 10 Tories won—just three behind the Liberals, who narrowly avoided a humiliating third-place finish—with many close races outside Montreal; they increased slightly in Atlantic Canada. Harper became prime minister-designate and delivered a late acceptance speech before a massive crowd in Calgary.

The NDP consolidated its rise in visibility and relevance and delivered impressive results, concentrated in Ontario and BC. In Ontario, 12 NDP MPs won, with eight from blue-collar cities such as Hamilton, London, Northern Ontario and Windsor. The other four came from downtown ridings in Toronto and Ottawa. It held its seats in Atlantic Canada and Manitoba, and elected 10 MPs in BC with growth in Vancouver, Vancouver Island and the interior; the NWT's seat was also picked up.

About 2.5 million people voted NDP, or 17 per cent, and of the party's 11 new MPs, eight were women. The party of Agnes MacPhail, the first woman MP; the first party with a woman leader and then the first to elect a second had 41 per cent women MPs—more than any party, ever. In total, it won 29 seats.

If Tories and Tommy did well, others had a difficult night. Predictions of Bloc supremacy proved wrong and Duceppe lost seats, finishing with 51; an Independent MP also won in Quebec City. Liberals suffered their second-lowest popular vote in history, falling to 30 per cent, and were surprised to elect 103 MPs, one of whom became a Tory within weeks. Liberals lost seats in Atlantic Canada, Quebec, Ontario, Manitoba, Alberta and the North, though they inched up in Saskatchewan and BC. For the seventh straight election, Liberals lost Quebec and ended five points behind the Tories in their popular vote. Only one in five Quebecers voted Liberal.

Martin resigned as Liberal leader on election night, fewer than three years after his juggernaut was picked to win the largest majority in history. Politics' new rules do exist and are real, as he can attest from essential retirement, but also can be put to progressive advantage. We need a rethink that strives to see more than what Liberals like to show. They need us more than we need them, and if we're going to shape the road ahead ourselves, we have to want to.

PART 2

SEVEN ELECTIONS THAT WRITE POLITICS' NEW RULES

Breaking the Liberal Hegemony Mirage
and Using Politics in Flux to Win

The Hegemony Mirage   15

CHAPTER

A WEEK AFTER ELECTION day, the reliable Jim Stanford wrote a *Globe and Mail* column called "NDP Gains: One Hand Clapping," which placed blame for Stephen Harper being Canada's first neo-con prime minister squarely at the door of the NDP. Among the party's sins, to Stanford, were pushing for an early election for a few more MPs, which it cared about more than Harper winning. Paul Martin would be proud, and Stanford's line is identical to the former PM's, just as his recall of the 1988 campaign is in lock step with the Liberal Party's. In the column, he suggested the NDP ban itself from describing the election as a high-water mark, even though it elected the most New Democrats ever.

"It's like a swift kick in the gut to those of us who poured our souls into fighting free trade," he wrote, as lingering hurt in progressive circles showed itself again, analogizing the 2006 election as a repeat of 1988's. It is important to note that Stanford's former colleague, Peggy Nash, is now an NDP MP. His approach isn't universal among Auto Workers, but also that we can't keep going like this. Blaming each other after voters defeat Liberals is no way to move forward, as progressives keep paying the highest price for the Liberal hegemony mirage: we keep losing. When lefties are angry at the lefty party *for doing better*, something, somewhere, is fucked up.

It's a mess, and lefty reaction to Harper's win puts us in the same box as after Brian Mulroney's re-election in 1988, which brought free trade with the U.S. When Tories start to take us in a wrong direction, we start to ask how Liberals lost and who's to blame. Conversation turns to what has to happen for Liberals to win, and the party soon starts scurrying away to rebuild its sandcastle on the beach, ready for the next Tory tide to take it out. The NDP gets lost in the shuffle as another election of solid growth is glossed over, partly because of the perception that it didn't try to Stop Harper.

King Canute telling the waves to stop didn't help him much, and the tempting push to stop something wasn't much use, either, in 2006. But there could be another way to look at things. It's at least worth double-checking to see if the scallywags are up to no good, which means stepping back in time again to see if what we're told happened in 1988 really did happen.

No question, Stopping Harper is a worthy goal, but how we replace him matters as well, and with Liberals down anyway, it's time to break hegemony. With so many big issues at stake, making progressive clout in Parliament makes sense. More blasphemy, but one look at the corroded, directionless hulk of the Liberal Party is surely incentive to ponder—even briefly—if we could do better.

The thought of lefties doing something ourselves is heresy to Liberals, who help widen our fissure by blaming the NDP for them sitting in opposition, with plenty of back-up singers on the left. But why agree, when we could instead break out of our cycle, and believe we can do more than beg Liberals to do better. That makes getting our act together to try for bigger wins important, along with a common frame in elections against which to push—as our American cousins do, but with a larger progressive majority to put it to work. We don't have to look south in envy. We could be asking how *we* can do the same thing here.

But we can't move forward until we look back, and double-check that the Liberal line on how the 1988 and 2006 elections turned out is correct—or horrors, a partisan untruth. From the Liberal Party, of all places.

The beginning is a good place to start, when John A. Macdonald won a majority, which was a regular thing in the late 19th century. Reaching into the 1930s, Robert Borden and Richard Bennett did as well. There wasn't an NDP to let Tories do it, and still, somehow, Liberals lost. Indeed, given that politics' new rules arrived in 1984 and began the Liberals' stretch of seven straight defeats in Quebec, it's fair to ask why there's no lefty anger at the NDP for *that* Liberal loss. It was, after all, the largest majority victory in history and Liberals were reduced to the rubble of a paltry 40 seats at Brian Mulroney's hands, but Stanford strangely excluded it from his analysis.

Perhaps New Democrats, as Stanford seems to believe, are guilty if Liberals only fare poorly, but don't implode. Or, Liberals could just lose elections as they have since Canada began, and 1988 was the second time politics' new rules deemed the party to be something other than a natural winner.

We need to see which is right, and it's possible the election that was an ominous precursor to 2006 was Mulroney's sweep of 1984, not the iconic 1988 version. To stop Liberals pulling our chain, tactics should flow with events, and not overlook as much as they'd like us to. There could be good reasons why the party's fallen on hard times, but we can't expect Liberal speeches on them. We'll need to see through the hegemony mirage on our own, instead of flagellating ourselves over what is the Liberals' problem. Not necessarily Canada's, as the two aren't interchangeable.

In Oz, the wizard wasn't as advertised, as even the challenged scarecrow discovered after looking behind the curtain. We can probe behind it as well, just to see, in the knowledge that replacing Liberals is easier to do when they are down—and set out to frame politics so they let us work together in elections. Our movement is built on two-sided arguments that don't work in to campaigns, and before rushing to rebuild hegemony, we could take a larger view of 1988 and see it as powerful incentive to fix the root problem: our lagging desire to do away with a dominant party of the meaningless middle.

After the 2006 election, the NDP can seem one-dimensional, always going back to the same well of us-versus-them class politics. And—partly by its own making, partly thanks to other progressives—it can be too one-dimensional. Good thing that dimension is key as Tories also know, and after a dozen Liberal years, little guys were looking for someone to stand up for them. To stop corruption that was stealing their money; to stop crime that was hurting their family; and to protect the pensions they worked hard for, or improve the social services that keep families from falling into the gaps. However Tommy or Tories said it, it was us versus them, with two sides. The natural way debates work, without all the mush found in the middle.

For a smaller party growing, two-sided debates are tough for the NDP, especially when it and Liberals sound the same. And though the party's class approach can seem limiting, it's also often a matter of phrasing. Dealing with the climate crisis without focusing on the oil industry's clout makes little sense, and it's often difficult to see where Exxon stops and the Bush administration begins at times. That's power-struggle politics, too. New Democrats often sound less flowery than Liberals on issues such as global warming, but they also have a broader prescription to fix it, and dare mention some of the mucky-mucks to blame.

Liberals don't do this because in large part they *are* the mucky-mucks, and their recent majorities were hands-off regulations. For more than a decade, Liberals chose not to force polluters to do better on toxics, emissions and efficiency. Both parties said they supported Kyoto, but one undermined those words by policy, as the price we pay for crowding one side of the debate mounts. Exactly like 1988, when two parties said they opposed free trade.

There's plenty of acrimony on the left about both partisan and non-partisan approaches to 1988, and the wound's yet to heal. The problem has also yet to be fixed, and the lack of a common progressive frame against which to push bedevils us still. The meaningless middle keeps getting in the way, and stopping the two-sided activism of the community, workplace or campus from rippling onto the Hill. The truer progressive party is also active on these debates, but faces the unnatural dynamic that turns two-sided debate into a multi-pronged migraine once it enters a federal campaign.

Fixing it won't just happen. It needs to be won, by cashing in on predictable Liberal decline. But whether the NDP is on the way up or Liberals are on the way down, there's always a reason why now isn't the time to keep the momentum—NDP rising, or Liberals falling—going. Liberals, not lefties, lit the fires that have left them a smouldering hulk, and we don't need to hope they will find water soon if we pour gasoline on. The Liberal dilemma could be its own, not ours, if we keep pushing it down, while building a party up to govern.

The first chance to shrink Liberals came around the First World War, before the CCF was born, when conscription tore the party apart, but also solidified its hold on Quebec. Its grip's long been weak there, and as Quebec leaves Liberals' column, it rewrites politics' rules along the way, which created the second chance to reframe politics following the 1984 election—the first of politics' new rules.

We won't win if we let Liberals or the Jims, Laxer and Stanford, explain politics' rules to us. Sometimes, Liberals are wrong, and if we never question if their version of how politics works is right, they'll always be hapless victims, not the bandits themselves. Elections will seem as things done to Liberals, who are entitled to win until someone else botches it up. We'll never find out if we only take their word for how politics' rules work.

Before going through it all over again, we should at least ask if it isn't overly self-serving for Liberals to explain away defeats by blaming those friggin' New Democrats. Losses are becoming more regular, after Quebecers wrote a new electoral map on which they're no longer reliable for Liberals. Unless we navigate this new map to present Quebecers with a third option besides neo-conservatism or separation, our majority is at risk. So time to debunk the hegemony mirage, myth by myth, back to 1988, when our progressive division got worse.

MYTH ONE: Liberals are Viable Without Quebec

Federal politics sometimes do fixate on Quebec, because it matters. For obvious reasons, yes, but also because its dependable support for Liberals is the sole reason the party is seen as a natural governing entity. As assumptions go, it's a precarious one on which to bet our majority's future, for Quebec hasn't held up its end of the bargain for more than a quarter century. As its support leaves Liberals, opportunity follows. With this in mind, we shouldn't see the 1988 or 2006 elections in isolation before moving ahead. We should see the period from 1984 as one before deciding, for the Liberal cloak is the emperor's. Their hegemony is a mirage.

That Liberals could be losers is crazy talk to many, who see the 1988 and 2006 elections as exceptions to natural hegemony, not politics' new rules. Perhaps not. In 1984 and 1988, Liberals were trounced, and fell far below their norms in both 2004 and 2006. Three of the four elections that surround Jean Chrétien's majority wins are Liberal defeats, while the fourth was a minority that did not last long. Just as Martin didn't control the House as the winter guillotine progressed, Liberal hegemony doesn't exist because Liberals say so. Quebec is why.

We've so far failed to present a third option to Quebecers and it caught up to us in 1988, when conservative integration with the U.S. took place because we couldn't outweigh the impact of the Constitution. The hegemony machine won't tell us that Quebec's votes were largely cast on the Meech Lake Accord, not free trade, but bothersome to it or not, there were still two elections underway: one in Quebec, and one for everyone else. Harper is trying to do it again, which makes Liberal–NDP unity outside Quebec matter less, for the Tory path to a majority runs through Quebec itself. It's a big nut that needs to be cracked.

But we were divided from counterparts in Quebec in both 1988 and 2006, and this failure, not a rising NDP, caused two Conservative victories. Seven million Quebecers carry more clout than the usual third party that Liberals are desperate to keep down. It can't get up, though, until Quebec's more on side as the cyclical progressive challenge is shown: If we are going to have a governing progressive option, Liberals have to go down. If they are left dominant, we'll keep seeing progressive people outside Quebec and those within on opposite sides—not on trivial issues, either, but the cornerstone of the election. In 1988, Quebec's unions supported free trade, and its mainly sovereigntist left embraced the Liberal scandal with infinitely more glee than progressives elsewhere. Tories, however, find common ground often.

The Tory–Quebec alliance has been around since it won Confederation, but 1988 marked the first time in the 20th century that it lasted through two straight elections. And as the free trade election approached, historical habit—not future possibilities—kept lefties apart, tragically in one of our landmark elections. Liberals were down following the 1984 election, but we were divided about whether to keep them there, and the fatal progressive error in 1988 was believing Liberals to be inevitably viable—and odds-on favourites to be the better bet to beat Tories. It wasn't true and Quebec, not Ed Broadbent, was why.

MYTH TWO: Liberals Have a Larger Pool of Votes than Tories

When Mulroney entered the election in 1988, he had the backing of the largest majority ever, which underlined that the biggest landslides are always blue: Only Conservatives have elected more than 200 MPs, and they've done it twice. The first was Diefenbaker's in 1958, then Mulroney's in 1984, with both landslides built on strength in the West and Quebec's rejection of Liberals. Like the 2006 election, Liberals were not a factor in these regions and the same was true in 1988. Masquerading as the Stop Harper brigade, Liberals mainly observe in the two regions that Harper needs to form a majority.

For all their puffery about being a natural governing party, Liberals have never built sweeping majorities, because large parts of the West can't stand them. The closest they came was in the post-war boom of the 1940s, with 190 MPs in 1949. In the 60 years since, Pierre Trudeau found bases within Quebec but lost handily elsewhere, while Jean Chrétien's majorities came from outside Quebec. Martin's fate has been covered and it suffices to say his story didn't end well, but the changes in Quebec that brought it about also help decipher, first, how free trade really came to be; and second, how to really stop a Tory majority now.

While Trudeau enjoyed Quebec increasingly united behind Liberals, they couldn't defeat a united Tory party outside it. They had help in rebuilding, though, in the fractured politics of the tumultuous 1960s. Following the Diefenbaker sweep, the Creditistes arrived on the federal scene in 1962 and won 26 Quebec seats, which became 20 in 1965, then zero in 1968. As Liberals welcomed voices on Quebec's leading edge into their ranks through Trudeau types, Creditistes suffered a corresponding drop in popularity.

This didn't happen after 1984, when Tories threw out the welcome for figures at the forefront of Quebec to join their caucus, which Lucien Bouchard found enticing when he entered Cabinet shortly before the 1988 election. The Liberals' star candidate in Quebec at the time was Martin, a shipping tycoon who had grown up in Windsor, Ontario. The Trudeau fumes were running out, and Liberal chances in Quebec were bleak. The NDP actually did much better than Liberals in Quebec and entered 1988 with a slew of high-profile candidates, including former Parti Québécois Cabinet ministers.

The 1984 election was a potential watershed and voters were unflinching in pummelling Liberals. Saving Liberals was impossible as the landslide took hold and progressive people outside the NDP didn't even try. With unemployment soaring and the recession of the early 1980s leaving scars, they were angry with Trudeau, too, and fed the scale of the Tory win that broke Diefenbaker's previous record from 1958.

The Diefenbaker sweep almost wiped the CCF out, and a similar fate seemed possible leading up to 1984, as New Democrats struggled to stay in double digits in polls. But in the election, the party turned back from the brink with a hard-hitting campaign that gave birth to Ed Broadbent's defining phrase of ordinary Canadians. In the biggest sweep in history, the NDP lost but two seats and elected 30 MPs, including a record 13 from Ontario, only a seat away from beating the Liberals.

In Quebec, Liberal punishment was magnified as economic troubles combined with anger at the province's exclusion from the 1982 Constitution. Of the 74 seats Trudeau won in 1980, new Liberal leader John Turner won only 17 as the Tories elected 58 Quebec MPs. Mulroney's Quebec caucus formed the bulk of the Bloc Québécois when it was created, with Bouchard as its first leader, after the Meech Lake Accord failed. This made politics' new rules permanent but hidden long after he left office, but they were quite exposed as he sought re-election in 1988. At the time, the odds were stacked high against him. Or so history said.

MYTH THREE: The NDP Not Doing Well is Why Lefties Reinforce Liberals

In the late 1980s, the last time Liberals lost consecutive elections in Quebec was more than a century before. The last time it lost it all, in the Diefenbaker sweep, the party regained its feet within an election. Liberal weakness in Quebec was alien as the free trade election neared, but its long stability drew many progressives into Liberal circles long before Mulroney was elected. The magnet was strongest in Ontario, which had yet to do as three western provinces did, and push Liberals aside as its dominant progressive voice.

Many Ontarians became Liberals by default, in much the same way that western progressives became New Democrats. Largely, because they saw federal Liberals as inevitable winners, due to strength in Quebec. Viability is a powerful motivator for progressives as well as values, and guides us to paths more likely to win. This creates conflict, as the better progressive option and the historically more viable one were not the same, and the only way to bring them closer together is to reframe. But as the 1988 election approached, history got in the way.

From Confederation to 1988, Liberals suffered consecutive elections without winning Quebec only twice.[25] After Wilfrid Laurier

25. The Conservatives won a majority of Quebec seats in 1867 and 1872. Liberals won one more seat in Quebec than Conservatives in 1874 before embarking on a stretch of three consecutive elections in which they failed to win a majority of Quebec seats. The third election, 1887, was Laurier's first as Liberal leader and the party fell one seat behind the Conservatives.

became leader in 1887 it had never happened, and as the free trade election loomed, Liberals had won the province in 25 of 26 tries, with the loss to Diefenbaker being the only exception.

In elections from World War Two to the Liberals' last win in Quebec in 1980, it averaged 56 Liberal MPs an election, or more MPs than either the Bloc or CCF/NDP has ever elected. It was a significant head start, and rarely could anyone catch up. As 1988 approached, only two majority governments since the advent of multi-party democracy had been of a stripe other than red, with the second one led by Mulroney, which was seeking re-election.

It turned into a quasi-referendum on free trade, and there's plenty of progressive critique of the NDP resisting a push to turn the election into a one-issue affair. Maude Barlow and former CLC president Bob White felt so strongly about free trade, that they helped make the election about it, with plenty of help—from the right. The Tories and Tom d'Aquino also wanted to focus on trade and the trifecta of themselves, Liberals and some lefties found common ground. Policy is everything on the left at times, and we're sometimes convinced that if we only spoke about it more, we'd win more. This might not always be true, and it's possible that voters have more criteria, but this means trusting the NDP is motivated well. And that its message—as the part of the movement with the broadest audience—can get things done, too.

Trust was hard to find in 1988, and goodwill harder in its aftermath. Lefties blame the NDP for not helping frame the election as one to Stop Free Trade, while New Democrats blame lefties for not helping make it about Stopping Mulroney, but the real problem was the meaningless middle. As long as it's around, progressives are forced to choose a party's message to reinforce. But why should we have to pick between Stopping Free Trade or Stopping Mulroney? If the only answer is that Liberals wanted to talk about free trade, it's one more reason for a rethink because in 1988, this allowed Mulroney to hide behind the policy, and make debate about it instead of him. History said Liberals *should* have contended for government in 1988, but they didn't. And not since Wayne Gretzky's rookie season have Liberals beaten a united right.

Some see Chrétien's majority wins and Martin's minority victory as the rule, with 1988 and 2006 being the oddities. But the Chrétien majorities are strange creations given the artificial circumstances then, which vanished as the right reunited in 2004. That done, the rules that began in 1984 reassembled in 2006 while Quebec's loyalties remained unchanged. The right may have united, but the third part of the Mulroney coalition didn't, which creates an eerie parallel between the 1988 and 2006 elections that makes our progressive problem worse.

In Quebec, Liberals won 12 seats in 1988 and 13 in 2006, although their share of the popular vote fell by almost a third in 2006. Across Canada, Mulroney won 57 per cent of seats in 1988, while his coalition—the Conservatives and Bloc—won 56 per cent in 2006. In between these elections, temporarily hiding politics' new rules, were three Liberal majority wins as the right wing of Mulroney's coalition remained divided from 1988. Reform did not win the fight against the PC Party until both were spooked into it, by what was then a Martin juggernaut.

MYTH FOUR: Liberals Can Always Get Back Up After Falling

As the right was fighting, Chrétien won majorities courtesy of staggering Liberal wins in Ontario, which elected 300 Liberal MPs compared to six who were not, over his three elections.[26] For more than a decade, 98 per cent of Ontario's MPs were Liberals, as politics' new rules delivered a temporary, but fruitful, gift and lulled many into viewing the 1988 election as a blip, which let the NDP's blip-like success explain what happened.

After the 1988 election, it's tough to fault people who saw two blips and concluded they brought about progressive defeat. There was little reason to question whether the Liberal frame worked, and even

---

26. John Nunziata was elected as Liberal MP in Toronto in 1993 but as an Independent in 1997 after leaving the party in protest over the broken GST promise. The other five non-Liberal seats were a Reform seat in Barrie in 1993; a PC seat in Markham in 1997; and two Alliance seats in the Ottawa Valley in 2000 as well as an NDP seat in Windsor. In 2002, Liberals lost a second Windsor seat to the NDP in a by-election.

less as the NDP came to power in Ontario in 1990 and largely failed. The fact is, we need to see Chrétien's majorities as blips instead.

The scale of Liberal dominance in Ontario during the right's squabbles is without parallel and almost beyond belief. While the hegemony mirage was most blinding, Toronto, which has rough-ly the same number of MPs as Alberta, elected one non-Liberal MP—a former Liberal-turned-Independent—while Alberta elected nine MPs other than Reform/Alliance.[27] Even in the largest sweeps, Ontario has elected around 20 MPs from different parties than the victor, but in the Chrétien years its largest opposition caucus was three out of 103.

Indeed, over the last five elections the NDP has come as close to electing an MP in Alberta as the Tories have to beating a Liberal in Toronto, as politics' old rules become less applicable.[28] It's no acci-dent that progressives from Toronto are among the least likely to see Liberal weakness or relish it—in a city where Tories are trounced—after being marinated in a sea of Liberal dominance for years. But this isn't seen elsewhere in Canada, or in Ontario itself.

Lovely though it would be, we can't wish Tory Blue Ontario away forever, and as the right reunited in 2004 the time came for Ontario to get back to normal. From Confederation through to the right's division, only Trudeaumania kept Tories from 25 or more Ontario MPs, and even then they won 17 seats. The Liberal run had to end sometime and it did, as politics' new rules re-emerged from a hibernation that made Chrétien look like an electoral genius. He may not have been so hot, and in 2004, Liberals lost 31 Ontario seats: 24 to Conservatives and seven to the NDP. By 2006 they lost 52: 40 to Tories and 12 to the NDP. Within two years, Liberal dominance in Ontario plunged, falling from 98 per cent to just over half. So much for the natural governing party.

---

27. If Nunziata is counted as a Liberal, Toronto elected its first non-Liberal MP since 1988 in the 2004 election in Layton. In Alberta, Liberals won eight times in Edmonton; the ninth MP was Joe Clark, elected as a PC MP in Calgary.

28. Edmonton-Strathcona, where the NDP almost beat the Tory by an identical margin as the Tory running against Michael Ignatieff in Toronto came to beating him.

Within Quebec, Chrétien's prowess proved more legitimate as Liberals slowly rebuilt from the decimation he inherited from John Turner. With each passing election, they gradually regained lost strength, and by 2000 managed to win 36 seats to the Bloc's 38.[29] Thanks to by-election wins and a Bloc defection, Liberals entered the 2004 election with the most Quebec MPs as the referendum loss began to put constitutional concerns on the backburner. Martin's early election call in 2004 in the scandal's immediate aftermath wiped out these gains, put politics' rules right back where they'd been and lets us look at the period as a whole—starting in 1984, not focusing on 1988 or 2006 in isolation.

For some, Liberals perhaps mounting a Quebec comeback may make it tempting to wait for a Chrétien-style resurrection, but things have changed since the Chrétien years, when Liberals were the dominant federalists against the Bloc. Even in Turner's time, they may have finished behind Tories twice but Mulroney wasn't committed to Canada's dissolution then, just as Harper isn't now, though we may not agree with his kind of unity. For the first time since the push for separation, the Liberal Party isn't federalism's voice in Quebec in sad testament to how far the party whose brand is Canada has fallen. Politics' new rules aren't mucking around.

Getting up could be tricky, too, with former PC Leader Jean Charest in the Quebec premier's office, where he refused to help Martin in 2006. Neither Tories nor the Bloc are going to help it rebuild in the scandal's shadow, and progressives might have better things to do than become the reinforcements. Unless we've given up trying to improve where Canada's at, reframing could prove more productive. After all, mention the Liberal record on an issue, and progressives rarely say it's good, but celebrate their demise and watch lefties howl.

In reply, Liberals point to being able to win in small parts of Quebec to make us overlook their record, and they're right, they can

29. The PC Party won a seat in Quebec in 2000.

win seats in Quebec. Unlike the NDP, Liberals are competitive in se-lect parts of Montreal and Ottawa's Quebec suburbs, but these aren't where Tories and the Bloc do battle. Quebec is also prone to volatility and often sees pendulum shifts, and if we tried to win with as much vigour as we fear Tories winning, perhaps we could lay some ground-work for change. That means seeing through the hegemony mirage first, and recognizing that even if Liberals could do well in Quebec again, it may be a long wait. After their last Quebec disaster, it took 12 years to regain competitiveness.

True, our most progressive province hates Harper's radical agen-da the most, but this doesn't automatically help Liberals. The Bloc's still there, as Quebec's dominant progressive party, and like the NDP, has plenty to say about the True Grit approach to global warming, a stratifying economy and ethics. If you're a lefty Quebecer, you'd have two choices: Harper's decentralization, or Gilles Duceppe's progressive values. Which would win? Well, that's the big ques-tion but Liberals haven't been close to topping polls in Quebec for some time.

This raises a clear question: Is Ontario's trend more sustainable than Quebec's for Liberals? If Liberals winning 100 seats in Ontario is likely, they're our default choice as the more viable option, no doubt, if we don't factor in possible Quebec fallout. But if their losing 40 or more seats in Quebec is a more likely forecast, we have a choice for our biggest progressive party, and can invite lefty Liberals to join us if it's the NDP as politics realigns.

MYTH FIVE: Non-partisan Pressure is Always Non-partisan

To choose out of reason, not habit, we need to unpack the analytical fu-sion among many progressives and losing Liberals that keeps our cycle chugging along—as happened in tough Liberal elections in 1988, 2004 and 2006. In each, Liberals and anxious lefties saw things the same way, with the communal view being greatest in Ontario. To start unpacking, the games Liberals play when Quebec shuns them need to be seen for what it is: an entitlement mentality that thinks New Democrats should prostrate themselves and give votes up as offerings to compensate for Liberal losses in Quebec. The NDP doesn't see itself as an electoral charity, and the two rarely get along.

Though their words often ring hollow, Liberal pleas when losing are sincere and the hunt for NDP votes is aggressive. And with the NDP out of the race for first, the idea of Liberals losing fuses with fear of a Tory win, and propels thinking like Stanford's. But what differentiates 1988 and 2006 from the usual Liberal campaign isn't that it tried to get votes, but that many lefties wanted the NDP to offer its up without a fight. This makes the cycle worse, too, as lefties who don't see getting more votes in elections as positive see things they care about get worse. Around and around we go, wondering why we're not getting ahead.

Sometimes, though, there's a sense that it's all right for the NDP to try and grow. Few progressives chided the NDP for going after Liberal votes in 1997, as it tried to recover from 1993's decimation that left it without official status.

Across Atlantic Canada in 1997, with Halifax's Alexa McDonough as its new leader, the NDP trounced Liberals and brought humiliation to senior Cabinet ministers in safe seats in New Brunswick and Nova Scotia. Her Atlantic breakthrough was historic for the NDP, and included winning the most seats in Nova Scotia, where anger at Employment Insurance cuts was so deep it didn't elect a Liberal MP. Official status returned in spades in 1997 with 21 MPs, up from nine and all at Liberal expense. Progressive people cheered as humbled Liberals, who embarked on NAFTA and hacked social spending and the CBC in their first term, took lefty punishment from the NDP.

Comparing 1997 to 2006, what differentiates progressive analysis isn't the scope of the threat. Reform's Preston Manning was also quite right wing and Bouchard had only two years before come within a whisker of de-Confederation. But Liberals could lose in 2006, making their weakness—not the attack's substance—key in how Jim Laxer and Jim Stanford remember NDP tactics in hindsight. This cycle needs to break. It's plainly silly for progressives to be only allowed to bash Liberal failings if they are going to win, but not if there's a chance of us doing better ourselves. Liberals always say Vote Liberal. In 1997 it was to deny Manning a say in a minority House, yes, even as those New Democrats and Progressive Conservatives they now chum around with were on the rise.

As Parliament was falling en route to the 2006 election, lefties tried to keep a minority going as long as possible. But in 1997, few were frenzied about the prospect of another Liberal majority. No Think Twice coalition sprouted to urge Voting NDP to win one of those precious minorities. Many criticized Liberal choices in office, but broad-based, non-partisan coalitions didn't gel to counter a Liberal message designed only to elect more Liberal MPs. Chrétien won only 155 of 301 seats, and had he lost only five more seats to anyone, or three to McDonough, a Liberal minority with an NDP balance of power would have come. In 1997, strategic voting was voting NDP across the board to increase progressive clout with no danger of Manning winning a five-party race. He won only 60 seats.

It didn't happen, underlining the selective non-partisanship often at play, and also the power of a Liberal frame. It's as if direct calls to vote for a party or not are needed only if Liberals need help, but not if they should be whittled down. With a stable Liberal minority government elected in 1997, it's hard to see $100 billion going to tax cuts—in 2000, with the surplus ballooning—with nothing for climate change, child care, cities or Aboriginal people, which all became so sacred later on. Unfortunately, in the most flush period we've had, Liberals had a majority meaning we got *only* tax cuts—and a reminder of why picking up the story where Liberals like is doomed. Let us create a climate crisis! Then let us fix it!

There were other examples in 2000 and 2004. With Stockwell Day leading the Reform Party, renamed the Canadian Alliance, Chrétien struck hard and to the right as he welcomed PC MPs into his caucus, and took on Day on tax cuts. It was naturally masked in progressive rhetoric, as his belief in creationism was also attacked. It's tough to see Trudeau waving a purple dinosaur doll to underline why someone shouldn't be PM because he believed humans and dinosaurs co-existed. Liberals did, though, as more important issues were left untouched. It's ironic they dared make the charge, co-existing as they were with Barneys of their own such as Tom Wappel, and it might not be so smart to help fundamentalists recruit by vilifying religion. But hey, anything for a wedge.

That's the problem with the meaningless middle. Many lefties are attracted to it because it often won, but there's the same kind of gold-digger on the right. But the lustre dims after a while, as it always does, which brings about possibility for realignment. If we let the Liberals' structural gluttony kick in again, it will move—as usual—towards the right, but use progressive language along the way. Over time, this drags debate ever more rightward. In the 2000 election, when Liberals made quick work of Day, their main plank was a bidding war with the Alliance on tax cuts. The NDP was alone among four parties outside Quebec in not promising at least $100 billion of a $130 billion surplus for tax cuts, as the centre drifted right.

It happened again during Paul Martin's leadership juggernaut. The would-be PM wasn't much interested in us as he swept to 96 per cent approval from Liberals, which explains his waffling avoidance on the Iraq War, equal marriage or Kyoto ratification and preferred priorities of closer ties with the U.S. and a much lower debt-to-GDP ratio.

Then Martin's electoral map began to shrink, and Liberals sought salvation in the same left they'd clearly said didn't matter. They're like Pac-Man, gobbling for gobbling's sake, and whether the hunt takes them left or right, who cares, let us get back to running the broad, deep trough of power as Liberals simply do. It's the entitlement mentality, which equates Liberal with governing. But this is also a party whose mission statement says it matters not where it stands. Progressives tend to mind more, and our values deserve more than being rolled out whenever Pac-Man sees more dots to the left than the right.

We should believe in the values themselves, and exact a higher price if Liberals want to claim them as their own. Or a more hopeful path: building a party that's more natural. The old adage that Liberals campaign from the left and govern from the right is true, but this puts us in the driver's seat because they can only rebuild if we let them, and see their lefty rhetoric when they're down for what it is: a partisan tactic. Imagine, and in an election, too.

The plaintive Liberal siren call is sometimes alluring, and Ontario's the most wooed by pleas to put aside partisanship and Vote Liberal to Stop Tories, which was for a decade a literal Liberal one-party province. To its west, Tories rose and next door in Quebec the Bloc was strong, and many Ontarians came to see Ottawa as theirs to defend from the regions and the Liberal-threatening parties they spawned. Yet wherever Ontarians looked around their own province, Liberals were under attack from both left and right. Just like 1988, as the disappointment cycle starts again.

MYTH SIX: Voting Liberal is Always a Good Way to Stop Something

Many progressive Ontarians see its voting patterns as interchangeable with Canada's in much the same way Liberals view their values as interchangeable with Canada's. Small c-conservative journalist John Ibbitson's book *The Polite Revolution* says it well. He is rare in seeing Ontario as a region of Canada rather than representative of it. We should listen to him, for the only way we can remove the Liberal Party is if Ontario sees itself as a component part of Canada. Progressives in Ontario need to trust their western cousins more, to Stop Harper where he can win seats and hopefully create productive, stable minorities along the way.

It's not a one-horse race, and as the West has long believed, thinking the NDP cyclically can't win is as curious as believing Liberals are born to. Just as Secretariat had never won a race until the first, many a legendary racehorse has lost the last few races and the Grits could be destined to join them in pasture. Whether that's natural or forced is the question, and to decide if they lost in 1988 or if defeat was foisted upon them by Broadbent, as Jim Stanford holds, we should at least ask if there's another way to see things than how Ontario did—as Liberals wanted it to.

We need to start in the here and now for what's to come may sound strange, like an NDP that is far more popular than the Liberals and en route to replacing them. Too few heretics want such a thing, but it appeared to be a turning point, which seems odd now mainly due to what happened afterwards. Before really looking back, we need to move these events out of the way, for they'd yet to occur in 1988. Starting with two terms of neo-con government from 1995 to 2003, mainly under Tory Premier Mike Harris. Its viciousness was nothing like the moderate Tory governments to which Ontario was used, and helped give birth to the bastard child of strategic voting.

Harris won in 1995 with 45 per cent of the vote, mirrored in 1999 when he won a second majority, much to the dismay of Ontario's slim progressive majority. In the 1999 election, many decided that Harris had to be defeated at any cost. This gave rise to an organized Stop Harris campaign that set a new standard for vocally advocating voting, essentially, Liberal to avoid another Harris win. It didn't work then, and doesn't work federally, because there's a critical mass of lefties who won't—no matter what—vote Liberal. And see nothing strategic in keeping progressive options small in a functioning multi-party democracy.

Led by many unions, the teachers most prominently but also some industrial unions like the CAW, it was called strategic voting— another poster child for the powerful view through a Liberal frame. That the Liberal Party is so entwined with what's allegedly strategic says it all.

That Harris followed the mostly disastrous first NDP government of Ontario only muddles things more. Bob Rae was unceremoniously flung from office in 1995 after a debt-ridden spell in the world's steepest recession since the Depression. The NDP entered office unprepared to govern, and was as shocked as Ontario's stunned voters when it won one of the largest upsets in history. It was a short-lived romance, and the centralized Rae government was humbled by voters who saw it as incompetent, and did itself few favours along the way. The economy was also a mess, as Ontario's workers were hit hard by free trade's arrival. Ironically, the party that opposed it loudest at the outset became a partisan victim of the fallout, a farce poetically brought full circle with Rae now being a Liberal.

MYTH SEVEN: The NDP Doesn't Grow Because it Can't Get its Act Together

The situation in 1988, though, was different. Rae was popular, hurt only by Liberal premier David Peterson being more popular. In the late 1980s, progressive people reinforced a Liberal frame because they wanted to, mainly due to its historic viability as the natural governing party. It also hurt the NDP, which at the time had built the most competent progressive government in Ontario's history.

In 1985, Rae anointed Peterson premier to end Canada's longest-serving political dynasty. After more than 40 years in power, Ontario's Big Blue Machine again won the most seats, but was ousted when the third-place NDP supported second-place Liberals in a written accord. In return for Liberals enacting NDP items, Rae gave Peterson support until 1987, which proved to be a progressive, productive and popular time. In the election called at the accord's end, Peterson won almost half the votes, and 95 of 130 seats in Ontario's biggest sweep; the NDP lost six seats to win 19. But in both seats and votes, the NDP beat the Tories, and was an asset to Broadbent as the election approached.

The NDP was a runaway hit on the national stage. In the summer of 1987, it peaked above 40 per cent and entered first place in polls as the stars aligned: Unpopular conservative governments ran BC and Saskatchewan, the party was doing well in Ontario and was newly viable in Quebec, with hopes for an Atlantic breakthrough. After connecting in the 1984 "ordinary Canadians" campaign, Broadbent was tops in popularity among the three leaders, with John Turner under unrelenting attacks from Liberals. If there was half as much muster on global warming as there was on ambition in the Nineties, the environment commissioner might not have called all those green pledges "confetti." Liberals cling to the impression of virtue on key issues—global warming now, and free trade in 1988.

The year before the election, the NDP won a trio of by-elections on the same day that seemed to show change was afoot. It won a tough fight with the Liberals to keep an NDP seat in Hamilton and observers were stunned by NDP wins in Tory bastions in St. John's and the Yukon. As the 1988 campaign began, the NDP was second to Tories in most opinion polls, and stayed there for the first few weeks of the seven-week campaign.

New Democrats appeared poised to defeat Tories in sizeable numbers in BC and Saskatchewan, and had a string of impressive candidates running in Quebec. Hopes of replacing the Liberals as the country's progressive voice were not foremost on New Democrat minds. For the first time and the only realistic one, the NDP entered a federal election to *win*. Leading opponents of free trade, however, were less than impressed and tried to defeat NDP MPs as Liberal candidates.

Barlow won the Liberal nomination in Ottawa Centre in 1987[30] to take on its sitting NDP MP, Michael Cassidy. Most of Ottawa's seats had Tory MPs, but Barlow, a longtime organizer for Turner, chose to fend off a Chrétienite for the downtown nomination as their bitter rivalry endured. Though committed to fighting free trade, Barlow was a Turner loyalist and followed none of what she later urged voters to through Think Twice.

When Tories threaten, the broader left often pressures the NDP, effectively asking the party to sacrifice growth for a larger objective. Liberals aren't subject to the same pressure, but as Barlow showed in 1988, neither New Democrats nor Liberals see agreement on one issue

---

30. Barlow won a nomination scheduled early to provide the best conditions for her, but the risk failed. The election did not come as Barlow hoped and was delayed. In the meantime the census-driven redrawing of riding boundaries occurred, meaning a second nomination on new boundaries had to be held. She lost the second nomination to Chrétien loyalist Mac Harb, who won the riding four times. The NDP's Broadbent in 2004 and Paul Dewar in 2006 defeated Barlow's campaign manager, Martin aide Richard Mahoney, in elections following Harb's Senate appointment. For fair disclosure, I came second in the June 1997 election against Harb, and in the June 2005 NDP nomination against Dewar. But at least I have never presumed to contest a nomination against Broadbent.

as sufficient to put aside partisanship. If it's fair to ask why the NDP did not cede to Liberals' tactics during 1988, it's fair to ask why Barlow didn't give way to a dominant NDP before the election began. Both left 1984 on roughly even footing, and saw the election as a fight for dominance; for the NDP, government.

It was a scrap. So partisan, Turner rejected calls for a non-partisan alliance against free trade during the campaign, rarely mentioned in Liberal revisionism. Lefties' failure to stomp on Liberals, not reinforce them, didn't help.

MYTH EIGHT: A Rising NDP Cost the Free Trade Election

As the election began, free trade was a focus of all three parties but the sole focus only for Liberals, who had nothing else going for them. Down in the polls, led by a leader who even Liberals saw as inept and facing a popular Tory constitutional deal in Quebec, the Liberals had nothing to lose. They lurched from the gate divided, and planned a mid-campaign coup to remove Turner if need be.[31]

Mulroney opened the campaign pointing to a rebounding economy and new deals to come in free trade and—to Quebec—the Meech Lake Accord. Personal unpopularity aside, Mulroney's Tories led the polls, while the second-place NDP had the most popular leader. As Tories stressed issues to avoid leading with their chin and focusing on Mulroney, the NDP showcased Broadbent to remind voters a PM was at stake, too. It's the only time the NDP has had a shot at framing what an election is about, and Liberal propaganda aside, the best way to stop free trade was likely a popularity contest between Broadbent and Mulroney. It wasn't progressives' fault that Liberals were in such a mess.

Turner's last gasp at turning things around and avoiding the fate of British Liberals rested on the leaders' debate and the last chance to break through. He did, and in brilliant form echoed by groundbreaking Liberal ads that showed the Canada–U.S. border being erased, put a

31. *Playing for Keeps* by Graham Fraser.

clear partisan stamp on the free trade debate and turned the election into a referendum on it. All aboard the Stop Free Trade train, perhaps, but there is another way to see things.

In making the election about free trade, Liberals created a divisive, two-sided debate, while the NDP ran on a broader platform focusing on Broadbent against a deeply unpopular prime minister. Turner's gambit worked, and thanks to historical habit of Liberals being contenders for government—even if they aren't—pushed a third-place party into second.

Without having elections where two-sided debates have more natural champions, parts of the left tried to jam a two-sided pole into a multi-party system. Together with Liberals, they turned the campaign into a free trade debate, which thrilled the Tories to bits.

Picking only one argument doesn't make much sense. Diverse progressives need many arguments, allowing lefties to have an election about Mulroney, and free trade, or the environment. Helping on one front while helping on another, which takes common frames against which diverse progressives can push. As long as the middle stays big, we'll regularly see the progressive party separated from parts of its base—without a progressive party in power.

In 1988, many Ontario lefties saw Liberals as the No side in a free trade referendum; and the NDP feared many of them were Liberals. It didn't work. Most of Canada had already chosen sides or was holding an election about something else. Saskatchewan, BC and parts of Alberta were NDP–Tory fights, while Quebec debated the new constitutional deal that Mulroney wrote.

Already doing well, Mulroney did even better as the NDP blundered on then-controversial language rights and sacrificed Quebec seats to save ones in the West. Broadbent's remarks on the language law had incensed the party's Quebec wing, doing very well, and the public fight that followed wasn't nice. In its first campaign as a Quebec contender, the NDP stumbled and, like Harper is discovering, growing in Quebec and the West at the same time is often tough. Politics' new rules were unfamiliar all around.

Mulroney handed Liberals their worst defeat in Quebec yet, with just 12 MPs. Outside of dependable federalist bastions in Montreal and the Outaouais region beside Ottawa, Liberals weren't a factor. Indeed, the stiffest opposition to Tories in parts of Quebec now dominated by Bloc MPs came from the NDP, in a hopeful flicker of life in the most progressive province. It got 14 per cent of the vote, and in 1989 Phil Edmonston became its first Quebec MP in a landslide by-election win in a francophone, rural riding.

On election night, Mulroney won a second majority government that stunned and angered many progressive people. The Liberal Party was not supposed to lose just as politics' new rules proved unfamiliar, with good reason. There had not been consecutive Conservative majority governments since John A. Macdonald's in 1891,[32] thanks to Liberals not losing consecutive elections in Quebec in more than a century. As Martin discovered, politics' new rules are unforgiving to Liberals, but they soon went into hiding as the Mulroney coalition splintered. They would not re-emerge until 2004, by which time the inevitably of Liberal election victory had become habit once more.

The Liberals couldn't resuscitate themselves following 1984 in time to win the 1988 election, which, despite 17 years of falsehood since, they lost all on their own. This is seen in the results themselves, which are as immutable as politics' new rules. Outside of Quebec, where trade dominated debate, Tories lost 47 seats and were defeated by a combined Liberal–NDP total of 114 to 106—113 to 81 if the Tories' usually dependable haunt in Alberta, where the NDP won its first seat ever, is excluded.

In the West, the NDP trounced Mulroney and won 19 seats in BC and 10 of 14 in Saskatchewan. Canada-wide, the NDP—sorry, Jim—won record highs of 43 MPs, and more than 20 per-cent voted NDP. It could have been even better, but lost six seats in Manitoba and Ontario as Liberals grew, and tantalizing common cause with Quebec

---

32. This doesn't count Conservative Robert Borden's second majority victory of 1917, when he ran as a Unionist with the support of pro-conscription Liberals. If Borden's second victory is deemed a Tory one, then it's the last consecutive Tory majorities.

fell just out of reach. Liberals weren't a contender, and finished with 83 seats—all but two from Manitoba-east—as the two parties showed starkly regional strengths. And a bit of foreshadowing: the NDP lost St. John's East in 1988, as Liberal votes went up and elected a Conservative MP.

In other words, if Quebec's left out and Alberta's also put aside given it hadn't elected a non-Tory MP in five elections, the truth comes out. To counter Tory sweeps of Alberta and Quebec, the Liberals and NDP needed to win 72 per cent of the remaining seats. They got 65 per cent. Only by winning in the deepest Conservative heartland could they have done it, without the benefit of a united right in Ontario.

The bunkum of how Liberals tell it is seen in the 10 closest ridings. Each was decided by fewer than 300 votes, and the net change was Liberals up four, Tories down one and the NDP down three. All the Liberal gains were in Ontario at both Tory and NDP expense, though they lost Ontario seats to Tories, while the NDP lost two in BC to Tories. That Ontario saw one thing didn't mean other regions saw it, too, and Liberals wishing this were untrue doesn't make it false.

Divided progressives did not re-elect Mulroney in 1988. Our Failure to find common cause with Quebecers did us in. Finding it won't happen overnight, but nor will the Liberals' rejuvenation in Quebec. The Bloc's not disappearing overnight, making minorities more likely than not and giving politics time to realign in ways that let us win more often. Crumbs don't have to be our fate forever if we go for the loaf, but history can only guide us so far to where we've never been.

To go further, we should listen to Stanford's sage words and deliver a swift kick to the Liberal Party to help politics realign, knowing that in ridings where two progressive parties clash Tories aren't going to win. Liberals' clinging to old rules helped Mulroney finish the job that Laurier tried back in 1911. We became more integrated with the United States in a wrong kind of globalization, not the more balanced kind that progressive people support. With Liberals weak again, let's not fall into the same trap. Instead, let's go west, which saw through the hegemony machine first.

Go West

16

CHAPTER

UNTIL THE BAND'S lead singer, African relief activist Bono, tired of Paul Martin's abandoning foreign aid, U2's songs were often Liberal anthems. It soon became unsustainable, not only because its star was publicly criticizing Martin, but also as the song "Beautiful Day" came to define his tenure less and less. In looking for a back-up, the party should have considered the Pet Shop Boys' "Go West." Its title encapsulates Liberal strategy as a century's dependable support of Quebec evaporated through the 1980s, 1990s and into the 21st century. The Liberals needed to find a new region to dominate. It was the NDP stronghold of the West.

Liberals went with something else, so fortunately "Go West" is available. We should have a listen, because the West, in both a Canadian and global sense, is well ahead of federal politics: it has no dominant middle. Unless we think the status quo works well, we should do what progressives do worldwide, and change things that don't work. To be progressive is to want change, not be stuck thinking that because something hasn't happened, that it won't. Liberals used to govern western provinces regularly until Tommy Douglas began removing them from office to bring better things in—such as universal health care, which Britain saw first.

The U.K. beat us by 20 years on health care, after its second Labour government took over after defeating Conservative Winston Churchill, following World War Two. Bye-bye British Liberals, hello sensible partisan arrangements and the voluntary progressive wins that followed. On one side of the Atlantic, the meaningless middle ran the show, while on the other, it was long gone. We know which side delivered the more progressive post-war government.

If we're going to break our cycle, we need to punish Liberals eventually for their long habit of voluntarily doing as they please, instead of what our progressive majority wants. But if we don't frame elections to let us Do Something, and instead focus on Stopping Something, our hopes won't get far—as we'll watch progressives win in other countries, using the kind of politics that comes when the middle gets smaller.

Australia's first Labour government won in 1903; Britain, New Zealand and Sweden first elected social democrats in the 1930s, and they soon became the norm throughout Europe and into Latin America, like Chile, where Salvador Allende was elected in the Seventies, before he was assassinated in the Pinochet coup. Progressive Chileans didn't give up, though, and in 2006 elected Michelle Bachelet as a new lefty president, while Canada still waits for our first progressive majority government—some 60 years after Britain, home of our political system, went for the loaf and won.

No contender for the Liberal leadership rivalled Churchill. True, Michael Ignatieff did push for global conflict like Churchill, but contrary to Republican rhetoric in Iraq, only Churchill was actually facing Adolph Hitler. But in 2006, you could be a pro-Iraq War star candidate for the anti-Iraq War champions. How sweet for the meaningless middle, offering candidates for every value, as votes flood in from every direction.

Perhaps Liberals can also explain why Mulroney fans in Scott Brison and Belinda Stronach are welcome, for either they have fundamental values, or not. Liberals love to cook up all sorts of alleged stark choices in election time, but nothing stops them answering a few, too. If Mulroney's vision was dangerous enough to stop Ed Broadbent from becoming PM, it can't be benign enough to be tolerated by those who fought it so bravely. Either it's dangerous or benign. It can't be dangerous in Tory hands, but benign in Liberal ones. The meaningless middle tries to make it work anyhow, as its dreary, dominant existence long has.

When Brison and Stronach bolted the Tories, their arrival was celebrated by Liberals as a masterstroke. Come to us, Mulroneyites, Liberals purred as neo-conservatism grew. Come join the Tom Wappels and a party whose unity failures keep begetting referendums. Toss in their record in majority governments, and a Liberal take-over seems kind of dumb. Indeed, it's the same madness that drove Liberal–Labour coalitions during the Depression as the CCF formed. History tells us that cozying up to the Liberal Party is unproductive. We should listen this time.

Bob Rae disagrees, and now that he's a Liberal, makes the case that the left should unite like the right did in 2004—namely, a take-over, which is good for him, but not for us as the situations aren't alike. First, the right was split because one party started to cleave, while the progressive divide is more than 70 years old. Second, the biggest progressive split involves Quebec, not the Liberals and NDP. Third, just as not all right-wingers voted Conservative after the merger, not all New Democrats would vote Liberal as their next op-tion. Not everyone can fall in love with the middle, and some NDP votes would go Tory.

And let's not forget. The right's divisions were restricted to Rae's Ontario, while the lefty split extends over seven anglophone prov-inces. Only Newfoundland & Labrador and PEI, along with anglo New Brunswick, have a clear preference for a dominant progressive party— the Liberals—but they account for 18 seats. Everywhere else is divided, and Rae's solution doesn't help.

South of the border and across the Americas, a dominant, truly progressive party allows for more unity, and for diverse tactics to be used in common goals. In elections, they try to help their party win, and in between use many ways to push ahead: the courts, peaceful mobilization and workplace bargaining—and perhaps urging their party to become more progressive still. But unlike the U.S., we have multi-party democracy and the system to use it on. With minorities likely, progressive parties don't have to come first to get influence—while building up a party to challenge for first.

Power's not a bad thing when it is used well, and wanting to win isn't shameful. Someone has to and it may as well be us. If this isn't where we'd like to end up, we are a sad, unambitious bunch to be sure, watching Harper's ilk grow from hapless to governing without thinking we can get things done in Ottawa, too. More Liberals hasn't worked before, and allowing the Liberal Party to instantly return to strength now has some problems.

If we allow Liberals to rejuvenate, the first hidden cost is that the Conservative Party will become more neo-conservative, driving more moderate right-wingers out. Ballast to counter radical Harper types will leave, and the Red Tory tradition of Joe Clark, John Diefenbaker and John A. Macdonald will become rarer. And with a weakened NDP as we rush to help Liberals, Tories' radical conservatism will drag the middle rightward. Having a bigger Liberal Party for a bigger Liberal Party's sake is silly, unless Brian Mulroney's friends become our friends when they put on the red button.

With politics in flux, though, parties that can elect MPs have more clout. If we use this period of flux to shrink Liberals and strengthen multi-party democracy, we might push a few moderate Tories back—to moderate the Conservatives. We can't stop Tories coming first in every election, and a more moderate Conservative Party helps in the long run. But unless we help make the meaningless middle less convenient for wayward moderates, there will be almost nothing left of the Toryism we might prefer not be in office, but which doesn't keep us awake at night. Sleeplessness is magnified by the alliance between radicalized Tories and their well-armed friends, the Republicans.

The second cost is that we'll accept defeat and fail to elect a Liberal majority. Presumably, if Liberals could win one, the leadership would not just have been a free-for-all and candidates after the prize for some time would have done more than watch. But no. John Manley, Frank McKenna, Allan Rock and Brian Tobin each took a pass on the leadership despite knowing that almost everyone who's been Liberal leader has been PM, often for quite a while. There they were, though, ambitious Liberals not going for it and along the way blaring that a Liberal majority is a long way away.

It wouldn't be the first time Liberals lost two in a row, and politics' new rules say it won't be the last. Liberals can tempt us with the political equivalent of Florida swampland, but we don't have to jump in and sink some more if we build a bigger, broader progressive party to win ourselves—leading a minority government, or part of one.

Lastly, Rae's track record on delivering isn't always so hot. His advice would make things worse and expand our already dangerous divide. This should worry progressives, and the notion that Liberal rejuvenation is wise needs its tires kicked because weakening the NDP could help elect more Tory MPs. To see how, we should head to the coasts, which are entering uncharted territory.

Liberals running to win in the West and New Democrats doing the same in the Maritimes is recent. The two parties don't usually compete on both coasts, but in 1997 Liberals had more MPs from BC than the NDP, while New Democrats did better than Liberals in Nova Scotia. Its unprecedented. And the Bloc's arrival in Quebec has panicked Liberals into desperately heading west to make up the difference.

The NDP isn't alone anymore in trying to win in a region— Ontario—that it hasn't cracked. The Liberals are at it now, too, throwing frantic Hail Mary passes west to try and keep the hegemony mirage intact. And if it's reinforced, gainful employment as an MP for many a western Tory comes along, as Liberal tactics splinter progressive votes where Harperites are the most likely to win.

As progressives pressure the NDP to avoid partisanship in Ontario, greedy Liberals look west and move the left's partisan divide in the opposite direction to the right-wingers'. In the four anglophone provinces west of Ontario, Reform/Alliance was the more popular conservative party and laid claim, while in the four anglo provinces to Ontario's east the PC Party was, as the right restricted its split to Ontario. In each election with a divided right—which allowed Jean Chrétien to pile up unwarranted majority wins—this regional rule was almost unbreakable. The only exceptions were popular Brandon, Manitoba mayor Rick Borotsik winning for the PCs, and Clark's personal win as PC leader in Calgary.[33]

Here's what faces us: the Liberals and NDP both elected MPs in BC, Manitoba, New Brunswick, Nova Scotia, Ontario and the territories in 2006. We're not concentrating the showdown in one province. We're spreading it, and as it grows further west, Tories slip up the middle and win seats they should not. It isn't as extreme as Chrétien winning a Fidel Castro-like 300 of 306 seats in Ontario over three elections, but western Tories aren't complaining much.

And let's not forget populism, which puts the NDP in competition with Tories throughout much of the West. There's a big anti-establishment vote out there, and it doesn't go Liberal. New Democrats don't compete with Tories in Toronto for many votes, but it's not always true further west. A big F-U has sparked many a Prairie fire, but none of the meaningless middle.

But as Liberals tut-tut NDP partisanship over lattés in urban Ontario, the Pac-Man gene hungrily tries to expand west. Never questioned and often cheered, it makes things worse, and drives lefties apart more. In Pierre Trudeau's last four elections, Liberals won only 21 seats in total west of Ontario. In John Turner's first election, his own seat in Vancouver and one in Winnipeg were the only of 40 Liberal seats west of Ontario; in 1988, the party fared only marginally better and elected eight MPs.

In contrast, the NDP dominated the West and showed how it had strengthened since Diefenbaker's drubbing. As Tories rose in the West in the late 1950s, the 20-year-old CCF crumbled and forced the NDP

---

33. The PC Party won seats in Quebec in elections during the right's division.

to broaden its base into industrial Ontario through an alliance with organized labour. Diefenbaker all but eliminated the CCF in the West, where it lost 10 seats in Saskatchewan, five in Manitoba and three in British Columbia. The NDP was formed with only five western MPs and three from Ontario.

In the second great Tory sweep in 1984, the NDP fared much better after emerging as the West's dominant progressive party with the structure to match. In 1958, the CCF had governed Saskatchewan for 14 years, and had run federally for only a quarter century, but as 1984 arrived, the NDP had run Saskatchewan for 28 years. It also governed BC for three years in the Seventies and was, in the third year of government in Manitoba, after serving eight years in an earlier term. It made a difference in beating Tories.

After the 1984 election, the NDP had 17 MPs from the West— more than Liberals kept in Atlantic Canada, Ontario or Quebec. It also picked up eight seats in Ontario as Liberals fell, while in the Diefenbaker sweep at least didn't lose its small Ontario rump. But it underlines NDP resilience to Tory surges in areas where it's strong. By 1988, the NDP beat Mulroney's majority in much of the West, as Tories and Tommy battled long before the 2006 election.

The NDP trounced Mulroney, winning 19 of 28 seats in BC and 10 of 14 in Saskatchewan while holding the Yukon, and picking up its first seat in Alberta. As Liberals rose in Ontario and Manitoba, largely due to an NDP humbling in 1987's provincial election in Manitoba, the NDP fell and lost three seats in each province. It also lost St. John's to the Conservatives, even though Tory votes fell.

The 1988 St. John's effect of NDP-held seats going Conservative as Liberal votes rise is why the NDP lost the six western ridings and Oshawa to Conservatives in 2004. These seven ridings cost progressive people the balance of power in the minority Parliament, and this trend will keep infecting the West until we reframe. This isn't the free-trade era, and there are many more NDP seats in the West now than there were New Democrat MPs in Atlantic Canada then. We need to chuck politics' old rules out.

If we don't, competitive NDP–Tory races will become more un-competitive and a Harper majority that much closer. Ontario's voting patterns are not interchangeable with the West's and because Liberals want to win more seats there doesn't mean we have to help. It makes for great rhetorical flourishes to head west and urge that people Vote Liberal to Stop Harper, but it's a reckless tactic designed mainly to Save Liberal Ass. Hello, Vancouver Liberal David Emerson and his contemptuous defection to Harper only weeks after being elected to stop him, as lefties sometimes believed the rhetoric more than its beneficiaries.

During the 2006 campaign, though, the NDP was severely criticized by the Jims—Laxer and Stanford—for going soft on Harper, and refusing to hyperventilate about his agenda as Martin did. This fed self-serving Liberal rhetoric that only they could be trusted to Stop Harper, and sent more charges of irresponsible partisanship the NDP's way. We need to see if this Liberal frame is right, and what was happening in British Columbia was telling.

In both 2004 and 2006 elections, BC was governed by neo-conservative Gordon Campbell. But don't tell Martin that the third-largest province was undergoing its own Harris-like transformation, since federal Liberal messaging dealt with the evils of Alberta's Ralph Klein, and the reminders of Ontario's Harris. Despite the push to Stop Harper, Liberals, funnily enough, didn't make any link with his ideological twin currently running the province. This *was* passing strange since Campbell is also aggressively privatizing BC's health system like Klein did, which allegedly fuelled Liberal vitriol against him.

If Liberals rejected neo-conservatism across the board, the sitting neo-con premier of BC should have been a prime target. He was spared, making Liberal rhetoric against neo-cons more convenient than ideological. Had Liberals not been an endangered species in Alberta, Klein may have been spared a bulls-eye, too. But only Klein and Harris, who hadn't been premier for four years, were objects of Martin's scorn for neo-conservatism. What bravery, to attack an ideology in a province where Liberals had scant hopes, and in another where neo-cons weren't even in office.

The explanation is straightforward, and Martin refused to attack Campbell for the same reason Layton did not eviscerate Harper, but did attack Campbell: Liberal and NDP growth rhetoric sounds different. Liberal messaging meshed closer with some progressive fears, but that doesn't make attacking Liberals interchangeable with helping Tories. Instead, it's why it's time to reframe politics, so we can take on harmful ideologies and elect more MPs who mean it. But not until we reduce the number of sides to debate, and let the larger progressive side actually be progressive, without the meaningless middle getting in the way.

That we wonder where Canada went at times is the steep cost of echoing politics' old rules. But if only Liberals cling to these old rules as we frame things to make it easier to say yes, our elections would likely change. We'd have elections about who should win, not who is likely to, leading to people voting Liberal because they want to, not bludgeoned into it in the contrived necessity to Stop Harper. Changing the voting system would help, too, but we can't get there as long as Think Twice protects the status quo, all because it's convinced that Canada votes in the same way Ontario does. It's time for a rethink.

In 2006, Harper won more seats on the Prairies with 36 per cent of the national vote than Mulroney won in 1984 or 1988 with 50 per cent and 43 per cent, respectively. It's an alarm bell that should spark us into action as the 1988 St. John's dynamic of Liberal votes electing Tories is now infecting the West. As further proof, consider dangerous shifts underway in Manitoba and Saskatchewan.

Manitoba's normally a very moderate place, whose voting patterns resemble Ontario's and Atlantic Canada's more often than Prairie cousins Alberta or Saskatchewan. It's also the only province west of Quebec that's not seen a neo-conservative government. Manitoba is not where you'd expect radicals to find broad appeal, but Harper did well there in 2006. Manitobans gave him two more seats than they gave Mulroney in 1988, while Harper received fewer votes. This shouldn't happen, but will keep up if only the NDP's tactics are finely scoured. Instead, both Liberal and NDP approaches to elections should be put under the microscope and the one found more wanting offered a swift—and collective—kick.

More troubling are Saskatchewan's developments. In 1988, the NDP won all of urban Saskatchewan and 10 of the province's 14 ridings. In 2006, it failed to win a seat for the second straight election and the province elected 12 Tory MPs. There are three possibilities that explain it.

The first is that the long-serving provincial NDP government, in its fourth term as 2006 arrived, is deeply unpopular and it's rubbed off on the federal party. There may be a grain of truth here. Saskatchewan once before went through a stretch in which the NDP was shut out there, ironically in the first elections with Douglas as leader in the 1960s; he was an MP from BC after losing his own seat. Diefenbaker, too, hailed from Saskatchewan, which may explain some of the problem at the time, as does the extremely long-serving CCF/NDP government as Douglas moved to the federal level. But Lorne Calvert's government is not loathed and the NDP being shut out is odd, given it got more votes than the Liberals.

The second possibility is that Saskatchewanians don't live in cities, and an NDP with a Torontonian as leader is repellent. This first rose as Layton ran for leader, yet strangely emanated from Toronto itself and assumed, personality aside, that anyone from Hogtown couldn't connect with Saskatchewan. In truth, he had much support among Saskatchewan New Democrats. Inevitably, this analysis either thinks the Prairies have no cities, or that the urban Prairies are massively different than urban Ontario, when a city is a city. If the NDP's opposition to the Iraq War, or support for Kyoto or equal marriage was the problem, Liberal votes would also likely have dropped, given all the hyperbole.

The third is that Liberals have infected the place, and split the progressive vote. Both provincially and federally the NDP's strength in Saskatchewan flows from cities, whose federal ridings are absurdly drawn like pizza slices. In both Regina and Saskatoon, there is a spot where four ridings meet and then expand outward to include towns often two hours' drive away. In typical elections, these ridings are contests that pit the NDP's ability to pile up a massive urban majority against the Tories' capacity to deliver a massive rural one. It's a different twist on the battle between Tories and Tommy. And made more difficult for Tommy when Liberals arrive in search of only urban votes.

Consider the impact of this Liberal invasion: In 1988, urban Saskatchewan elected eight NDP MPs, while in 2006 it elected seven Tories and a Liberal. And like Oshawa, the gap between the winning Tory and second-place NDP grew from the 2004 to 2006 elections, while Liberal votes fell nationally. This shouldn't happen as Liberals are thrown from office, but it did, as Liberals getting in between Tommy and the Tories is helping Harperites win.

Tragically, the march continues unquestioned. Worse, it is reinforced by Think Twice and the Jims who are so used to Liberals being a natural governing party that new rules have gone unnoticed. We need to change this quickly and the power's in our hands. Our values don't flow from the Liberals down but from progressives up, and if we decide the NDP can help reframe politics to do better, we can give Liberals a firm push, by simply questioning its frame. With some gusto.

Coalitions such as Think Twice don't help. They validate the Liberals' hegemony mirage, tactics—and record. Sometimes, even the most objective arrows can't pierce, no matter how right they are.

In the dying days of the 2006 campaign, *Toronto Star* and *Le Devoir* columnist Chantal Hébert wrote that Think Twice was blinded to NDP chances in the West, and overlooked the almost certainty of a minority being elected—while ignoring Martin's ideological bent and policy incoherence. She held that toeing the Liberal line ignored unique progressive opportunity. It was a magnificently blunt evisceration of the logic at the coalition's core.

In response, Maude Barlow wrote that Think Twice was strictly non-partisan and concerned only by the imminent election of an extreme Conservative PM, which the coalition urged voters to reconsider. It's tempting, considering her own partisan history, to accuse Barlow of being an outright Liberal, but this is deeply unfair. Her response wasn't based on a great love of the Liberal Party, but rather a faith in its frame of how politics' rules worked.

Together, we can reframe that, but only if progressive people outside Quebec truly unite the left in a common effort. If we want to win, we'll need to first go west to duplicate its achievement in shrinking the Liberal Party away from dominance. Because it can't infect the only region where it is habitually weak and where Tories traditionally face off against Tommy.

Wrong Kind of Blue State

17

CHAPTER

O NLY ONE NORTH American leader is putting a million solar panels on roofs today. On a continent with 440 million people rapidly changing the climate, there's a lonely pioneer aspiring to fight global warming on a scale that matches the problem. He isn't Canadian. But we can't ask why if all that matters is Stopping Harper. Multi-party democracy lets us ask why. It helps progressive people, unless the kind of binary, two-party debate we see in the United States is something we want, too.

The rapidly greening politician is Arnold Schwarzenegger, the Republican governor of California. Under his leadership, California has passed some targets for climate-changing emissions that put Canada's—Liberal or Conservative—to shame. Their targets are more ambitious, their timelines shorter, and despite how greenly we like to see ourselves, California's record of voluntary wins is longer.

Hang on just a minute. A *Republican* governor doing something more progressive than Canada? Well, yes. After more than a dozen years of Liberal majority government, the Terminator is doing better than we are. Nor can it all be chalked up to California's hedonism: nine other states are trying to sign on and six of them also have Republican governors.

Red states doing better than our red state under Liberals sums up life in the hegemony mirage, where to be Canadian is to be progressive and to be a Liberal a progressive Canadian. Global warming is only a looming catastrophe and before rushing to rebuild the Liberals, we could always ponder how it is that Arnold is doing better than we are. Heavens, we could ask why the Liberal Party dares claim to be green.

So thumbs up to Schwarzenegger for leading—and following. The solar roof idea came from Japan, and in 1994 it launched an ambitious program to solarize roofs and along the way take the lead in the emerging solar energy business. A year before, Liberals were elected to a majority government pledging to cut climate-changing pollution by 20 per cent. Thirteen years later, with emissions soaring and Bill Graham comparing global warming to the end of days, we still can't manage to connect Liberal with polluting.

But facts don't lie. The actor-turned-GOP governor went from releasing *Last Action Hero* in the year that Jean Chrétien became PM to pulling well ahead of Canada after Chrétien had gone. Indeed, as Schwarzenegger was fighting the Bush administration in court over California's tough new standards, Liberals adopted the voluntary standards that Bush wanted. During the 2006 election, Elizabeth May attacked New Democrats for daring to criticize *this* Liberal record as the two-party debate kicked in.

If Harper is bad, Liberals are good. If the Americans are bad, Canada is good. Canada is progressive, therefore Liberals are. And so political debate goes, marching down a binary, sometimes Orwellian path and moving ever so reliably rightward with each step. That Belinda Stronach, the moderate right-winger, is more often than not seen as progressive just about says it all.

Stronach shows how few questions Liberals really have to answer from the left and why we can't afford not to reframe. And the best way to see why is to look south. Nancy Pelosi becoming speaker of the House after the Democrats regained control of the Congress in November 2006 is gleeful stuff, but before thinking that voting

Liberal to Stop Harper is inherently strategic, we should double-check. Few need convincing that Democrats are better than Bush, but that doesn't make Democrats automatically progressive—just as the moderate-right Stronach doesn't become progressive by becoming a Liberal.

Neither Stronach nor Liberals seem to mind, and she's at home. Together, they don't question why manufacturing jobs are evaporating or whether more women in poverty has something to do with changes in E.I. rules—there's no need to, if everyone becomes progressive just by joining the new Liberal club. If the transformation is helped along and people like Stronach become new "progressive" champions, the Liberals will look more and more like America's Democrats as will Canada's political terrain.

Rejoice in the return of Brian Mulroney's Tories, from whose ranks Stronach sprung. Scott Brison had left long before and soon settled into a party where everyone's welcome. As a Tory, he opposed Kyoto, but was the Liberals' first environment critic after they lost to Harper—as what actually *is* progressive gets lost in a U.S.-style rush to Stop Harper.

Yippee! Liberals think after cashing in on Democrats' wins in 2006 and inviting former Vermont Governor Howard Dean to speak at their leadership convention. How anti-Bush and in binary-land, how progressive, as Liberals try to import the very kind of American debate we don't want. It would be the big surprise in a box of Crackerjack for progressives after it happened, but nothing would make Liberals happier than talking about Canadian values in the kind of system the Americans have.

South of the border, "liberal" is a dirty word, dragged around Republican Web sites like a Tory child pornography press release to write off progressive options. To be *liberal*, Republicans sneer, is to be anti-American, echoing the kind of mantra that makes "Liberal" often interchangeable with "Canadian." But as we muse about how unquestioning Americans can be about where their country is heading, we should probe how it is that Liberals can appear progressive with an eerie lack of inquisition. Like our American cousins, we have our buzzwords, too, but the word's not liberal in Canada. It's left.

To be left is often to be a pie-in-the-sky nut talking on the fringe until it's time to save a Liberal, or until something comes true. Climate change started long before Stephen Harper became PM, and as the threat expanded, Liberal failings hid in plain view without the furore over imminent destruction that came after a Tory win. Liberals low-balled federal budget surpluses for years to justify policies that increased poverty, but it needn't have been.

Lefties actually called budget surpluses better than banks in the Liberal years, and solid work is done at places such as the Canadian Centre for Policy Alternatives. They're undeniably left, but not crazy, and being further left than the Liberal Party might be where progressive really lives. It's a debate we can't have as long as all that counts is not being Conservative.

But size counts and because they're bigger, Liberals often decide what the progressive side of debate is. Maybe that's natural, but if left unchallenged, we'll squander the benefits of vibrant multi-party democracy, and, along the way, undermine one of its pretty good ideas: voting for the person you agree with and want to win. That's what strategic voting advises. Don't vote for what you *want*, vote for what you *don't*. At a rare moment when progressive citizens have real clout, we're told it's strategic to ask for a crumb, not a loaf.

As long as the Liberal offer is the best thing going, progressives risk abandoning aspiration by telling other hopefuls to fear. Canada has its buzzwords, too, and should Liberals come under lefty scrutiny, the first reaction is to marginalize those who ask if we can't do better. Republicans call them *liberal* ideas; Liberals call them *left* as a no-need-to-explain proxy for unworkable. As California powers ahead on global warming, Canada tries to stop electoral debate about why, all to protect a falling Liberal Party. George W. Bush would be proud: You're either with us or not.

Thank goodness for multi-party democracy and hope for debate that's broader than why Harper's blue emissions are more dangerous than Liberal red ones. His scariness can't only be because his targets to cap emissions end in 2050; that was the Liberals' target date, too—not that you'd know it. Faraway nonsense instead of immediate practical steps doesn't help the crisis, but as long as Liberals are the good guys—not the polluters—politics can't aspire to what's possible or take a broader look than Canada's long-standing lust to be better than the Americans.

This isn't to say that the NDP is automatically the answer, but that without parties to reward for good progressive behaviour, debate will shift to the right. Arcane, maybe, but Belinda Stronach's politics are identical to Brian Mulroney's and if we don't rethink how what's good enough has slipped, we can't have our necessary chat about how we've veered so far right that Republican governors are more progressive than we are. It also makes progressive Liberals both the solution and the problem.

Progressive Liberals—MPs and staff alike—regularly urge New Democrats, in hushed but honest tones, to keep up the good work. When there's a large question at stake, the NDP, being a separate party, has the liberty to say publicly what many progressive Liberals say privately: No to Iraq, for example, which progressive Liberals then use as leverage within their party to stay out of the war. Sometimes it works and sometimes it doesn't, but no matter. Progressive Liberals are there for the long haul, no matter how often their party shows it does not listen.

As long as pressure is put on New Democrats to help progressive Liberals, and not on progressive Liberals to help New Democrats, we'll be stuck in our loop. Take Liberal leadership candidate Carolyn Bennett, who is a true believer in child care, but stuck around through budget after budget of losing. The kids who were first promised a program were in high school by the time something arrived, and it says something that progressives focus on the 12th year when something happened—not the 11 years when it didn't. That's not splitting hairs. It's why California is doing better than Canada on the climate crisis.

Unless there's some broader progressive agreement that Liberals are bad, we will never have the sense that we can do a bit better. If all that counts is a Liberal government—no matter how timid—Canada will keep winning symbolic victories and keep watching Kyoto-free places actually deliver more on the problem behind the treaty. New Democrats suffer for it, but they aren't alone. Civil society does, too, as a two-party state grows and then, just as everything cumulates and Liberals lose once more, the issues that were so important to kick up a fuss over aren't important enough to punish Liberals for failing on. In practise, it turns the NDP into a useful ruse to try and push a reluctant Liberal Party leftward.

Within non-partisan circles, progressive Liberals are coveted for their influence. It's partly a logical fit, and helps explain why May supported a government that always managed to put progressives in the environment portfolio and conservatives in files big enough to thwart them. Over time, it becomes a treadmill, where the beleaguered progressives within the Liberals need help—no matter how little influence they've managed to show. And each time we decide that all that really counts is helping progressives within the Liberal Party, not those outside, we shift debate to the right. That might not be so strategic with 70 per cent of voters supporting different parties and Liberals morphing before our eyes.

We've dangerously let politics become about the Liberal Party. Unless we're absolutely convinced that spending the year following Liberal defeat asking which new Liberal leader can Stop Harper—and *not* asking if Liberals deserve to be returned to office so soon—we run the risk of only asking how they can reclaim the Hill. Not what they do afterwards. An era of minority governments makes that debate limiting, but it's our lot as long as Liberals are the Sun God of politics, expecting all to encircle without probing if the orbit really works. Galileo was onto something. And after politics followed a Liberal trajectory during the Chrétien–Martin 15-year-long feud, our debate sank so low that we're voting for Brian Mulroney's policies to *save* our values. But don't worry, we're told. With a new leader, the Liberals are ship-shape and ready for us to trust with our values again.

When Stronach bolted from Harper's caucus in 2005, she was often seen as having made a principled choice, driven out by unbending neo-cons. Her defection, like Brison's and other former Tories, was presented as more proof of how scary the Conservative Party had become under Harper. Hail to the moderates, the chant often went, as Liberals threw their doors open to right-wingers. Fair enough. But why didn't any MPs leave the Liberals for following their own wrong direction—as if only Tories, not progressive Liberals, should defect when parties morph rightward.

Global warming can't both be humanity's biggest threat and also not important enough for any Liberal to bolt the party for failing. Two Liberal MPs resigned when Jean Chrétien broke his promise to abolish the GST, but none did over not lowering climate-changing emissions. That doesn't add up, but as long as all that counts in the end is keeping the Liberal Party big, we'll all keep being stuck in unproductive loops. Some of us will be in government but marginalized, some outside government and marginalized there—as progressives everywhere get the sense that Canada's missing some progressive potential.

Consider former Liberal Cabinet Minister Lloyd Axworthy, one of the vanguards of the party's left flank. In office, his party embarked on steep—and often unnecessary—cuts to social programs and allowed Canada's voice in the world to wither. He is more eloquent out of office, which is sad.

New Democrats and non-partisan progressives weren't the only ones who didn't win much during the hegemony years; progressive Liberals lost, too. Before forming the cavalry to rush off and rescue them, politics in flux might provide a fix in a *different* party that could also win. But as long as politics asks how many Liberals will win, not how many progressives, we'll never know.

Progressives need to punish governments for failing and offer alternatives to do better. Without competition and realignment on the left, politics will keep shifting to the right. A divided right accelerated things and eventually dragged the Conservative Party the wrong way. The Liberal Party kept up, however, and is now a place where Mulroney Tories are mainstream. We do indeed still have a largish Liberal Party, but it's much less liberal—and increasingly ever less likely to aspire.

It's funny how a Liberal retirement often triggers some of the good stuff. Pierre Trudeau's peace tour around the world came as a swan song in his final year as prime minister, but his government allowed cruise missile tests only a few years before. Jean Chrétien's legacy hunt was often progressive—the Iraq War or championing African development—but while in unfettered majority governments, Canada's role in the world shrank. Like child care, if we only celebrate what Liberals do before they lose instead of ask where that purpose was just after they won, Canada will keep lagging under nominally progressive governments. What does it say that Liberals critique Martin's bungling of a scandal more than they critique Chrétien's bungling of the climate?

Multi-party democracy lets us do something about it and elect Parliaments with more progressives to push for and implement more change sooner. They help us ask what's possible, not only what is offered, and create the chance to have politics that aspire. Changing Canadian politics presents possibility as well as danger, but to realize it, we have to hope that it's possible to do better than we have.

Monique Bégin did just that. She was the Liberal health minister behind the Canada Health Act, but didn't stop at asking what the rules let her do. In the dying days of the Trudeau government in 1984, she rewrote them. At the time, Ottawa had no way to stop people from paying out of their pocket for necessary care because of doctors' extra billing. Instead of hiding behind impotence, Bégin wrote new rules that looked forward and she won—by asking what she could do, not what her predecessors didn't.

Europe has long asked what is possible and out of chaos began to build ways to let progressive ideas win. Europeans didn't have to. They wanted to. And as the European Union grows, it doesn't ask its new members to accept only rules that make trade easier; it makes new entrants do better on many fronts before they can join.[34] Europe enjoys market economics, but still manages to keep living standards higher for more working people. It's attractive and countries clamber over each other trying to get in, but before getting access to the club, they need to improve their own domestic laws. Turkey, for example, has ushered in a raft of civil liberties reforms to help get a chance at better trade; former Soviet bloc countries moved from repressive states protecting to minority groups in a historical blink of the eye.

As the EU helps its business trade, it also helps less well-off members compete on a more level playing field—not by lowering the bar, but often by raising it. Ireland, Portugal, and Spain received often-generous help as a more progressive integration pushes living and environmental standards up. Ireland is an economic sparkplug, in part, thanks to it; Portugal has just changed its national building codes to require solar power as it rushes to join the world's green energy revolution, while Canada lollygagged for a decade.

While in Europe minority rights are won because they are wanted, Liberals here waited for years until courts made them do it. Each year that progressive Canadians spend pushing Liberals to do better is another year when Europe pulls further ahead because it *wants* to.

Comparing ourselves only to the United States creates a false impression that Canada is at the front of the pack. We are on creating a country that's diverse and open-minded, but we aren't on sustainability and we lag well behind innovative economies in the United States, Japan, and Europe. A solar panel that works in Berlin will work

34. *Why Europe will Run the 21st Century* by Mark Leonard.

in BC, and a fuel-efficient car in Osaka will also run on the streets of Ottawa, but if all that counts is ratifying something that Americans won't, progressives are denied politics that aspire because it works for Liberals. By echoing it, we become backwards Oliver Twists, doffing our cap to the Liberals and politely asking after long years of knowing the answer, "Please, Sir, may I have some less?"

With politics changing along with the climate, asking how to win less is limiting, but as long as all that counts is doing better than the Americans, that's where we end up—equating progressive foreign policy with not invading Iraq. Lost in the chest-beating was that Canada was solidly among the global majority, what with Iraq's grand coalition boiling down sadly to two. Canada wasn't ahead of the pack; we were mainstream, which caps possibility for a country that longs to play a larger—and leading, not merely mainstream—progressive role in our world like Europe does.

Europe is enthusiastically multilateral, which doesn't make it either neutral or pacifist. It wants to work with others on fixing big problems, and regularly sees security issues to extend beyond the usual. For many progressives, Afghanistan is worrisome not because we are in Afghanistan so much as where we are not. It's unbalanced, and Canada seems to hop to it on multilateralism only when it's American-supported multilateralism, not the broader kind that Canadians like. We want tragedies in Rwanda or Sudan to count, too, and saw a glimpse of it in Kosovo in 1999.

With a humanitarian crisis unfolding in the Balkans, the EU, U.S. President Bill Clinton, and Canada responded through NATO to militarily intervene, and progressive Canadians supported it. It's the kind of approach most of us are comfortable with and takes a broader look at problems to include humanitarian ones that worried for no reason other than people needed help. Key is that Europe asked what it could do, not what it hadn't done yet. It aspired for more and applied the same kind of common sense that it does to the climate crisis where it is the world's progressive superpower—asking what it can do, not what the Americans haven't.

Deliciously, debate in Europe is multipronged. Each member country has multi-party systems and most of them also enjoy often workable proportional representation. In countries with PR, parties of the centre-left and centre-right compete with arrays of smaller, more ideological parties on the margins of left and right and often sizable Green parties thrown in. Europeans get all of the advantages of two-sided debate, but without an encompassing, empty middle; each side tends to mean it and newer ideas can gain by being rewarded at the polls. Here, large brokerage parties such as the Liberals like to pick priorities in secret after the election.

In Europe, the deal-making on policy is often public—through coalitions in minority situations—while in Ottawa, it's behind closed doors during each majority government. Secretive backrooms exist in Europe, too, but thanks to more diverse politics, they are not the only haunt for debate. It's heresy, all of it, to the Liberal Party, which says we need large brokerage parties of the middle, forcing progressives to work within the Liberal Party to make gains and lowering progressive bars along the way. They rarely advertise that progressive Liberals have to compete behind closed doors with the right-wingers, or the hangers-on that predictable wins bring in the Joe Volpes.

Volpe, the leadership candidate shunned after taking donations from children of well-connected friends, was Paul Martin's *political minister for Toronto*. The poster child for what is wrong with the Liberal Party, in fact, doled out Liberal favours in the most Liberal part of the country, all, apparently, without anyone wondering if it was a good idea. It's into these backrooms that Liberals try to push debate by asking progressives to sacrifice one more time to keep multi-party democracy down and the Liberal Party up. To help keep Canada Canadian, even when we're doing worse than the Yanks.

And then there's America. In 2006, Democrats swept back and controlled both houses of Congress. Progressive Canadians were gleeful as our cousins handed George W. Bush a thumping and retook Capitol Hill for the first time in a dozen years and, looking on, cocked a smile as Donald Rumsfeld walked the plank. Finally, that elephant we're in bed with whittled its radicals down to size, making it only a matter of time before we get rid of ours. Right?

Democrats lost control of Congress in 1994, a year after Liberals gained control of Parliament. If the binary code is right in equating Stephen Harper with Bush and Liberals with progress, Canada should be far ahead of the United States. Arnold Schwarzenegger thinks otherwise, but as long as we compare our symbols to American symbols, the hegemony mirage will say that Canada is progressive by dint of the president being conservative. And that Canada is greener because we signed onto Kyoto while Bush did not—just don't ask why our emissions are rising faster.

As long as that's the paradigm, progressive people can't ask tough questions that contradict the frame. For example, the U.S. has long banned some of the world's most toxic chemicals like flame retardants. It took a Conservative government here to follow suit, meaning for a dozen years the Liberals let the Americans do *better*. Yes, I said it: Harper did something good, and in progressive circles, them's fighting words. As the binary march towards American-style debate continues, we risk judging ideas based on their source, not their content. Harper's ideas are always dangerous while Liberal ones are more in line, and Canada is better because we are not American. It's not always so clear-cut.

Americans enjoy stronger protection of drinking water than we do; they have often-tougher rules on toxics than we do; and the U.S. had laws to protect endangered species long before we did. And regional groupings of states are trying to honour Kyoto without Washington. Pacific states, northeastern states, and some in the Midwest—along with some 200 cities—are ushering in some innovative stuff to cut emissions growth. In Canada, Liberals gave us a TV ad challenging Canadians to pitch in and do our bit, while American governments challenged themselves to get going. Why didn't Canada's Liberals?

There are other examples, too: A Republican Congress failed to abolish America's affordable housing program as Canada's Liberal Parliament did in the 1990s; and American public transit was federally funded before it happened in a minority Parliament here. Sometimes, Canada was more progressive—child tax benefit—and Liberals did shore up the Canada Pension Plan, but it wasn't interchangeable. Being Canadian didn't always mean being more progressive.

On trade, Liberal prime ministers were interchangeable with Democratic and Republican presidents alike for a decade, pushing for more NAFTA-style integration. But the problems with NAFTA or some of the more progressive kind of trade that's possible was left aside in the race to replace Paul Martin. Shouldn't natural governing parties at least have a debate before asking us again to let them be our progressive champions facing some big questions?

Our progressive American cousins know where this ends up, and before letting it happen here, we should imagine the depressing life in a deep blue state. You sit there, unloved and unattended, because Democrats are fighting states over the Republican swing vote. You're sometimes taken for granted and might wonder where a more progressive Democratic Party went, but have to vote for them anyway because George W. Bush is such a fright. It creates common tactics that excite us when Republicans lose, but that isn't the same as progressives winning when they do.

If multi-party democracies don't stop and ask if these binary choices are real, we'll keep being stuck in the wrong kind of blue state. We will celebrate being better than Bush without asking why Arnold Schwarzenegger is doing better than we are, and celebrate Liberals coming first because it means Harper didn't. Eventually, we will be like the depressed progressive in a U.S. blue state, wondering where real debate went and unable to mount pressure to put it back in balance.

Multi-party democracy provides more options because it lets progressive pressure be mounted on a system that allows it to work. Unlike the U.S., our toolbox includes minority Parliaments that make progressive wins easier by empowering more parties. If medicare can be born during a time of flux with Liberals weak, this could be a time to hope that we can do better. With the Terminator doing better than Canada on fighting global warming, it's at least worth a rethink about what's really strategic.

Alberta and the Betamax Lesson

IN THE MID-1970s, electronic giants Sony and JVC did battle over the new arrival of video players. Sony made Betamax, while JVC pumped out VHS in one of marketing's most famous fights. JVC won, and Sony's bid to control the marketplace by open-sourcing Betamax technology lost, as more and more companies climbed aboard the VHS train. It's too bad, because VHS was rotten, but in the end Beta was only embraced by the television industry.

It just became popular to use VHS. And the more it was used, the more popular it became until few people asked if it was better. In the big scheme of things, a couple of decades of using an inferior video player isn't the end of the world, but that might not apply to our government. For almost a century now, we've kept voting Liberal, and the more we do, the more popular it becomes, so when the chips are down we often have a tough time asking if the habit's really worth it.

We can't ask that if elections aren't about Liberal failures in lefty eyes. And if we listen carefully to Liberals in elections where defeat stares them in the face, the dominant message isn't their goodness, but that something is so bad it must be stopped. This bad thing is never their record.

Come election time, Alberta usually fits the bill and is routinely vilified by Liberals. Odd, for a party so Canadian, that its ticket includes exploiting tensions, but also important if we are going to reframe. Particularly in Ontario, we aren't going to get far without trusting cousins in other regions—like the West, which is often attacked only because it happens to include Alberta.

That's a Liberal frame of how Canada works, and as sure as they will go hunting for NDP votes, a modern Liberal campaign isn't complete without healthy lashings of Albertaphobia. We've seen it in the ritual frothing against Ralph Klein in each of the last three elections, and the character assassination of Stockwell Day's religious beliefs when he made his federal debut in 2000. Alberta's the monster under the bed for a Liberal campaign, and they love to demonize it as they shuck for votes in Ontario—while doing sweet nothing to prevent it from privatizating health care or helping prepare for its oil running out. That's some time away, but Alberta's looming water crisis isn't and if water really is the new oil, maybe building firewalls around a parched province isn't such a good idea.

One way or another, the oil industry won't run the energy show forever, and again like Liberals, it's only a question of how much damage it can do beforehand. And Liberals have much in common with the Alberta they malign, showing a healthy addiction to tar sand oil over the last decade. They helped (in a harbinger of trouble to come) pawn it to not one, but two, superpowers in China and the United States. As our currency becomes a petro-dollar, emissions soar and water dries out, that we've not had a good chat about this is a problem. This doesn't mesh with an enemy hunt, however.

To Liberals, if Americans aren't to blame, it was those right-wing loons in Alberta. Listening to them, one might not know Alberta's public health care reforms are among our most innovative. We're unlikely to hear that it's Canada's leading renewable energy producer, with exciting projects such as Calgary's light rail system, which is powered by wind. Alberta has good ideas and bad ones, which makes it like every other province. If we'd like to shrink Liberals, Alberta's will need to be judged on their merits, instead of dismissed because it elects herds of Tories. Vilifying it isn't likely to return fewer right-wingers, but we've got to stop buying into the Liberals' enemy machine.

The 2006 election wasn't a promising start, and Stephen Harper often came under progressive fire for being an Albertan. Buzz Hargrove provided the clearest example, and in his infamous campaign-ending event with Martin when he suggested that people vote for the Bloc, essentially said Albertans' fondness for individualism made them un-Canadian. This earned a public rebuke from Alberta's unions, which had a point, for Harper's hometown is Toronto. It's also difficult to see why Klein's government made Alberta that much worse than Ontario given Ontarians had twice elected Mike Harris.

Granted, Alberta is rather dependably blue. It hasn't had a true change in government in almost a century, and rotates through right-wing ideologies rather than try a real change. Federally, it is a bastion of conservatism and clean sweeps of the province occur often, though Edmonton has pockets of resistance. Another part of Canada reliably delivers bushels of conservative votes, but is obscured partially by being part of Ontario. It exists nonetheless, and a great band of blue stretches from the Ottawa Valley down to the southern shores of Lake Huron.

Ontario and the West resemble each other. Both have large spots of blue with the West's sometimes seeming larger due to Alberta being a separate province. If Ontario were carved into four provinces like the West, it's a fair bet one of them would vote like Alberta. Ontario is no more or less progressive than BC or the Prairies, and Ontario lefties need to de-link progressive and Liberal. Western progressives often aren't Liberals, but can beat Tories, too. To unite the left, the flag on the legislature—indeed, provincial boundaries themselves—may not mean much. With Canada's politics splintering, one Albertan's advice helps ask if voting Liberal really is all that strategic.

🍁   🍁   🍁

Joe Clark once famously described Canada as a community of communities. It's helpful to reframing politics that, instead of being caught up in federal politics' contrived provincialism and regionalism, to focus on the kind of communities that make up an increasingly urban Canada.

With our votes split all over and with minorities more likely, a progressive electoral map might not have six regions—BC, the Prairies, Ontario, Quebec, Atlantic Canada and the North—but three: West of Quebec, Quebec, and east of it. Whether a lefty lives in Ontario or Saskatchewan doesn't matter much. We're in the same boat together, making Alberta a progressive ally in a time of flux.

East of Quebec is largely not a lefty battlefield. Atlantic Canada wouldn't necessarily balk at a dominant NDP, but old-time voting habits are only gradually changing. More and more, Nova Scotia is voting more like Ontario and Manitoba than other Atlantic provinces. The 18 seats in Newfoundland and Labrador, PEI and anglo New Brunswick aren't showing signs yet, and this small pocket is a straight Liberal–Conservative fight for now.

But in Nova Scotia, change is afoot. With broad support in Metro Halifax, some rural towns and industrial Cape Breton, the NDP has been stronger than its Liberal counterpart for some time. As the province undergoes a change in dominant progressive party, it has also elected a rash of minority governments and the NDP has been productive in a loose relationship with moderate Tories. Federally, Atlantic Canada is mainly loyal to tradition, but Alexa McDonough mixed things up with her debut as NDP leader in 1997.

Though often mocked for running in Halifax, where McDonough formerly led the Nova Scotia NDP, sometimes as its legislature's only woman, she stood firm. When elected in 1995 to succeed Audrey McLaughlin, she was adamant about running at home and many, believing it unlikely she could win, questioned her call. The NDP had elected Atlantic MPs at times, and on Cape Breton with some regularity in the 1970s, but never had more than two at a time. In his four elections as leader, Ed Broadbent won only three seats in Atlantic Canada and none since 1980, except for the telling St. John's seat in a by-election.

West of Quebec's a progressive battleground, though. And its 23 million people from the Ottawa River to the Pacific and Arctic Oceans make two-sided races for government—not multi-sided Parliaments— a poor fit. Though NDP encroachment into Atlantic Canada since 1988 didn't cost the Liberals a single seat, the Liberals' unquestioned march west has not been so forgiving to the New Democrats.

From 1988 totals, the NDP is now down nine in BC and 10 in Saskatchewan. It is also down one seat in Alberta but up one in Manitoba, which deserves an asterisk since the 1988 campaign followed immediately after a messy defeat of the province's NDP government. Briefly, the NDP fell to third place in Manitoba as Liberals temporarily soared. But as time progressed things normalized, and Liberals are again a rump presence in the Manitoba legislature.

Liberals haven't taken root beyond select parts of Vancouver and Winnipeg, however. They have become fond of ritzy neighbourhoods, though, and as Tories become more radical, Liberals become more Tory and keep soaking up the hoi-polloi refugees. And along the way, became the party of The Establishment.

Across Canada, most gentrified neighbourhoods outside of Alberta have Liberal MPs. In almost every major city, the most-connected parts of town—Westmount, Outremont, Rockcliffe, Forest Hill, Rosedale, Wellington Crescent, Point Grey—all have Liberal MPs. These moderate-right urbanites used to be Tories, outside of Quebec, but no more. Politics' new rules have changed the old axiom that New Democrats are Liberals in a hurry, and the most recent majorities show Liberals in a hurry now to be Tories. None of Mulroney's policies that earned him such loathing was reversed by Liberal majorities that followed. That was their choice, and now it's time for us to make ours—strategically.

Clark's take on Canada helps, and breaks down the region west of Quebec into five kinds of communities. The first is most likely to go Tory, and its towns dot the rural landscape across the south. Both the Liberals and NDP won seats in rural areas, but towns such as Bracebridge, Camrose, Comox, Grande Prairie, High River, Pembroke,

Penticton, Souris, Steinbach, Strathroy, Swift Current and Viking are most likely to vote Tory.

Every democracy has a functioning conservative party that enjoys strong support in areas like these, and as long as Kentucky and South Dakota, the Australian Outback and Sussex in England are safe for those countries' right-wingers, we can't stop ours from winning seats they get to mainly mail in.

But we can stop them elsewhere, starting in the two big cities. Toronto and Vancouver have more than 70 seats, and are both surrounded by sprawling suburbs: Mississauga and York Region in Toronto, or Burnaby and Richmond in Vancouver. There are also many medium-sized cities such as Calgary, Edmonton, Hamilton, Kitchener, London, Ottawa, Regina, Saskatoon, Victoria, Windsor and Winnipeg, with between nine and three ridings a piece.

Throughout the region, smaller cities such as Abbotsford, Barrie, Brandon, Kamloops, Kingston, Lethbridge, Oshawa, Peterborough, Prince Albert, Prince George, Red Deer, Sarnia, Sault Ste. Marie, St. Catharines, Sudbury and Thunder Bay form one riding, or join with surrounding rural areas in two ridings that split the main city in two.

In the far north, places such as Fort McMurray, Iqaluit, Kenora, La Ronge, Prince Rupert, Thompson, Timmins, Whitehorse and Yellowknife sit among resource towns and often smaller but more plentiful Aboriginal communities. They form huge ridings, sometimes bigger than France or Germany.

It's a progressive battlefield, and Liberals and New Democrats fight throughout. In 2006, only 13 per cent separated the two parties nationally—skewed in Liberals' favour, with more votes in Quebec. That's an I've-drunk-the-Kool-Aid hegemony, and removing Liberals boils down to wanting to. But it's going to happen only if pressure is applied to changing something, not protecting the status quo. If we see more wins becoming possible in this realignment, now's our time.

If we ever had elections where it's permissible—positive, even—to vote for parties you want to better, some Liberals would win and good for them. The benefits of multi-party democracy don't end if the biggest party changes, but multi-party democracy only works with, you know, multiple parties. There'll be none of those productive minorities without larger third and fourth parties. They'd also likely become more stable—like Nova Scotia's—if more common. It all makes strategically voting Liberal often unstrategic with so many different kinds of races underway in elections.

Screaming Stop Harper on this battlefield is a de facto call to Vote Liberal, given history and how elections are framed. It also lets Tories win seats they should lose, leading to Edmonton, Oshawa, Peterborough and Saskatoon having only Conservative MPs. As Canada becomes more urban it shouldn't become more conservative, but the trend could be snapped if we saw through the hegemony mirage instead of reinforcing it.

Liberals are vulnerable, and their true weakness is seen when ridings basically safe for one party or another are taken away. This leaves 68 ridings won by 5,000 votes or fewer (listed in the appendix). If we look at them, the allegedly strategic path of Think Twice was anything but, starting with seven ridings where three parties were within 5,000 votes. Liberals won more than others, but either the Liberals or NDP could have swept all seven.

In the remaining 61 seats, 15 were NDP–Liberal races, 10 were NDP–Conservative races and 36 were Liberal–Conservative races. The NDP won seven of 15 contests against Liberals but just two of 10 versus Conservatives. When the three-way races are included, the NDP won only 17 of the ridings decided by 5,000 votes, and lost head-to-head contests with Tories in six cities, five in the West proper. All of the NDP's urban races with Liberals were in Ontario, where Think Twice's prominence was largest, but whose purpose was unclear. Ontario's big cities are the least likely of anywhere to elect Tories.

In other words, there were 29 NDP MPs elected, plus 21 ridings where the party ended up within 5,000 votes. New Democrats weren't fighting for a few more piddling seats: they had legitimate shots in 50—15 of which were losing NDP ridings within 5,000 votes of a

Tory. What's strategic about not wanting those kind of progressive wins in a minority Parliament?

It's explained away any number of ways, but Think Twice's advice to Vote Liberal ends up seeing Liberals defeating Tories and New Democrats as better than NDP candidates defeating Liberals and Tories. With no party able to win a majority, the obvious question is why? Particularly, given Liberal surges in the West hurt the NDP in its traditional region of dominance. New Democrats don't need Liberal advice on how to beat Tories in the West.

Whichever parties' message Think Twice reinforces, Tories won't be the only victim. We're not servants who have to rush to help, though, and could have more shades of grey available to us than we think. With Liberals helping Tories defeat New Democrats in more than 10 ridings, and minorities in the offing, why underline the Liberal line that elections are all about coming in first?

Swing voters between Conservatives and Liberals aren't going to be impressed much with another lefty Liberal endorsement. Swing Liberal–NDP voters might be, or New Democrats might be driven into becoming swing voters. The only people who pay any attention are questioning progressives, too often beaten into being fearful than encouraged to hope. I know I'm odd, but if none of your neighbours is a raving right-winger, and a Tory didn't win the 'hood even as Brian Mulroney swept the country, maybe, just maybe, it's not so strategic to vote Liberal to stop them.

In a *Globe and Mail* column after the election, Hargrove claimed that strategic voting worked because in the 43 ridings where the CAW endorsed New Democrats, they largely won. Undeniably true. It's also true that Oshawa, which with Windsor is where the union has the most clout, re-elected a Tory MP. If the call to vote strategically isn't a blanket call to Vote Liberal, Oshawa might perhaps have voted New Democrat given it was on the list of ridings where you vote NDP without bringing on Armageddon.

When unveiling Think Twice, Hargrove was asked why he was urging people to Vote Liberal. He said that he couldn't understand why everyone kept thinking it was partisan. I couldn't imagine. Generously, it's similar to why Maude Barlow ran as Liberal: Ontario's proximity to Liberal hegemony guides many of its lefties onto the most viable path they see, leading to contortions like Hargrove berating the NDP for not being left enough, while stumping for Liberals.

Like Barlow's response to Chantal Hébert, Hargrove didn't believe Liberals were the best progressive option, but did believe them when they said only they could Stop Harper. And, I suspect, realizes his members are nowhere near in love with doctrinaire socialism as he is.

Hargrove was challenged vigorously by other union members in large NDP rallies during the campaign, but his take on things, not the thousands of workers who filled halls to defeat Liberals, perfectly fit the Liberal frame of how politics' rules work. No surprise, then, the NDP was asked how it could be so nasty to Liberals more often than Hargrove was asked why Liberals deserved the support.

The notion of large-scale strategic voting, putting aside the inherent linkage of strategic and Liberal, makes sense only if there's a Liberal Ontario and a Conservative West. Then, Ontario is obliged to overlook progressive failure on Liberals' part to give them enough seats to withstand a Tory surge heading east. That New Democrats can beat both Liberals and Tories is glossed over, and if we want to elect more productive governments we'll need to combine the two regions.

Liberals doing poorly might only mean that they won't win a majority, or—treasonously—never recover hegemony. Tories and Tommy have battled often, and Tommy's proven effective in winning more than his fair share. Still, not all Tories can be defeated, and in rural ridings can win no matter what we do.

This leads to a difficult choice, but a key one if we're going to put our majority to work. Nobody's wailing much about Liberals' decline in rural Quebec, and while rural races are often decided locally elsewhere, Quebec is different. Rural ridings west of Quebec often vote differently than cities, but Quebec's don't fit into the same mould. In Quebec, a community's size isn't as large a factor in how it votes, just as its dominant provincial parties don't fit the usual ideological divide. The Parti Québécois is both its largest progressive party and sovereigntist one, while Quebec Liberals are the dominant conservative and federalist option. This odd arrangement is also seen federally, in its three kinds of ridings.

The first type of Quebec riding is strongly federalist and found in the narrow strip that runs from downtown Montreal westward through the Island of the Montreal, ending in the Gatineau area opposite Ottawa. The second is found in the remainder of the Montreal area except west, which with a few exceptions is neither a federalist heartland nor sovereigntist hotbed.

The third is best described as everything else, and Liberals are in big trouble in a provincial election if they are not far ahead in public opinion polls. With the massive majorities its dependably federalist ridings produce, the party wastes many of its votes in ridings it has already won, needing large victories in the popular vote to be competitive with the P.Q. for government.

In each of the 1984, 1988, 2004 and 2006 elections, Liberals failed to win seats in any part of Quebec beyond the narrow federalist strip. Before Mulroney's coalition splintered, the remainder of Quebec was solidly blue though the NDP appeared viable in 1988. In the 2004 and 2006 elections, the "everything else" region was Bloc turf that Tories are encroaching on. Though the Liberals can win more seats in Quebec than the NDP currently, they aren't factors in most of rural Quebec, where the Bloc and Tories compete. We don't need to know much more about how Quebec's ridings vote beyond knowing that urban areas outside western Montreal and Gatineau have a lot in common with rural areas, making rural Quebec much more important than rural ridings elsewhere.

Quebec's cities, however, are very much like those elsewhere in a ringing endorsement of Canada being a community of communities. Quebec City could be Halifax or Victoria, while gritty Trois-Rivières resembles Hamilton, Prince George or Sydney. From college cities like Sherbrooke to resource outposts in Sept-Iles or the large Aboriginal population, if progressive people outside Quebec could form a common frame to push against with our counterparts there, our majority would be unbeatable. Seeing the Bloc as an ally is risky. Until further notice, its prime purpose is separation, not progressive wins.

Problems would also have come if either Harper or Martin had won in 2006. Harper's are clear, but Martin's two-decade dither on climate change, incoherence on Quebec, U.S. relations, let's-make-a-deal attitude to equalization, or turning the Charter into a prop would have been interesting, too.

Citizens outside Quebec would also likely have had a difficult time explaining to Quebecers why we didn't mind Liberals trying to buy their love. For Ontario, an explanation might also have been due about how bad it had to get, exactly, before it craved a fresh start, too. Hallelujah for multi-party democracy. And back to Hargrove again.

His third campaign stop with the Liberals came in Strathroy, Ontario. It's a town of 13,000 people in the London area that elected a Liberal in the first divided right election of 1993, and re-elected her since. It was here that he endorsed and unendorsed the Bloc. Nominally, he went to salute a $60-million investment in a local auto plant, which is about $1.34 billion less than what the oil industry gets in direct federal subsidy a year.

Brilliant. Let's give more money to the money-printing companies drilling for what we say we want less of, and let the Big Three automakers stay addicted to large cars that we'll be buying less of, not helping them change. Oil reserves aren't about to pick up and move to Mississippi or China, while our manufacturing base—pounded by a dollar driven high by oil—isn't quite so immune.

Liberals don't want these debates, and as long as they are the bigger "progressive" party, we won't have them much. Another lop-sided trade with South Korea might loom, we might keep failing to build greener cars here, but elections won't talk about them as long as the goal is stopping something, not winning it. Like Elizabeth May on climate change, offering better progressive ideas for auto policy than Liberals isn't seen as that interesting when the CAW president is urging the re-election of the long-serving governing party, as he did in Strathroy. If space isn't created, it can't be filled—defeating the very benefit of dynamic multi-party systems: the ability to make change.

In Hargrove's words, Strathroy was a riding where the NDP had no hope. He went to urge Strathroynians to Vote Liberal to replace its Liberal MP, Rosemary Ur. She opposed equal marriage and was one of the more vocal opponents of gun control. Like hordes of others Liberals keep in their ranks, she's not progressive and the ambitions of Liberals like her need to become their problem, not ours. The seat was lost by more than 9,000 votes in the end, as Hargrove found the most cameras going to urge everyone, everywhere to Vote Liberal, to save Strathroy. After some clarification, this included people in rural Quebec, who were invited to hop on the red *Titanic* sinking like a stone.

Hargrove insists he went to tell only Strathroynians how to vote. They have local media for this, which reach fewer people than the 32 million available viewers, listeners and readers who could take in his advice. There were so many races at play, a simple message to Vote Liberal didn't apply across the board. But history and politics' old rules lend credence to it, and it is magnified.

The *Vancouver Sun* is broader than the *Brandon Sun*. The *Toronto Star* reaches more people than its Sudbury namesake; national papers and networks cover even more ground. People don't need to follow Think Twice's advice for it to do the most damage, and help frame the election as one where a smaller NDP grows only at Liberal expense. Instead of helping to Stop Harper, the NDP is sometimes wrongly seen as a Harper Helper.

The U.K. has a similar group to Think Twice, and in its recent election built elaborate Web sites to advise the like-minded of how best to stop British Tories. While in Canada, navigating the 68 close ridings west of Quebec was left up to voters and reporters, in the U.K. every riding's voting history was put on a Web site. In most cases, its advice was to vote out of choice, not strategy, as most ridings were either safe for one party, or a Labour-Liberal Democrat race a Tory couldn't win. Think Twice didn't take even this basic step, and its Web site was all about why we needed to Stop Harper. More hopefully, if our pressure can sway elections to help Liberals, we can also bring about positive change if we'd like.

Change would also become structural given new electoral financing laws that make the Liberal Party, the most reliant upon large corporate donations before new laws, evermore dependent upon $1.75 a vote in public subsidy. Were progressive pressure applied to shrink Liberals, they would become increasingly more incapacitated to run the usual Cadillac campaign, as more progressive entities grow in clout. Liberals are already in the poorhouse, and we can keep them there—instead of pumping the strategic bounty that $1.75 a vote brings into Liberal coffers in elections' dying days. The NDP and Reform Party were both funded mainly by small, individual donations, but Liberals are having a tough time adapting.[35] Oh well. It's not progressives' fault, but the party's.

It's another good reason why we should kick 'em while they're down, and trust that we can do more than squabble over how to get our hands on Liberal crumbs. To go for the loaf, we need to trust people like us in other regions. They're the reason we are the majority and we don't need a Liberal interpreter to speak with them. Instead, we should remove the confusion the meaningless middle creates. So let's do as Rae suggests and unite, but recognize that what's strategic for him isn't necessarily so smart for us. Like the right, we did indeed leave the 1990s at odds, but our division was different.

---

35. In 2005, Liberals raised half as much money as Conservatives from donations and had fewer individual donors than the NDP. Before the change in electoral financing, the NDP—contrary to perception that it was fuelled only by union donations—didn't only have the largest percentage of its funding coming from individuals of the three federalist parties. It raised more money, period, from individuals than the Liberal Party and before the change in the law, 70 per cent of NDP finances came from individuals.

The *No Logo* Divide

19

CHAPTER

THE TRAGEDY OF OUR progressive majority not applying itself to Ottawa is underlined by Canada producing some of the
world's foremost progressive people. Stephen Lewis stirs people to
act worldwide against the AIDS scourge, David Suzuki is a clarion
voice on the urgency to deal with climate change and Maude Barlow
is loathed by some of the world's nastiest entities, while respected by
some of its most innovative progressive people.

Our hopes echo regularly in the world, but we often live under
governments at home that turn a blind eye to the crises of our time,
or make them worse. And as the century began, no Canadian voice
echoed around the world like author Naomi Klein. In 2000, she published *No Logo*, which became a world bestseller and influenced the
movement against the wrong kind of globalization.

No Logo was translated into more than 20 languages and excites
many people still, often further to the left. In Klein's home country,
however, we've yet to use her main point to create conditions that let
progressive people co-operate in elections, which is tragic. Progressive
Canadians are among the world's most able to find common frames
with other progressives against which to push, but live in a country

where Hamilton, Prince George, Sydney and Trois-Rivières see politics so differently, they voted for four different parties in 2006—three of them, allegedly progressive.

But are they? We have yet to send our first cheap AIDS pill to Africa, years after Liberals pledged Canada's help. We choke on emissions rising faster than the Texas oil man's in the White House, becoming an oily Colombia, feeding the Americans' dangerous addiction. And we're unsurpassed in our zeal for the kind of trade agreements we know hurt the environment, workers and our ability to write our own rules through elections. Our largest failing, however, is that while we bemoan the wrong kind of globalization's impact upon democracy around the world, many progressive people think our domestic national politics are largely not worth much time.

Today, it's common to hear lefties say the only politics that count are local or global. Many proponents are drawn to city politics, where a tangible impact is seen, and leading the way is Ottawa city councillor Clive Doucet who, despite living in the nation's capital, says the federal government is irrelevant. He is collateral damage from the deep frustration at not applying our majority to Parliament. For many, often the main purpose of federal elections is to stop something worse from happening and then re-focus elsewhere. This needs to change if we're going to participate in the world with a government behind us, and build a country at home that reflects what we tell the world Canada stands for.

Clearly, more politics matter than either local or global. Almost all progressive people have a strong opinion about Stephen Harper, just as opinions run strong about recent elections in Venezuela or the United States. We clearly do care who wins, and shouldn't let frustrations such as 1988 or 2006 leave us bogged in thinking that the best we can do in the Americas is watch progressives majorities remove conservative leaders and elect progressive ones. We should decide to join in, but only by seeing more opportunity than danger in Liberal weakness.

It isn't simple and inevitably needs some blunt partisanship to declaw the Liberal Party while it's weak. We're going to have to find common project with progressive Quebecers, too, but thankfully *No Logo's* basic premise still works. It's too bad it leaves the impression that partisan politics are passé and seemingly newer, seemingly more exciting forms of progressive activism will inevitably take over. Reading *No Logo,* you'd think that Canadians can only work around the world for change, and not in Ottawa. But Klein's key point can be made more empowering: by seeing Canada as a two-sided argument that a progressive majority can win.

That's what her book, which described the then-nascent "anti-globalization" movement, holds true for the world, and there's no reason it can't work at home. If we think we have a progressive majority, we should put it to work. We don't have to argue about whether electoral politics really matters, or how best to finagle progressive votes so Liberals can be punished without being harmed. Instead, we could set our sights higher and pack the punch that one of the world's most progressive and open societies can. In short, we should demand the loaf after growing frustrated at crumbs.

Think Twice is wrong in overlooking politics' new rules. Maude Barlow, Buzz Hargrove and Elizabeth May see partisan politics through a Liberal frame that doesn't want to see the opportunity that Liberal weakness brings. But there is another part to politics' new rules, and Think Twice's principals aren't wrong always. Around the world, non-partisan players are organized and effective. And as politics sorted itself out after 1988, it's merciful that partisanship isn't the only part of Canada's new rules.

Following the Second World War, conservatives were on the outs in American politics and removed from mainstream thought. In response, the pariahs built institutions to promote conservatism. From think tanks to foundations, infrastructure emerged to help further conservative principles which, while not necessarily agents of the Republican Party, both gave birth to Republican agents and helped negatively brand progressive ideas.[36] These grew and became more

36. *What's the Matter with Kansas,* by Thomas Frank; and *Rescuing Canada's Right,* by Adam Daifallah and Tasha Kheriddin.

ambitious, and today help divide America on everything from faith to global warming. Karl Rove's daddies, if you will.

We've already got this kind of progressive infrastructure in Canada, on everything from economics to social policy to the environment. What we don't have, and won't get until the Liberal Party is a lot smaller, is the essential two-sided frame against which to use it. The apparent Republican electoral genius has helping hands to provide the kind of external validation that Think Twice largely provided to Liberals, as progressive people emerged from the 1990s on different tactical sides. Partly, due to the state of the NDP as the decade began.

As the 1993 election approached it was desperately weak, bordering on dead in Ontario. Bob Rae was convinced he could bring Ontario out of recession single-handedly, and fared badly. In its only election with Audrey McLaughlin as leader, the NDP lost official status, won only 6 per cent of the vote and elected nine MPs. Rae, endless constitutional wrangling and a miserable economy compounded McLaughlin's woes, just as Brian Mulroney's repulsion made Kim Campbell's spell as the first woman prime minister brief.

Nasdaq was about to rise on the dot.com bubble, and old rules appeared to rewrite themselves everywhere as voters handed the PC Party the world's worst peaceful defeat ever. As Mulroney's coalition splintered into regional rumps and three parts, Campbell was left holding the smallest and lost 293 of 295 seats including her own. If anyone had said in 1989 that the parties of Mulroney and Ed Broadbent would be unable to reach Parliament's magic number of 12 for official status, they would have been scorned. But it happened, as two of the three old-time parties had 11 MPs—combined.

Jean Chrétien became PM with 177 MPs, Lucien Bouchard controversially led the opposition with 54 MPs and the new Reform Party under Preston Manning had 52, with an Independent MP from Quebec. Canadians had returned a Parliament without a progressive English voice, which Barlow helped provide throughout the 1990s. But as bad as the 1993 election was for the NDP, its result would still cause excitement in Green circles in an uncomfortable reminder of how low some sights are set facing the calamity of global warming.

As the 1990s ended, Barlow was often called the unofficial leader of the opposition, as vigorous resistance to rightward Liberal policies came from outside Parliament. Her organization, the Council of Canadians, was formed in the mid-Eighties when she helped propel the fight against free trade, and a decade later was a gnawing progressive problem for the government. After Chrétien implemented NAFTA—which expanded 1988's free trade deal—she wrote *Straight Through the Heart: How the Liberals Abandoned a Just Society*. It was a stinging condemnation. She didn't hide her disgust.

After losing a Liberal nomination in 1988, she continued to be one of free trade's most vociferous opponents. Turner's debate with Mulroney may have managed to avoid humiliation for Liberals, but the most memorable were outside the partisan arena. Barlow and business advocate Tom d'Aquino squared off on more integration into the United States in eloquent, gripping and engaging terms. Canada debated a clear, two-sided question and Barlow did well for progressive people. Quebec's complications tragically re-elected Mulroney, and free trade became law.

She never looked back. The Council of Canadians grew through much of the 1990s and broadened as the decade progressed to cover many issues with a corporate angle such as energy, genetic engineering, water ownership and trade. She has written more than 15 books, the latest a denunciation of the continental integration talks among Canada, Mexico and the U.S. that Paul Martin began as PM. Other topics included health privatization, the bulk export of freshwater and media concentration, all of which were growing concerns without much hindrance—often, help—from majority Liberal governments.

Liberals aggressively pursued the wrong kind of globalization that Barlow, the Bloc, NDP and progressive people saw as overly generous protections to corporations to do as they pleased. The rapidly growing agreements dominated much of the decade's debate. In Vancouver in 1997 and Quebec City in 2001, summits turned ugly and police reaction to overwhelmingly—though not entirely—peaceful protests triggered investigations and outrage. In Calgary in 2002, police took a much different approach and few problems emerged as the G8 Summit in Kananaskis took place an hour away in fortress-like conditions. The cops were no longer the only problem. Widespread concerns about the armed encampment and civil liberties grew.

Global gatherings of leaders became focal points for the anti-globalization movement that *No Logo* described. It was released in the aftermath of a 1999 meeting in Seattle that was the first time broad and citizen-driven activism dominated a gathering of governments. Large protests took place. Thanks as well to African and European governments inside the summit, Seattle failed to bring even more of the wrong kind of globalization. Later meetings attracted large protests, too, which were now predictably violent and sometimes fatal, as news began to focus on how (not why) protests were occurring. But news was generated. And potentially exciting alliances were forming at home and around the world, which fuelled opposition to George W. Bush, the radical new American president.

This kind of activism didn't come with the internet and has long played a crucial role in Canadian politics. It was similar, for its time, to how women won the vote in the early 20th century. The CCF itself flowed from large-scale showings of unrest, like the legendary 1919 Winnipeg General Strike. Buoyed by the energy and common sense of purpose, workers and progressive clergy came together, and by 1933 the Co-Operative Commonwealth Federation was born as lefty hopes transcended the decades. Seven have since passed, but the dream of forming progressive government that was the genesis of the CCF has yet to be realized—as the tactics, changed by technology and demographics, battered Bush shortly after he kind of won.

Initially, he was seen as a bit of a boob, who had a dubious win rigged by Republican officials in Florida and a helpful ruling from the U.S. Supreme Court. His new oil- and coal-reliant energy plan, instead of Kyoto, made progressives worried about the new Republican president's impacts on Canada and the world. This view lingered for a year or so, but wasn't the case as Bush arrived in Alberta for the 2002 G8 Summit, wooing world support for his path ahead. It ominously appeared to be a fundamentalist-fuelled Republican invasion of the Middle East dolled up as U.S. foreign policy in response to a tragedy.

The terrorist attacks of September 11, 2001 on the United States shook much of the world, and transformed many Americans along with Bush's presidency. In the year following, the Bush administration's foreign policy became sharply more aggressive and its view on the world instantly more black-and-white, as progressive people worldwide worked hard to introduce shades of grey to it. Part of the Liberals' response was to go to Afghanistan, and shortly before the 2006 election, begin the combat mission in Kandahar. Eight of 11 Liberal leadership candidates opposed extending the mission, which their own government began less than a year before without any Liberal hullabaloo, or a democratic vote.

Another Canadian development was to join Bush, Britain, Australia and other western nations and pass sweeping new security laws like America's Patriot Act, which raised significant civil liberties concerns. Progressive people fought these laws and were in lockstep with the Bloc and NDP, which opposed them, as the NDP had the Liberals' War Measures Act. Bloc and NDP MPs dug in hard, and collective pressure moved Liberals as far as a sunset clause for the Draconian law the government itself eventually admitted went too far. It has yet to be changed, though it is linked to the torture of Maher Arar in a Syrian gulag, and related police raid on journalist Juliet O'Neill's home.[37]

---

37. For fair disclosure, the RCMP used this law to deem me a security risk at the G8 Summit. I worked for Greenpeace and, together with a photographer for a labour magazine and several reporters for urban weekly papers, was denied accreditation for the media centre based on this risk assessment. None of us promoted violence. In my case, Germany's Greenpeace magazine, which is sold on newsstands in that G8 country, provided accreditation. But despite this apparent risk, within the year, they gave me a House of Commons security pass that allowed me to enter Parliament free of metal detectors or frisks, and the kind of pass I had let me be within steps of the unguarded door to the House floor and PM. At the G8, the leaders were an hour's drive from the media centre in Calgary. I met the Liberal who made the security risk call—stamping on several outlets' press freedom—on a TV panel in 2003. After letting me know, he joked about it in a commercial break.

The path to progressive victory didn't always seem to follow Douglas's ballot box route, and as the sense grew that we were getting somewhere, less energy was paid to elections. Often, Liberals seemed to be going in the right direction, though the benefits for people or the environment weren't that apparent. At times, a contest seemed to be underway for primacy of tactics, as 1988's scars remained. The Douglas frame saw Barlow often as an example of the impediment she represented, as a Liberal, to finally removing the party. Her Liberal frame saw New Democrats as dividing progressive votes, allowing free trade to pass, and exposing deep flaws in the partisan route. Despite working together often, and many invitations to Barlow to become an NDP MP, their tactics never converged.

Part of the price is paid on issues like global warming, which the NDP hasn't been able to make headway on. Majority Liberal governments have dismal records on many fronts, but punishment for their dirty secrets is rare from broader progressive circles, despite the NDP and non-partisan groups often agreeing on realistic demands, on climate change, for example. Through a Douglas frame, Liberal pollution means punishment's due, but in the timid Liberal and Ontario frame, this risks electing Tories. And dare we think it, angering Liberals who helped pollution soar.

The NDP's often left at the altar come election time: right on the issue, but wrong on tactics. Over time, it feeds the sense that the party cannot win, which is well illustrated by the feeling that Broadbent was the right man to lead the country, but in the wrong party.

Take climate change or child care. On both, 11 years of Liberal majorities made things indisputably worse, and neither eventual plan was close to the original promise, or what progressives wanted. But it was often better than nothing, creating the difficult debate where Liberals and Tories fight over the principle—Kyoto, yes or no—while Liberals and New Democrats scrap over the details—a real or fake plan? This often leaves an impression that the NDP is mostly kumbaya-chanting perfectionists or Liberals in a hurry, and hinders us from doing better if the Liberal plan is seen as good enough. Eventually, though, desperation leads non-partisan lefties to challenge the NDP for harming even timid steps ahead, instead of punishing Liberals for waiting decades to begin them. Or never get going at all.

Desperation is incentive to reframe, and recall the two victories—equal marriage and a new budget—in the 2004–2006 minority Parliament. They show that both partisan and non-partisan triumphs can excite. In a Liberal frame, a key reason why the NDP budget was good was that it protected steps ahead already contained, and was a dual win. Through a Douglas frame, equal marriage is a tribute to queers' tenacity, and not due to NDP votes any more than Liberals deserve credit. We like both kinds of victories, which is powerful reason to reframe—to let diverse tactics be used in common purpose.

This is already underway with Quebec, where common cause is often found by non-partisan progressives on many issues. Queers aren't alone in finding common project, and unions try to push ahead in Quebec and Atlantic Canada on Employment Insurance, while many green groups have alliances in Quebec, too. Child care came first in Quebec, and provided a beacon across Canada, as Saskatchewan's health care progress did decades before. These are exciting and potentially powerful, but can be made more potent through a Douglas frame that sees a partisan component as essential to big wins. Certainly, activism doesn't need partisanship to work, but either Parliament or the courts is needed to finish most jobs.

It's also fair to be appalled by Douglas's partisan and electoral fixation sometimes. Parliament Hill is often an irrelevant place that is consumed with David Dingwall's chewing gum as larger questions such as pollution, manufacturing job loss, or the grinding hopelessness of many Aboriginal people are ignored. Here, Douglas needs a hand in focusing debate on what's often more important, which can't always be done by a party alone. Tactics can be complementary, even if partisan politics or issue-based focuses don't always appeal.

Too often, differing views start to apply motive to other progressives as charges fly back and forth. Accusations that the NDP's tactics are irresponsible and that it helps Harper is one example; calling Barlow a

Liberal because she used to be one is another. New Democrats wonder why Barlow writes books but doesn't pass laws, while she may ask if the NDP has read them. This isn't getting us far, and Barlow is no more a Liberal for seeing the world than she is for growing up in Ontario and seeing it as more viable because, well, it used to be until Quebec left. As she saw events grow and link worldwide, there was little reason to probe whether 1988 was a blip for the Liberals or for the NDP. She came to view Canada's problems as linked to the world's and was not wrong.

After the 1988 election, the Council of Canadians and similar groups began to fight global problems they saw as the root of domestic ills. But even when Canada made a big progressive choice on Iraq, we hardly did so with vehemence. Despite how we often like to see ourselves, we weren't North America's leading opponent to the war. That honour fell to the conservative Mexican government of Vincente Fox, which bellowed opposition in contrast to Chrétien's muted, if correct, disagreement.

Mexico sat on the U.N. Security Council, which determined whether Bush's plans would receive global approval, and despite being equally entwined with the U.S., minced few words either speaking in Mexico City or at the U.N. It soured formerly amiable relations between the two, but for a reason, unlike Martin gratuitously attacking Bush during the 2006 election over global warming—with a record that in many ways was worse.

We're becoming a leading global hypocrite. Canada has plenty of symbolic progressive victories—and real ones, such as Vietnam, Iraq and equal marriage—but increasingly define ourselves by what we say we stand for. How we put those values into action is often quite different, or invisible, and as climate change shows best, we're perilously close to urging the world to do what we keep delaying. Canada's at risk of becoming Liberalized: asking the world to judge us on what we say, not what we do.

Throughout the 1990s, particularly when the NDP lacked official status, progressives showed spunk in trying to force Ottawa to better match rhetoric with policy, which often came via non-partisan, issue-based activism. This spark was appealing to unions, which had seen setbacks like manufacturing job loss, declining real wages for working people and shrivelling union density throughout the *No Logo* years. As they approached the 2004–2006 Parliament, the apparent inevitability of broad, issue-based activism caused many, notably the CLC, to become much less partisan in applying pressure to politics. The apparent inevitability of Liberal wins brought on a bit of a rethink, even from those formally aligned with the NDP.

Canadian unions weren't alone, and their American brethren underwent a similar introspection when several quit the CLC's sister organization, the AFL-CIO, in 2005. Nor was the CLC's new approach popular all around, and deep divisions emerged at its 2005 convention, including fisticuffs as Duceppe spoke and unleashed a torrent of abuse towards the NDP. Years of majority Liberal rule did damage to Canadian workers and middle class, whose insecurity grew as pensions, E.I. and quality jobs became scarcer and less reliable. We're hollowing out, and poverty is on a disturbing rise, partly because a majority of unemployed workers have nothing between paycheque and welfare, thanks to the Liberals' E.I. reforms which even major banks say cut too deep.

Relying on Liberals to push ahead is a non-starter. Since 1988, their dominance meant no economic issue was as debated in Ottawa as Iraq, Kyoto, Star Wars, equal marriage or either the Meech Lake or Charlottetown constitutional deals. The exception was tax cuts, which though inevitable given the size of the surplus and occasionally progressive—indexing tax brackets to protect workers from inflation—on which we got clobbered in the 2000 election. With climate change, child care, cities, and education needing solutions after seven years of promises to do something, Liberals spent $100 billion on tax cuts. Like most of us in the 1990s, unions were losing, which made some question the strong Douglas Socialist frame they had used for decades.

Hargrove not unexpectedly divided labour as the "Buzz Off, I'm voting NDP" buttons sported at large rallies in the 2006 election demonstrated. To some Douglas Socialists, he's a class traitor, but this label is unfair. Like other Ontario progressives, such as Barlow, the CAW's proximity to Liberal hegemony makes it want perfection from the NDP before it can support it. Without it, Hargrove sees little reason to sacrifice what his frame sees as pragmatism in getting things done with governments that are, usually, Liberal. It helps explain the oddity of his often vicious attacks upon Alexa McDonough for being a socialist sell-out, while being at home at Liberal campaign rallies.

The CAW is also unique among unions. It's almost exclusively Ontario-based, given the centre of the auto industry, and, given cars' relatively recent history, only grew significantly after the CCF was formed in the 1930s. During the 1950s, the communist wing of the UAW (prior to Bob White creating a separate Canadian entity, it was a joint Canada–U.S. union) used to wait until shortly before election day before endorsing the CCF to try to drive moderate votes to the Liberals. It's long demanded the party lurch further left and punished it for refusing, but shies away from punishing Liberals because it doesn't believe the NDP is viable enough.

This catch-22 is now a cyclical loop, which unless broken will keep us stuck with the Liberal Party being the not-Tory governing option forever, and to break it we need a big, non-judgmental progressive rethink in which motivation, not outcome, is key. Hargrove was clearly motivated by his members' well-being and the state of the unionized auto sector shows he was right to worry; CAW locals in London, Oshawa and Windsor gave the NDP their full support. The union is also credible economically in our largest manufacturing industry, and has shown pragmatism in dealing with troubled Big Three automakers, where it applies little of the dogmatism it demands of the NDP at the bargaining table.

But Steelworkers, by far unions' strictest Douglas Socialists, win change, too, though are less profiled. The landmark Westray bill—to hold executives criminally liable for gross health and safety violations following a tragic mine disaster—is now law thanks to them. While busy passing the bill, though, Steelworkers helped elect NDP MPs in Hamilton, Sault Ste. Marie and both northern Manitoba and New Brunswick, often felling Liberal Cabinet ministers.

Enter Elizabeth May, former president of the Sierra Club, who stepped down shortly following the 2006 election after being the most reliable validator of Liberal policy for years. She's both the most and least partisan Think Twicer, and torturously criticized the Liberals' green record while urging people concerned about humanity's future to vote for them. Her cozying up to those in charge has long been controversial and was attacked in the 1980's book, *Cloak of Green*.

Australian scientist Tim Flannery's book about climate change, *The Weather Makers*, is worth a read and if only half of what he says is true, utter fear should propel us to find common project with Quebec within Canada. Now. Unfortunately, Canada, the largest exporter of oil to the Bush administration and home to reserves on par with Saudi Arabia, didn't read Flannery criticize our Liberal government with the gusto he used for conservative regimes in Washington or Canberra. But at global Kyoto conferences for almost a decade, our Liberals were lumped in with Australia, Russia and the U.S. as prime culprits in weakening the essential agreement. May would no doubt agree, and worked in a government that was often much greener in the late 1980s.

In the last Conservative government, she worked for the environment minister and in 2005 her Sierra Club named Mulroney the greenest PM ever, primarily, to recognize his sterling work on acid rain and leading role in the landmark 1992 Earth Summit in Rio. With the science of climate change in question, our Tory government was ahead of its time in urging action, and hosted the world's first major conference in 1988. Like South African apartheid, where he differed with right-wing allies Ronald Reagan and Margaret Thatcher, Mulroney was sometimes quite progressive on the world stage. Unlike Martin, he also opposed missile defence in Reagan's Star Wars program.

But Mulroney's legacy is not all so green, and our climate-changing pollution is soaring, partly thanks to free trade. Oil production, not consumption, is behind most of our emission growth and NAFTA has made Canada the tiger in the Bush administration's tank. The NDP's alleged role in helping pass free trade scars progressive people in the re-think we need, but if it's fair to dwell on 1988 as the NDP's concerned, what about May? She helped Canadian energy policy be written in Houston by working for the Tories who threw our oil industry wide open for integration. Everyone has tactics, and hers involved close ties with two of our most conservative leaders: Mulroney and Martin.

After becoming a Liberal MP in 1988, Martin was the environment critic and condemned Mulroney's targets as being too timid. As Liberals prepared for the 1993 election, Martin co-wrote the ground-breaking Red Book, which at the time was the first detailed—and, with Liberals out of office, ambitiously progressive—platform that included a 20 per cent reduction to climate-changing pollution by 2005, actually a weaker target than Mulroney's. Liberals also promised to clean up the continent's worst toxic waste dump, found literally in the middle of Sydney, Nova Scotia, in its infamous tar ponds.

Martin's budgets cut environmental spending in larger relative terms than almost any other program. Even after the deficit was long vanquished, Liberals expanded incentives for fossil fuel exploration rather than aggressively investing in renewable, cleaner and more job-intensive energy production. For a decade, the tar ponds had none of their toxics removed, letting Martin the leadership candidate repeat his promise from 1993 to do something. In between, May went on a hunger strike to urge that Liberals clean up Sydney, which has cancer rates that boggle the mind.

Then 2005 came along, and with it the verdict on the 1993 Red Book promise to cut emissions. Liberals hadn't fared well. The promised 20 per cent cut was a 24 per cent increase instead, while the Americans were up by only half as much, although remained slightly higher on a per capita basis. A dozen years after first promising a plan to cut emissions, Stéphane Dion released one in 2005 that plainly failed to honour Kyoto. Eleven environmental groups, the Bloc and NDP condemned it as too weak; May applauded.

She also congratulated Dion for objecting to Bush's plans to drill for oil in an Alaskan wildlife reserve as he dodged whether drilling was wise in the delicate, earthquake-prone area off BC's coast whose drilling moratorium was under review. Or as our own North is being turned into a resource free-for-all, expanding drilling for gas in the Beaufort Sea, as emissions soar. These problems were swept under the carpet as May provided a steady stream of green reinforcement for crumbs. But fret not. Alaska's caribou will be harmed by global warming, but Canada let Bush have it about their wildlife reserve.

In one laugh, Liberals did the opposite of what May demanded, and refused to follow California's lead and impose tough efficiency controls on cars. Instead, Liberals adopted voluntary targets for an industry voluntarily building more polluting vehicles. Curiously, the Sierra Club congratulated Liberals for *not* bringing in mandatory standards, then criticized Stephen Harper when he *did*. It's ponderous, but environmentalists like May are timid in trashing Liberals, even when they flatly tell good ideas to go away.

Perhaps she's a sycophantic Liberal, but this doesn't explain her helping make a Tory government greener. May also criticized the Liberal record during the election and announced she was voting Green. In explaining, she said that in her riding Liberals were going to win, so it was okay to vote Green, which is an odd way to grow a party. Years of playing Ottawa's inside game had caught up, and May hovered on becoming its toy, convinced the only pressure worth mounting in the capital was within the governing party itself. Always the happy warrior no matter how bad the facts were.

In a minority House with both the Bloc and NDP pushing for far more aggressive reductions to emissions, it is likely this was unwise and certain that it made environmental debate more difficult. Some probing of what she actually supported and why can't hurt.

Because it's odd, less than a year after urging more progressive unity in Voting Liberal, May now believes the solution is to divide progressive votes further. And strange, that after more than a decade of hob-nobbing with Liberals whom she says put our planet in peril, her most stinging words are for the NDP. Stranger still, for she holds Douglas up as her own icon, but the NDP's the only federalist party she's not helped. Like many progressives, she takes a large progressive party for granted, as speaking about a problem becomes more strategic than trying to enter office to fix it. It's kind of politics as debating society, where lefties speak loudly from the sidelines in the hope an adult in charge will hear.

The people running the show rarely do, and through the 1990s and into the 21st century, federal politics saw some debates, but not much action. The deficit was dealt with, mainly by Mulroney. Then what? Years of housekeeping, absent of ambition or vision, followed by un-imaginative tax cuts that may well have been good to an extent, but who knew, given federal politics had only a superficial debate over purpose for our booty. Author Linda McQuaig has kept pulp and paper workers busy with her stinging condemnations of Liberal economic and environmental choices in majority governments. It's a library crying out for a reframing, as Liberal choices swept Canada ever further away from the kind of place we burst to tell the world we are.

At the height of the hegemony mirage in the late 1990s, the NDP grew slowly, the Bloc's raison d'être shrank and the right limped along divided. Around the world other citizens were engaging in real debate, while Ottawa didn't see much of it at all. Gradually, the capital's relevance declined as it came to be where Liberals went after they were elected. Basically, to do as they please, as electoral greed filled the capital, while the task of doing something lay there, fallow.

Debates swirled around Canada and we took part, but the sense that purpose had been sapped from national politics set in. At the

2001 NDP convention, an idea known as the New Politics Initiative was put forward to wrap up operations and form a nebulous alliance with non-partisan groups. No longer able to make a solid case for Douglas's ballot box path, a shortcut was proposed to ally with non-partisan groups to make co-operation easier—without reframing partisan politics first. Forty per cent of delegates voted for the NPI as desperation to get something going was high, but tellingly placed most of the blame for missing spark before the NDP, not the majority Liberal government in office and drowning in cash.

Progressive people blame each other too often for our failures. The NDP did not lose the 2006 campaign because of the Think Twice coalition, just as Stephen Harper did not fail to become prime minister because the Liberal Party lost all on its own. But look at what's hidden in the collective finger-pointing: a progressive party intact and on the rise, with potential allies in the non-partisan sphere, too.

In the U.S., pressure on Democrats to do better on health care, trade agreements, Iraq, or global warming comes mainly from outside the party, but not here. The Liberals expanded the very trade agreements that propelled Barlow's activism. These deals also ship our manufacturing jobs abroad, and Liberals refused to protect pensions or invest in key industries as Hargrove craved. May asked for emission cuts, and got a crisis instead. The Think Twice coalition's rallying cry in the 2006 election? Four! More! Liberal! Years!

It's backwards, bordering on nuts. Progressive Americans urge the Democrats to be more progressive, and help create space into which better ideas than Bush's can move. In Canada, some expect the NDP to be able to create progressive space all by its lonesome—as leading lefties say that Liberals should win again. There's nothing strategic about undermining progressives' ability to punish parties that move in the wrong direction. But this requires that parties be rewarded for wanting more progressives things done, or doing them. We won't get our act together until there's common pressure in a common direction.

Realignment might beget realignment this time, not a return to hegemony. Liberals are down and Harper's decentralism is replacing

Liberal scandal as a prime clash with the Bloc—who fight back with the same kind of values we want. There could be something here, no? Perhaps, a chance to create the conditions for elections about more than stopping the worse from beating the bad could be afoot. We don't have to listen to Stephen Lewis or David Suzuki plead for action. We could invite contemporary icons to write the odd law if we seize possibility, and reframe.

André Boisclair's Global Generation

20

IN AUGUST 2003, a faulty power plant in Ohio had a mishap and thanks to a massive and intertwined power grid, blacked out the northeastern United States. Along with the rest of Ontario, Ottawa lost power, too. It was a revealing sight. On the south bank of the Ottawa River, there was pitch-blackness, while the northern Quebec side sparkled brightly into the night. But the electricity that powered Gatineau couldn't make it across a river—in a capital supposed to symbolize common projects, and put there by Queen Victoria to help reduce tensions. Parliament was silhouetted in the blackout by the power it couldn't get from Quebec.

Down the highway, coal-fired power plants dot southern Ontario and generate 20 per cent of Ontario's climate-changing pollution. And when they belch, smog blankets the province from Lake Erie to James Bay, spreads into Quebec and plagues the Maritimes. Something's wrong when every city east of Windsor is choking on air it can't breathe, while the provinces to Ontario's east and west are North America's largest hydro producers. But like Ottawa in the blackout, hydro from Manitoba or Quebec can't replace the coal that kills thousands. We stopped building a country at the railway, and forgot about other links that help greenly move Canada ahead.

Ontario Premier Dalton McGuinty's answer is to say that his province pays more to Confederation than it gets. Toronto's bank towers apparently don't suck wealth from elsewhere and deliver it to Ontario, as premiers nickel-and-dime Confederation into meaninglessness. To Stephen Harper's ears, it is music and his solution is not for Ottawa to help provinces build together, but to take less and leave each to their own. It is the real conservatism at play, in a country so provincialized, its capital can't use power from a province across the river. And Nova Scotians breathe Ontario's smog because Manitoba can't send hydro east.

Everywhere you look these days, someone's predicting global warming will be this century's big test. They're right, but there's a problem in getting the federal government to green up because Canada's greenest citizens mostly speak French, as our most dangerous progressive divide lingers. Harper's response to these solitudes is to try and make the federal government weaker for everyone, which is a Quebec boon for Conservatives, perhaps. For the oil industry, certainly.

The more provinces strengthen, the less we can work together on the nub of the climate crisis: energy and efficiency. With each step towards an emaciated Ottawa, provinces without large oil reserves see their citizens become less able to write laws affecting the oil industry; and provinces without much manufacturing unable to combat smog. If it's every province for itself—including Alberta and its looming dryness—a weaker federal government makes putting our hopes into action almost impossible. Without taking a broader approach, we risk evermore fragmented progressive politics outside Quebec without being able to work with Quebecers on common crises.

As long as the Bloc is around as a sizeable party and the right stays united, minority governments are a pretty good bet. Changing politics makes more stable minorities more dependable and likelier to deliver progressive wins, particularly with politics in such flux because of Quebec.

With the national question returning, the Constitution also comes up. Boring, maybe, but important, too, not only for enshrining rights, but also for helping keep us stuck in provincialism that doesn't let us deal with what's heading our way. Not talking about it won't make it go away, and with Quebec's votes so important, the dry task of figuring how best to work together may be worth another look. Quebecers have twice already said no to separation, and could be open to finally getting something done.

Harper hopes so, and looks to Quebec's desire for autonomy to give him a key to its heart. Letting Quebec go its own way within Canada could work, and may, unless we offer something better. Some autonomy is important to Quebec, but there's also a large chunk of Europe buried in the province's hopes. Allowing Quebec to go its own way on some things, but protecting capacity for the big stuff— foreign and environmental policy, and socioeconomic direction—may have appeal. It could be a pipedream, but Quebec won't cope with a climate crisis well without it. And if it withdraws from national debate, neither will we. It's fodder for a rethink nonetheless.

For 70 years, the NDP's not cracked this nut. It's the flipside of the hegemony mirage, and Quebec's 25-year-long allergy to Liberals places the emphasis emphatically on the mirage part. But the NDP won't govern until it or a cousin can elect large numbers of MPs in Quebec—a project made easier by a larger NDP outside Quebec. But the NDP can't grow elsewhere with Liberals in the way, and is hurt in growing inside Quebec because it's seen as too small. Growth solves many things, and waiting for NDP perfection to help it sprout is likely unwise.

Policy isn't always a magic bullet, and size often counts. To be sure, the NDP has its problems in Quebec, where it finds plenty of company with Liberals. Both parties have been torn apart by the Constitution, which has seen Conservatives reach three agreements with Quebec as Liberals wait for their first. Progressive reframing isn't just possible, but imperative, for neither the NDP as it is nor Liberals as usual can help create conditions for more progressive unity with Quebec, although the NDP's long history of factionalism appears to be waning.

In January 2003, the party had a unique kind of leadership race. Usually NDP races are ideological, with candidates becoming proxies for whether the party should try to win, or elect only a sizeable conscience in Parliament. Indeed, through much of the 1970s, 1980s and 1990s it was split by stark ideological debates. The left-leaning Waffle movement, headed by Jim Laxer—who ran for leader once—was evicted in the 1970s. In the 1980s, bitter debates occurred during the Cold War over NDP support for leaving U.S.-dominated military organizations NATO and NORAD, which Broadbent opposed.

In the late 1990s, Alexa McDonough tried to re-energize the party, both through outreach to progressives outside of the NDP, but also to Liberal and wayward PC voters who—after Mulroney began to eliminate a deficit, which Liberals and a global economic rebound turned into a giant surplus—expected fiscal responsibility. This came to be known as the third way and was widely interpreted as the New Democrats abandoning progressive principles, like Tony Blair's transformation (or destruction, depending) of the British Labour Party.

Buzz Hargrove led much of the assault on McDonough, in a squabble that became bitter and personal. Hargrove saw her as a quasi-Liberal in the same way many New Democrats came to see him as one, as he opposed her policy changes, chiefly balanced budgets, which the NDP adopted in both 2004 and 2006 elections more stringently than McDonough.

Despite this, the race to replace her wasn't ideological, but tactical, and flowed from the controversy around the New Politics Initiative. The two leading contenders, Bill Blaikie and Jack Layton, are similar ideologically, though Blaikie's stern, but correct, opposition to the NPI created a sense he was more conservative. He's not, and the main difference was that Layton wasn't an MP and planned on keeping it that way until the 2004 election. He often stressed other ways of growing the party, similar to NPI's but not identical. It helped make him a candidate of renewal, which was what the NDP was looking for.

In contrast, Blaikie is Parliament's most intelligent performer and a powerful orator, and saw being an MP as essential to the party's continuing to return to viability. Though they stressed different issues—Layton focusing on seemingly newer areas like the environment and cities, with Blaikie stressing more traditional NDP concerns for working families and social services—each agreed with the other's prescriptions.

After Layton won, New Democrats did what Liberals haven't in more than 20 years. They got along. All six leadership candidates—the others were Lorne Nystrom, Joe Comartin, Pierre Ducasse and Bev Meslo—ran in both 2004 and 2006 elections. Unlike the bitter Turner–Chrétien, Chrétien–Martin, Martin–Sheila Copps affairs, New Democrats didn't engage in civil war after electing Layton. That Liberals did makes them riper for removal.

But the race put reporters to sleep. One of the most telling impressions was a journalist commenting after one of the dozens of leadership debates. "I can understand why someone would ask about the plight of Tibetan monks," he said, "but what I can't understand is why the candidates try to outdo each other in how much they know and care about the plight of the Tibetan monks." New Democrats, like Reformers and the Bloc, love their policy.

The quip is revealing in the same way the McDonough–Hargrove squabble is, for the NDP's in a bit of a bind. Hargrove's bang on in saying we do not need another Liberal Party; that's why Douglas types try to defeat it. McDonough was right as well, and working people don't like seeing fiscal irresponsibility at play; neo-conservatives Harper, Gordon Campbell, Mike Harris and Ralph Klein were all elected on a wave of anger that included treating workers' money with respect.

The same is true in Britain, where the loony left Labour Party of the 1970s and 1980s was trounced regularly by Tory Margaret Thatcher. In contrast, Blair—and I'm no fan—has won three majorities and despite many failings, was quite progressive domestically early on, and has moved ahead on issues such as global warming. With Britain's Labour Party being dominant, however, it debates its ideological bearings with more relevance than the NDP can. And there's still a spirited bunch of truer Labour MPs, who kick up more of a fuss than lefty Liberals did over the last decade.

Whatever one thinks of New Labour, Britain's key difference is that the party's purity matters. The same is true in the U.S., where Democrats see a similar contest between the centrist Democratic Leadership Council of Bill Clinton and the lefty populism of the Howard Deans. Whichever side or combination of them we think is better, the debate within British Labour or the Democrats matters. In the NDP, it's less relevant as perfectly illustrated by Think Twice, which saw policy matter less than winability in echoing the Liberals' message.

It's backwards. The purity debate needs to happen after politics is reframed, and the decades-old NDP purity obsession only underlines that it's not a path to win. The Liberal record shows non-partisan activism wanting, too. The solution might not be a purer NDP, but a bigger one, but that's tough when its prime rival is reinforced by those, such as Hargrove, who seem to want purity above all.

The NDP's in a box, and loses some progressive support if it takes a run at Liberals, but can't gain broader support by going further left than voters want to go, or should. It's most severe where Liberals dominate since if people want only to win, they could always Vote Liberal. Partly as a result, the NDP is often the haunt of folks who dislike victory, and prefer vehicles to lobby or debate. The further the NDP is from government, the worse it gets, and Ontario is hit harder than western provinces, where the party is usually a governing one. Whining versus winning: it's another way to keep lefties apart, as we cede power to Liberals or Tories along the way.

How—or whether—to fix this is hotly debated within and beyond the NDP, and suggestions often become loaded with connotations as the left does well. It's often surreal, with most anglo lefties feeling enough ownership over the NDP to know what it should do, but also feeling that it is the NDP's job alone to do it. If we really want to do better together, we're going to need to smarten up and see it as a collective project, which isn't the same as thinking that only partisanship matters. It also means being honest that a party that can win elections is needed if we think the path ahead can be more hopeful than feared.

It's a field filled with bruises and loaded terms like the third way, but objectively the NDP didn't abandon values in embracing fiscal responsibility or a more realistic view of the benefits of enterprise; Tommy Douglas himself powerfully supported balanced budgets, and markets can both exist and be shaped. It may surprise Hargrove to learn he himself has proposed a third way which makes sense. It's best described, though, as a *troisième voie,* in a view of Canada for which Hargrove was criticized when he first suggested it.

In 2005, Hargrove called on the NDP to cede Quebec to its dominant progressive party in the Bloc Québécois. This earned him another round of attacks from New Democrats for undermining a progressive federalist option's capacity to reach Quebec. The thinking that led him there is covered in Part One, namely seeing the Bloc first as a progressive party and then as a sovereigntist one. It overlooks a not insignificant part of the Bloc's agenda, making it problematic to current politics or future wins, but it wouldn't, if the vehicle in Quebec were both progressive and federalist.

Inherent to Hargrove's thinking is that the party through which Quebec applies its majority federally might be different from provinces or territories with anglophone majorities. He's right, and if Quebec wants a progressive federalist option, it's almost certain that it will be formed in Quebec, not imported. This is not to suggest that the vehicle cannot be the NDP, only that Quebecers will decide.

Liberals have their preference for uniting the left, but the winningest unity is found in a federalized Bloc—or healthy chunks of it—progressive Liberals and NDP, who are almost in lockstep in approaches to almost every issue. Getting there is uphill, but not trying guarantees we won't arrive, partly by shrinking Liberals down a bit to shake some progressives loose. As for the Bloc, it's seen defections to federalist parties before, and if we put our minds to building a progressive Canada, defections to federalism could again plague the Bloc.

Countries like ours already have similar arrangements to what Hargrove proposed. Belgium has separate progressive parties for its two linguistic groups, while in Australia two conservative parties divide activities on an urban–rural split. For all intents and purposes, the parties on Belgium's left or Australia's right are the same and deal with issues jointly in the countries' legislatures. Other diverse countries such as Brazil or the United States have a common progressive party, both of which have significant wins under their belt. Both models appear to work.

That the NDP today represents ridings as diverse as downtown Toronto and the Western Arctic, anglo- and francophone parts of Atlantic Canada, and suburban Vancouver alongside poverty-stricken areas of Winnipeg indicates common parties can work well if we'd like. The choice, however, is Quebec's to make, and progressive Quebecers have their own view we need to respect. We're starting to find our way, though, and tactics used in the *No Logo* years include alliances with them. Many lefty structures, from the green movement to Oxfam to the student movement, respect Quebec's difference, while allowing joint progress: autonomous to an extent, but still part of a bigger pie.

Indeed, non-partisan infrastructure, built to connect with diverse people on common issues, makes it easier to speak with like-minded Quebecers. If there's benefit to working with Quebec's progressives within Canada to apply our majority to Parliament, they're going to have to want it. But we don't need Quebec MPs to ask, and could start tomorrow with what we have if we liked. This will mean making a case for Canada, which is less dicey a proposition than allowing neo-conservatives to make change we don't want. If we're out to really Stop Harper or his successor, common cause within Canada will need to be found with counterparts in Quebec.

People like André Boisclair, who's doing much the same thing with atypical sovereigntists in Montreal. There, the Bloc and Parti Québécois are desperately trying to expand their electoral base into new and potentially fertile ground in the city's diverse population. Like all of Canada, demographics are changing and Quebec is becoming more diverse—and in the process, much more global in outlook. He's a member of Quebec's global generation, and the P.Q. asked him to lead them into a possible third referendum because of it.

Anyone reading this can think of someone like Boisclair. He just turned 40, grew up in the age of immigration, technology and a Canada—Quebec, specifically—that is a model of successfully becoming one of the world's most open countries. We're not tolerant in Canada. We're increasingly accepting and celebratory of our diversity, which should make us ask why Boisclair can speak with people who came to Canada about leaving it, but we can't find common project with people like him.

In the NDP caucus there's Nathan Cullen, in his thirties, bilingual and as comfortable at a First Nations ceremony in his sprawling northern British Columbia riding as he is at a Pride Day parade or a Sikh festival. Liberal Ruby Dhalla is a Sikh-Canadian doctor from Toronto who supported equal marriage; the Conservatives' James Moore from Vancouver is a wondrous moderate who also supported equality. The Bloc's Maka Kotto is an actor from Cameroon who sometimes flies home in the summer to make a film.

The former NDP president, Adam Giambrone, is trilingual and when not busy as a Toronto city councillor is an archaeologist in Sudan. Naomi Klein excited young people around the world and her ideas resonated internationally. Rick Smith heads Environmental Defence, and is among the non-partisan community's most strategic, and bilingual, thinkers. And they all, with Boisclair, likely get some American news from comedian Jon Stewart's *Daily Show,* which sadly overly gushed about how lefty the Liberal Party really is. There are tons of people like them—everywhere, and Liberals didn't create their outlook. Progressive values flow from the bottom up. They aren't property of the Liberal Party.

Let's not live in a country where people like these can't figure out a way to respect the differences they all celebrate, while protecting common ways to put our majority to work. Nor is the open-mindedness only a generational thing. Instead, let's ask why only Tories can change a country that revels in its diversity, and remains appalled at our long failure to embrace sustainability or reconcile with Aboriginal people.

Progressive people can change it, too. The bright, creative and strategic people we all know can use this moment to set about achieving more, and strive for the loaf after crumbs for so long. It's not as if wanting better has never been done. John A. Macdonald found common project with Quebec. Tommy Douglas demanded and achieved more for working people. Pierre Trudeau provided us with a purpose and equality. And René Lévesque inspired Quebec to build a society in its own image—while giving Canada a second chance in his *beau risque* of attending the 1982 constitutional talks. History matters to where we're at, and as we watch Harper serenade Quebec once more, it's troubling that it is on Tories' side in making the courtship work as we wait patiently for our first date.

One way or another, progressive people will work with our allies in Quebec on common issues. The only question is if we will do so as citizens of a common country with a federal government with the capacity to implement our hopes, which will require compromise if desired. Whatever progressive people choose is not simple, but if we want to protect and empower our majority we're going to need our counterparts in Quebec. And they've proven more open to Tories' wooing than Liberals' on nationhood.

Politics' new rules are born of constitutional debates and progressive people have struggled to find a common frame with counterparts in Quebec. We can't reframe without drilling into why Liberals lost in Quebec, why Brian Mulroney won or the lure of Harper's decentralization. Whether progressive people found home in the Liberal Party or the NDP, neither party was unanimous on the two constitutional offers. But before going on, a brief recap of how the sponsorship scandal came about, via the constitutional debates that shape our new electoral map. This is as fun as a root canal. Apologies in advance.

Following the 1980 Quebec referendum, won by the No side 60 to 40, Trudeau set about taking advantage of his second chance. He had retired following the 1979 election defeat, but the unexpected fall of Joe Clark's Tory minority within six months triggered an encore.

In 1982, the Constitution was approved without Quebec agreeing by all-party consensus, but notably Lévesque was an active partici-pant in the talks. Provincial governments supporting Trudeau were all led by non-Liberal premiers: six Tory provinces, two NDP provinces and Social Credit in BC[38] Federal New Democrats and Tories both split. Ed Broadbent's tone was closer to Trudeau's than Clark, who was closer to nationalist sentiment in Quebec, though both supported repatriating the Constitution from London.

Then, progressive sentiment mirrored the divide within the NDP more acutely than it did within the Liberals outside Quebec, and New Democrats were the more divided. Longstanding sympathy to the unfair treatment of the francophone minority compelled many anglo lefties outside Quebec to fear recriminations so soon after the 1980 referendum. It led to supporting the idea of patriation and the Charter, but opposition to approving it without Quebec. Others said the Charter was too weak, mainly around equality section protections for women, Aboriginals, and lesbian and gay people. Guess not.

The Liberal Party almost entirely supported Trudeau, but the NDP was less supportive of Broadbent's decision to roughly endorse the gov-ernment's direction and a party convention at the time was a brutal, tough affair. Saskatchewan Premier Allan Blakeney's justice minister, Roy Romanow, helped broker the deal that delivered the Constitution in the famed kitchen cabinet with federal Attorney General Jean Chrétien and their Tory counterpart in Ontario, Roy McMurtry.

Together, Blakeney and Broadbent stared down a hostile con-vention holding out for Quebec's support or a better deal, or both. Broadbent won the day, and worked with Trudeau to strengthen many of the Charter provisions used today.

But Trudeau's approach hurt Liberals in Quebec, and Mulroney's sweep of the province in 1984 was helped along by a sense of aban-donment after Lévesque's controversial decision to participate ended

38. Alberta, Ontario and the Atlantic provinces had Conservative governments. Manitoba and Saskatchewan had NDP governments, with Social Credit serving as the dominant right-leaning party in British Columbia until the 1980s.

in isolation. As prime minister, Mulroney delivered on his promise to bring Quebec into the Constitution through the Meech Lake Accord in 1987, which marked a dramatic shift in governments' approach to Quebec.

The shift was reciprocal in Quebec City after Liberals beat a divided and embittered P.Q. in 1985, the first election without Lévesque as leader. Quebec's new premier, Robert Bourassa, was empowered to seek a new deal, Mulroney's majority depended on one and the Accord emerged.

Unlike 1982, the federal government couldn't bring about constitutional change without Quebec, and all 10 provincial legislatures needed to agree. As the three-year period to approve the Accord began so, too, did changes in governments.

A Tory government in New Brunswick and the NDP in Manitoba were defeated before their legislatures could approve the Accord. The elections couldn't have been more different, as Liberal Frank McKenna won every seat in New Brunswick, while Manitoba Tory Gary Filmon eked out a minority ahead of the usually moribund but now soaring Liberals under Sharon Carstairs, as the NDP sunk to third. In Newfoundland, a Tory government fell and Liberal Clyde Wells won a majority.

This created delays in approving the Accord as the growing clout of Liberals in provincial legislatures changed the approach of their governments. This Liberal division towards Meech Lake was a switch. In 1982, the constitutional split was bigger in the NDP, but the Liberal Party—entering a leadership race to replace John Turner—tore itself apart over the issue, which some saw as a direct assault on Trudeau's vision of a strong central government.

As Chrétien, Carstairs and Wells dug in one side, Bourassa, Ontario Premier David Peterson and Martin dug in on the other. In a particularly ugly display in a Montreal debate among Liberal leadership candidates, young Liberals supporting Martin, mainly from Ontario, jeered Chrétien with loaded language and called him a sell out.

Sailing wasn't much smoother within the NDP. Progressive people were discordant everywhere during the Meech Lake debate. Within the Liberals, the debate was over the strength of the central government, while the Accord's failures on Aboriginal and other equality issues dominated New Democrat concern. NDP MLA Elijah Harper's holding of the eagle feather during votes, denying unanimous consent for Manitoba's legislature to approve the Accord in its dying days, symbolized much of the progressive concern with the agreement.

The Accord failed at the worst time, on Quebec's Fête Nationale weekend, which coincided with the Liberal leadership convention. By the end of the weekend, Mulroney's Quebec lieutenant, Lucien Bouchard, who had left the Tories some time before, and other Quebec Tory MPs had formed the Bloc Québécois with two Quebec Liberals, including Martin's future Quebec lieutenant, Jean Lapierre. It was a weekend that underlined politics' new rules and which creates many challenges to applying our majority's clout.

In 1992, another try at bringing Quebec into the Constitution failed, as a referendum to approve the Charlottetown Accord lost. In spite of, or because, all three parties and every provincial government supported the deal, Canadians rejected the Charlottetown Accord by a 54 to 46 margin, with Bouchard leading the No forces in Quebec. Preston Manning soared to prominence as the loudest English voice against it.

Turnout was high as citizens told politicians they'd had enough. British Columbia voted no with the largest margin, 68 per cent, and the only western province to reject the Accord less vehemently than Quebec was Saskatchewan where 55 per cent said no. Ontario barely voted yes as did three Atlantic provinces, with Nova Scotia narrowly rejecting the deal. In Quebec, 57 per cent voted no.

In 1995, a second Quebec referendum was held, which appeared set to break up the country as the Yes side was leading well into the night. Media reports say Chrétien was in tears as the country seemed lost, and the eventual result was a statistical dead heat. Turnout soared above 93 per cent, and the No side eked out a narrow, 50,000-vote win. In the aftermath of such a close call, Liberals began the sponsorship program to try to increase Canada's visibility in Quebec. Events move forward, and it's in nobody's interest but Liberals' to think they had a standing start in the 2006 campaign.

They didn't. And eventually, we're going to have to speak with our counterparts in Quebec on progressive terms, whether Liberals like it or not. The Bloc was born by constitutional debates, and its presence on the federal scene makes minorities now more likely than not. Politics is changing, and we limit possibility by only looking at the races that the Liberal Party wants us to. There could be more options, and larger rewards.

Navigating a path to create a common frame in elections to let Canada's progressive punch really work is our majority's biggest challenge. It's also our largest reward. But if Elijah Harper's eagle feather epitomized progressive dissent during constitutional debates past, a wind turbine may represent hopes now. Let's hope, for we can't green up without help from people who crave sustainability, too: Quebec's progressive majority.

We only have a progressive majority with Quebecers as part of our national debate, so we're going to need to find something beyond simple autonomy within Canada. The most progressive province might be open to different overtures, focusing on what we'd like to do together, to move ahead on the values we share. Hope could be out there, if we set our minds to finding it, and perhaps like Lévesque before, former P.Q. environment minister André Boisclair might be up for a *beau risque* of his own. And if not him, someone like him who sees the potential a progressive Canada really has.

If we'd like to replace Harper with the structural capacity to move ahead, we'll need a federal government powerful enough to act, but flexible enough to attract Quebecers to it. If Europe can move ahead after centuries of bloodshed, a progressive, peaceful place should at least try.

No More Crumbs

21

CHAPTER

A CROSS THE AMERICAS, throughout Europe and in the South Pacific, lefties have partied on election night. They won, right-wingers lost, and there are few Latin Americans who could relate to progressive Canadians arguing whether elections matter. It's a cottage industry here, and as we talk around the elephant in the middle of the room, its calf won—partly because Liberals lost, and partly because Stephen Harper built a party that wanted to win. We should, too.

Partisanship, many spit. It's a dirty word these days, as we think of the nastiness that party politics often entails. But partisanship ended the Third World blight of millions of people without health care in Britain, it stoked the fight against apartheid in South Africa, and fuels the hopes of many in Latin America, tired of a modern feudalism that keeps most people down. Even Elizabeth May's now on board a partisan train, which isn't a dirty thing. It's the core of why the wrong kind of globalization is wrong. Because elections do matter, and for all the badness that politics brings, it still gets big things done even if it frustrates.

We argue over whether we want to, or if there's a party good enough to support. We share a destination, but often bitterly disagree on how to get there, mainly because there's no clear option. In part, because we've not built it. If governing is our goal, we're going to need a party. And if it's not, we really do need a smack to begin the progressive rethink we've put off for too long. I'm no sycophant for the NDP, but after its biggest changes to public policy in a generation, that we didn't try for more in the last election—whether it pissed Liberals off, or not—is a progressive problem. Unless we want to win, we won't.

The NDP has failings as any party does, but its key problem is size. It's not big enough to have winning infrastructure, but it's too big to be the debating society that many of its members would like. And the smaller it is, the more space its crazies take up, driving other progressives away. But where to? The key Liberal failing is also size. It's too big and has grown too fond of winning for winning's sake to notice that it covers too much ground, which is why the meaningless middle's splintered everywhere else. Eventually, the shapeless blob loses whatever meaning it had, and people in politics for something find more comfort elsewhere.

We've yet to do this in Canada, and partly as a result suffer a crisis of political homelessness, as moderates of the centre-left or centre-right have nowhere to go. The Tories are too radical to tolerate, and the NDP too one-dimensional and too small to govern. This leaves the Liberal Party, and the inevitable failure that comes from believing the blob represents anything beyond an amoebic commitment to self-reproduction. Every decade, it cleaves, then rejoins, then cleaves again, sometimes reflecting on how desperately urgent it is to act on the crises of our time. We can do better. We can reframe politics so it works better for more of us.

Whether that's true divides us, and it's particularly bad in Ontario, where faith in the NDP is often hard to come by, sometimes with good reason. Not far away, however, is a place that better represents Canada and whose government is very much in line with the kind that most of us want.

Many Ontarians see their province as most like Canada, but there are others in the running, and Manitoba's very much what things could be like if we applied our majority. Apart from language, it's mainstream Canada. It's mainly urban, but has large rural areas. It is mainly European of many ancestries, but has thriving multicultural communities and a significant Aboriginal population, both in Winnipeg and further north. In short, it reflects the country it sits dead centre of, but Manitoba's demographics don't make it different. Its government does, and while it should be greener, it's pretty good.

The difference between applying our majority to politics and not is best seen by comparing Manitoba's NDP governments to Liberal governments in Ottawa and Ontario, as the three jurisdictions have almost identical structures. Only since the arrival of the Bloc federally in the 1990s has the usual three-party affair Ottawa knows well not looked like what's long been the case in Manitoba and Ontario.

Other provinces—Alberta, Nova Scotia and increasingly Quebec—have multi-party systems, too, but they're not the same. Alberta's dominant party provincially has changed only in name and scale of conservatism, and it is the long haunt of Conservatives whose evolution from Premiers Peter Lougheed to Ralph Klein mirrors Ontario's from Premiers Bill Davis to Mike Harris. And Lougheed showed more concern about the impact of the tar sands on Alberta's water supply than either Liberal PM, or any leadership candidate, did over the last decade.

Quebec is different for a host of obvious reasons, while Nova Scotia could be like Manitoba soon as provincial New Democrats are in the process of replacing Liberals. This leaves Manitoba, Ontario and Ottawa as the petri dishes for a reframed politics, and our interests win hands-down in Manitoba. Gary Doer's government, like those led by Howard Pawley and Ed Schreyer before, represents what federal Liberals portray in elections but whose record shows is a bit of a lark. Indeed, Manitoba's NDP governments are quite similar to minority Liberal–NDP experiences that pleased us a lot, and which voting reform could make better still.

Progressives like governments with NDP outlook tempered with realism. In Manitoba, lefty infrastructure has long since been in NDP hands provincially, while in Ontario the lack of reinforcements for the provincial NDP was clear. Ottawa, too, is a Liberal town and weaning its infrastructure from the teat will take time, but we know—surely, if we've learned anything—that we won't be at the front of the Liberal line if they manage to get back. Their friends got their goodies for more than a decade, while it took one year of a minority for us to get above the radar—just like the dreary Liberal majorities that came before, which is sad, for long frustration has made many lefties give up on governing as a goal.

Or at least in Ottawa. City halls are a different story, where innovative, progressive ideas work and progressives think elections are things to win. Most city elections are non-partisan, and let people of all parties use common frames to build cities they like. Joe Clark advised us to see Canada as a community of communities, and it may be time to listen. To empower the kind of politics we see municipally, instead of relegating cities to the third tier. In Calgary, Montreal, Toronto, Vancouver and Winnipeg multi-partisan coalitions elected progressive mayors as an urbanizing country started to think that cities matter more. Maybe they really should matter more, to help us better reflect the urban country we now are.

To make this happen, we need a party, otherwise, no federal government. But in our way, in part, is that partisanship is sometimes frustrating—repellent, even—to some progressives as our disappointment exacts a toll. It's worst in Ontario, where the experiences of the Rae government didn't inspire faith in the NDP. But parties sometimes fail. Maybe it was the leader, the party, or just the time, but parties are neither pure nor perfect.

What does it say, though, that one term of provincial government that went badly defines the NDP, but four terms of federal government that let emissions soar doesn't define Liberals? Unless we have stopped taking our own hopes seriously, we need to stop seeing literally one of the world's most polluting entities as an imperfect—but mild and harmless—governing option. We need to have the courage that fellow progressive voters want to do better, too, and build a progressive option we can have confidence in.

Progressive capacity to punish the NDP is well known, and some-times deserved, but what of Liberal failings? Is it enough to go to the screening of Al Gore's cinematic debut[39] and spout that the envi-ronment will define this century, without asking why urgency was so lagging in office, or inflicting punishment for the neglect? Attendees of the Liberal leftifest in Mont-Tremblant, Quebec in spring 2006 think so. But before rejuvenating the Northern PRI, we should remember the leftifest had a prequel in Aylmer, Quebec in 1990. Then, the out-of-office Liberal Party set out to champion the environment, too, and now 16 smoggy years later thinks it doesn't matter that it failed.

We're not Pavlov's pets, and don't have to bark when Liberals ask us to, unless we mysteriously conclude that Liberals mean it this time. Instead, we could set out to join the rest of the planet we'd like to pro-tect and create the kind of party that many of our progressive cousins worldwide enjoy.

These cousins have also suffered disappointments from their pro-gressive parties, but in perspective the Ontario NDP's failings pale to British Labour's decision to help George W. Bush invade Iraq, or events in New Zealand. There, the Labour Party was the victim of a right-wing coup that ushered in some of the world's most Draconian conservative policies in the 1980s that gutted social programs, priva-tized almost everything and turned the country into a guinea pig for the latest right-wing fad. Its last Labour prime minister for a while was Mike Moore, head of the World Trade Organization during the Seattle demonstrations that epitomized the *No Logo* years. The radi-cal reforms were blindly celebrated by neo-cons worldwide before the impacts became clear. For that matter, long after they were.

What's hopeful about New Zealand, Britain and Manitoba is what happens if the dominant progressive party fails or grows tired. Unlike federal elections, which currently result in Conservative governments of nastier stripes after Liberals inevitably lose, this rarely occurs in these three jurisdictions that mirror what Canada could look like if we reframe.

39. *An Inconvenient Truth,* his film on global warming.

In Britain and Manitoba, Liberals sit between the Tories and dominant Labour or NDP, as the case may be. Should, for example, Labour become too conservative, Liberal Democrats become powerful voices against the Iraq War and Britain's largest source of new ideas like European integration, greening up or voting reform. If they're good, either the Labour or Conservative Party scoops them up and enacts them, as federal Liberals were forced to when the Saskatchewan CCF developed public health care. If good ideas are ignored, multiparty democracy allows the largest party to change, as also took place in Saskatchewan, where provincial Liberals were less receptive and were replaced by Douglas.

There's some truth to the old saying that we get the government we deserve, and it's counter-productive not to punish parties that don't do what we want. But without a progressive alternative Liberals know will defeat their MPs, their usual why-bother approach makes sense. Ours doesn't. Few of us would suggest that Blair be unpunished for joining Bush in Iraq, but many are attracted to rewarding our Liberals for joining Bush on climate policy. It's a sneakier alliance, but numbers don't lie, and the dirty little secret is that global warming gets worse when they are in office, and worse when they're not.

We need a progressive alternative big enough to hurt when Liberals fail, and positive enough that people looking for something better can vote for it. Without this option, we'll moan about the Liberals' direction but when the chips are down, vote to reward it nonetheless, and start moaning a few hours after the ballots are counted. But they are already down, and now it's time for a switcharoo, to build a progressive party big enough to govern—and using federal politics' latest period of flux to make it work.

In Manitoba, which is rare in having no successful neo-conservatives, a marginally electable Liberal Party is a public service. It has all the pluses of Britain's situation, but also the benefit that should the NDP fare badly, a moderate alternative exists for disgruntled progressives. This also keeps Tories less radical, and the last Manitoba Tory government under Gary Filmon did less damage than conservatives elsewhere. When there are more than two players, it's harder to veer to the hard right, but if the dominant player is in the middle, also tough to move it closer to what we'd like—because the dominant progressive voice in federal Liberals rarely means a word it says.

When Rae was trounced, Harris won on a wave of populism that the established, recently-in-power Liberals couldn't match. There was no contest for the protest vote. Manitoba's NDP had a similar rough ride in 1987 when Pawley's government fell to third, but neo-conservatism didn't flourish. Instead, the Liberal Party, which hadn't governed in almost 30 years, soared from one to 20 seats holding the Tories to a minority. Making the middle less dominant is good for progressives in the long run, and makes it less likely that neo-cons will be elected due to outrage, not ideology.

But New Zealand's Labour Party remains a shining example, and after disappointing most progressive Kiwis, it was rebuilt by them and Prime Minister Helen Clark now leads a competent progressive government in its third term. It also has sensible proportional representation that, despite some complications lately, resembles most of Europe in how its politics are structured. This isn't the case in Britain or Manitoba, but may well become our future, and again New Zealand points the way.

There, there is a Green Party that unlike Canada's can elect MPs and which can press action upon the Labour Party and continue New Zealand's long record of sustainability. A smaller party to the left of Labour is also common, to keep the dominant party innovative and stop it from straying too far to the right. If we'd like, New Zealand also has overlapping ridings for Aboriginal people, with the results clear in how it is reconciling with Maori people, which puts Canada's record to shame.

If progressive New Zealanders can fix their Labour Party and prosper from it, there's no reason progressive Ontarians can't move out of the Rae years, look at the federal NDP and ask if it is viable with progressive Liberals in it. This works well around the world and in three western provinces, and the solution to our constant frustrations in Ottawa might lie in following suit by using this period of flux to grow a dominant, truly progressive party that can win.

Either way, a modern Liberal convention is like a job fair. It's inevitable that the progressive people drawn to the Liberals because of its apparent mainstream electability would quickly depart if it suffered. Rae may believe it is an acceptable home due to his own experiences in the NDP during the 1990s, but he led the party and isn't blame-free, either, and should provide a better explanation why Doer's party is not his own. In doing Liberals harm, we stand to gain the best of them, without them taking all of us.

This brings us back to the Think Twice coalition and why its Liberal frame is incongruent with Douglas's. Simply, its three principals are strategic people who want progressive wins, but aren't convinced the NDP is viable enough to get them. The NDP doesn't agree, and the core conflict boils down to what's the best we can do? The Douglas frame says govern, while a Liberal one advises us to lobby those in charge. Without resolving what the goal is, more disappointment looms.

Think Twice and the NDP mainly agree on policy, however, and despite the fascination with asking whether the party is left enough, this wasn't the problem in 2006, as neither it nor the coalition was a model of progressive purity. The NDP shows it each time it fights an election since a party can't be a perfect vehicle for any ideology and none is, including Bush's Republicans, whose ballooning deficits are anathema to conservative principles.

The partisan, electoral route is imperfect, but so, too, is Think Twice. Every time a Liberal frame was reinforced, a more progressive path was made more difficult. Nobody stressed a vision of progressive perfection. Everyone—Maude Barlow, Buzz Hargrove, Jack Layton and Elizabeth May—tried to highlight what they saw as the path to do better. But conflict resulted and as lefties do well, the aftermath of another Conservative win is spent blaming each other for how it happened. We've got to break this cycle.

The great tragedy is that they're all right and it's only a question of when. The people who were wrong were Liberals, and if we're going to stop frustrations such as 1988 and 2006 from happening again, we need to do what wasn't done following politics' new rules arrival in 1984. Remove the Liberal Party from dominance. *Now.*

As Liberals were falling and minority government was approaching its end, how progressive pressure was applied was the wrong tactic. If Paul Martin had been told by progressive people to compromise, the election would have come later than it did. His argument would no longer have fit the dominant frame, just as the NDP's did not, which helped create the sense that the election was early—as if the timing of the election, not the Liberals' behaviour in office, was really what did them in.

Liberals didn't deserve another government, and if we're as angry as we say about global warming or a growing gap between have-more and have-less, deserved to lose. The Liberal campaign also wasn't so great, and would likely have been as bad no matter when it took place. Martin was capital-W weak, and reversed himself on every item of conscience he claimed to have and ceded to public pressure five times. A later election would have happened because Martin would have had no choice but to compromise—as he always, and predictably, did. We didn't want to pressure Liberals, just as we didn't in either of the last two elections that Conservatives won.

The core problem in 1988 or 2006 wasn't a rising NDP, but the lack of a common frame to push against reliably together. And there are many who are further left than a dominant party vehicle can—or should—go, and others who think the *No Logo* years are the path to progressive majorities being applied worldwide. They're both helped by a dominant, truly progressive party, even if they dislike either the NDP or electoral politics, or both. Perhaps temporarily, they should see the NDP as it asked them to see Harper in November: As a short-term ally for a larger objective. A one-night fling, so we can reframe to help bring more debate really onto our turf.

We should also probe the Green Party, which would like to join, or replace, the NDP as a smallish but electable voice that a minority House might empower. If May's non-partisan activism didn't help us pollute less, it's not automatic that her new partisan take will. And if she helps Greens grow, she'll meet the same problem that has plagued the NDP for decades if Liberals are left dominant: those partisan Greens, tut-tut, out for a few more seats, unconcerned with a radical right-winger winning...we know the rest. Meanwhile, emissions will grow, we'll fall further back from innovative energy economies elsewhere, and we will keep on not governing.

May likely has it backwards, for every successful Green Party in the world is only successful with proportional representation. The key for Green growth isn't to win one seat, somewhere, but to change the voting system to really empower the party. That can't occur through the Liberals, whose hegemony rests on politics' old rules, but can with the NDP. Two parties want PR, but one has 29 MPs and one has none, with May's own Sierra Club ranking the Greens and NDP as almost a dead green heat in the last two elections. That should be common ground enough—particularly if Voting Liberal was acceptable, with their pollution record—to find a way to work together. If it's kosher for her to criticize NDP partisanship, what of her own newfound variety?

Global warming is the crisis of our time, and her partisan ambition should take second place to creating the kind of politics that let us do something about it. Bright shiny new parties often appeal, and it is possible that better debate would result if they grew, but we should focus on a prize bigger than having another lefty party that can't win. We need a new voting system, but also a new dominant progressive party because our cyclical failure needs breaking, and politics in realignment help.

The NDP's a lot like Lego, and every now and then another block is added. Originally, the base was western farmers, workers and progressive clergy and they kept it going for about 20 years as the CCF. The next bit was Ontario's industrial unions that gave birth to the

NDP, which grew again through the 1960s and 1970s, and seemed set to add Quebec—a vital piece—in 1988. It's now stalled at the second stage. And it's unlikely to grow in Quebec without growing outside of it, making now the time to add another piece to the largest progressive party we've got. Imperfect, yes, but easier than starting from scratch.

Alliances between social democrats and environmentalists govern Germany and Sweden regularly, with often impressive results. Whether sustainability is social or environmental, progressives need larger parties that care about both. The problems are also linked, and environmentalists won't get ahead if we only focus on jobs, and working people will suffer first if we don't take the climate crisis seriously, as hurricane Katrina so vividly showed. The two need to work together, either in one party or as separate ones in a PR system, which leaves basically two options for the NDP.

It could end ties with unions, which has good and bad aspects for both, but severing ties altogether and taking a piece away likely won't help growth. Or it could keep diversifying, with help from lefties tired of falling back or who've concluded the Liberal Party is structurally unable to win for us. The NDP needs to grow and add a part, in small-l liberals who have concluded the big-L Liberal charade is too hollow to support. It is like Lego, and if we want a bigger progressive party we are going to have to build it, to mirror the clout social democrats and environmentalists use in Europe to great effect. But the meaningless middle needs to go first. Taking lefty Liberals as welcome refugees, of course.

Politics' new rules are already reframing politics and we can help—questioning Liberals' line on events and keeping the party down when it is. We'll need to defeat Liberal MPs to have larger progressive parties but also welcome progressive Liberals into it if they can see it is viable. Politics can't be about protecting the meaningless middle forever, and if we feel let down after a long enough list of failures, an era of minority governments is a good time for a spanking.

So let's dismiss the nonsense that the NDP—without the balance of power, and facing a nationalized Bloc and reunited right—could have stopped the 2006 election. And instead turn attention to the Liberal Party, which voluntarily engaged in corruption that endangered federalism, opted to call the 2004 vote in its aftermath, and then promised an early election in 2006—all to fit its own scandal's timing. It also chose to break its progressive promises from 1993 to 2004, and progressives everywhere deserve better, with possibility presenting itself.

It's possible that Gilles Duceppe and André Boisclair will stay strong, and expand into Montreal. This could lead to Quebec formally separating, taking our progressive majority with it. More likely, it would birth such a loose alliance with Canada that we'll keep a progressive majority, but lose a federal government to use it. That's likely, too, if Harper reaches them first, which risks making our government too neutered to let us work in the world, for the kind of country we'd like to live in.

Or our majority can try to find a way to build a country that reflects us as progressive people, who live in common communities. If we're as global as we'd like to be, we limit ourselves by not finding a uniquely Canadian way that respects Quebec's hopes and our common capacity to dominate federal politics.

Harper's currently trying to import the American system of quagmire, and is appealing to Quebecers' long alienation to help. He wants, mainly with Senate elections that cement regionalism, to build into our system exactly why it's been so difficult for progressive Americans to move ahead. We'll have more squabbles between the Senate and House, and more elections with the illusion of citizen control, while creating governmental gridlock that prevents much from getting done.

The feeling the American federal government is less powerful than ours doesn't ring true. Congress deals with everything from school teachers to highway speed limits in much the same way Parliament attaches conditions to health care. Canada is already the world's second-most decentralized country after Switzerland, and Ottawa's relevance fell during 12 years of Liberals.

Progressive Americans can't do much about this as the votes of lefties in New York City, California or Chicago are wasted in presidential campaigns, thanks to a two-party system and the ancient Electoral College. Our multi-party system provides possibility, though, and inherent to applying our majority is finding common cause with Quebec, which will eventually mean bringing it into the Constitution it never signed.

This creates the chance to perhaps write a progressive Constitution that truly puts the power of our progressive majority to work. The norms of the 1860s, when the current division of power was designed, don't have to constrain us forever. Instead, we could look forward and implement an innovative Constitution that reflects the challenges the 21st century will bring, and the kind of country we now are.

We'd hopefully axe the Senate to stop U.S.-style gridlock moving north. It's also likely inevitable we would join Australia in trying to end the insult of a foreign, hereditary royal family that lets sons rule first. Instead, we might want to add a Canadian head of state to a Union Jack-free flag and Constitution found in Ottawa, not London. It could also tweak the division of powers, making Ottawa, cities and Aboriginal government more relevant and provinces wield a bit less clout.

Powerful provinces don't make such sense in a world where real decisions are truly global and local. With regional trading blocs and an inevitably more entwined co-operation on environmental, health and human security concerns, bogging Canada into a series of provincial fiefdoms will likely keep us at the back of many packs. Allowing more common approaches makes sense, as does helping cities decide more for themselves in a country that keeps urbanizing, and becoming more diverse.

Stronger federal and municipal governments put Canada's values better in action in the world, while better reflecting those values to people who call it home, too. If we like the kind of politics—as we appear to—that elects innovative municipal governments, the world's second-most urbanized country after Australia should design a Constitution that empowers them. Quebec's differences will have to be respected, too, given they are why the possibility presents itself, but autonomy is possible on many issues such as culture, language, or education, while protecting our ability to work together.

Then, we might build structures with the next Democratic president and progressive Americans who let us beat continental neo-cons together, and push for more of the right kind of globalization. Helping businesses trade isn't its only point, and rules that protect people and the only planet we have can work, too. We don't need to look longingly at Europe for an example of how things may work and regret we are stuck on a continent with the elephant. Instead, we should remove the elephant's calf in Stephen Harper and do what we can to help our progressive cousins south of the border lop the mother down to size a bit.

If Saudi Arabia can carry clout in Washington, why can't its largest supplier of oil also extract some conditions, or, more hopefully, work with our progressive cousins south of the border to create the right kind of integration for our planet and those who work on it? Linking Kyoto with foreign aid allowed the European Union to win Russian approval for Kyoto. If it's the kind of globalization we want to support, we could try to forge a more balanced kind of deal: providing secure energy in return for using less of it. We're facing the same changing climate together, and drilling Canada's supply out faster because we can won't help much, with Alberta's water supply paying a high price, too.

This brings us back to 1988 one last time, when a kind of integration into the U.S. began that moves in the opposite direction of the more progressive integration Europe enjoys. We should imagine what would have happened then if the frame that progressive Americans enjoy now were in place. How would things be different if we had one, too. But as many as we wanted: Hargrove asking whether workers deserve fairness. Barlow asking if democracy is worth protecting. May urging cleaner air. Broadbent asking if Mulroney should be prime minister. Quebec aspiring to its hopes with a question it decides.

If that's something worth working *for*, we'll need a truly progressive party to get there, to both benefit from and encourage all types of lefty activity, partisan or not. When this happens, Canadian cities elect progressive mayors, Chileans elect progressive presidents, and Manitobans—with Quebecers—elect progressive premiers. And Tommy Douglas brings universal health care to Saskatchewan after removing the Liberal Party that wouldn't do it voluntarily. When it doesn't, we know the failures that follow, and we should change that because there are too many of us not to move ahead on the issues we all care passionately about.

We shouldn't fight over how best to get the crumbs Liberals throw our way. With politics realigning, its new rules create opportunity to demand the loaf that our majority makes more possible. We might not have another time to keep shrinking the Liberal Party down, while keeping a meaningful way to join a global conversation that is much more important than it was. And work at home for the kind of country that we know 140 years of intermittent majority governments from the Liberal Party of Canada didn't build.

It's time to tell Liberals that we're tired of crumbs. This is a time to hope.

Rethinking Progressive **22**

CHAPTER

O NCE IN A WHILE, something makes you look at things differently. For me, it was in a damp, drizzly, so-*that's*-why-a-dry-cold-is-better spot on the Dutch coast in November 2001. It was a meeting for some of Greenpeace's global communications staff. Partly, to discuss winning Kyoto ratification, two months after the Twin Towers had fallen on 9/11. I'd never thought I was like the Americans, really, until people from about 30 countries began to talk about what the attacks meant for environmentalism.

Even today, being told that 9/11 shook the world brings on a bristle. It actually shook part of the world. Children scouring dumps for something to sell in Manila kept working. Kids being drafted into killing squads in Colombia didn't notice. Islands in the South Pacific kept sinking. At the meeting, an Indian noted that help for victims of 1985's Bhopal chemical disaster, which killed more people, still lagged. The office that covers Israel and Lebanon asked what we thought it was like talking about desertification there.

As we spoke, I found myself empathizing with the American. He tried to explain to lefties from around the world—no fans of many U.S. policies, they—what 9/11 meant for his country. I shared his sense of the tragedy's scope, and how it had changed debate at home. I also related to the dismay at what his government was doing to our planet. After digging in its heels to weaken the treaty, Canada had yet to even ratify Kyoto—eight *years* after our government promised to cut emissions by 20 per cent.

It wasn't that I didn't yearn for politics like the folks from Germany or sympathize with realities around the world. Like America, they just weren't Canada's realities. By the time we finally—begrudgingly, well, at least we got the thing weakened beforehand—ratified Kyoto in December 2002, I was working on Jack Layton's leadership campaign.

Jim Stanford is to blame, in part, for *Dead Centre*. He signed off his post-2006-election column by hoping we'd get our act together by next time. I agree with him—and funnily enough, I did for large chunks of the election, too. We would e-mail and phone early on. Then the e-mails stopped and the columns began. What's sad is that we saw eye-to-eye for the most part—until we just didn't see tactics in the same way. No, not one bit.

Our problem was that we saw the Liberal Party differently. He saw it as an occasional helper. I saw it as a party that doesn't play nice. And it's true, New Democrats do dislike the Liberal Party more than the average progressive because they are the ones fighting them. That's valuable. And without partisan New Democrats to let elections bring change, we'd have fewer progressive wins. Collectively, we can't keep taking the party for granted.

Hitting the reset button each time the NDP starts to show real growth doesn't make much sense—as if Liberals changing a leader with a record like theirs is all it takes to rev up the hegemony machine again. It doesn't seem sensible that momentum's defined as the Green Party hitting eight per cent in a poll—not the NDP doubling its caucus or tripling its vote. To me, at least, it seems there's a more viable growing option. And Dennis Young, a long-time New Democratic strategist, underlined for me how relativism can sometimes fail.

We were working together when Pierre Trudeau died. Like a good chunk of the office, I was crying. Dennis was sceptical about the myth. I asked why. He said that during the War Measures Act, he was fearful his student activism would earn him the kind of lock-ups that were going on in Montreal. The Trudeau I remembered was not his Trudeau, as two lefties used generational frames. We can't push history aside whenever Liberals say it's time to hit the reset button—what happened before counts.

History guides Eugene Kostyra, too, a roly-poly trade unionist and former Manitoba NDP Cabinet minister I had the pleasure to work with. As a driver, he is not so hot and hitching a ride is terrifying. His mini-van would careen across the centre line on the way from Winnipeg's North End to the office downtown. Detours were common, too, as a city steeped in the history of change had a tour guide who just wouldn't keep his eyes on the road.

To Eugene's right was a place where they organized for the general strike of 1919. Just around the corner was where J.S. Woodsworth schemed. Eugene would point them out, regaling the history that helped build a progressive province, lurching the steering wheel as we hurtled back towards the office. The bar there is called the 1919 Club as the past breathes through a movement—not to reminisce, but to win again.

Winning is trendy in the Americas these days. But not soon enough, and as George W. Bush was up for re-election, I figured if Republicans worked here, I could head for the closest swing state. I made some phone calls for John Kerry and was reminded just how widespread are our progressive fears. The people in his office in the little town in northern New Hampshire I ended up in were just like the woman I ran into on the lawn of Parliament Hill during Bush's visit weeks later. Layton was due to speak and I went to the protest beforehand. She asked if he would denounce Bush as a war criminal. I said I doubted it.

We had a fascinating chat about political parties and movements. About the different jobs, responsibilities and limitations each has.

How it's important to have progressives to elect, but that when things aren't going well a protest to challenge a bad frame is important. When I was told there'd be a last chapter due about the new Liberal leader, I looked forward to writing about Bob Rae. Because he writes about the progressive world of the mid-1990s and then freezes it in time to analyze today's.

Around 1995, I got my first e-mail address. Today, I bank online. That decade when computer use sky-rocketed, when immigration hit record highs, and when deficits stopped being our number one problem? Rae says it doesn't matter. That what happened during a decade when we globalized doesn't count. And there progressive analysis has stuck, in 1995—the year that Rae left office and of the last Quebec referendum.

Young adults in Montreal today sometimes refer to Ontario as Canada—as in "you're from Canada" or "I'm going to Canada," when they mean Ottawa or Toronto. It's funny in a way because southern Ontario is one of the last places in Canada that romanticizes en masse about having a strong Ottawa. It's the kind of flag-waving that fuels the Liberal Party but after a decade of it, our federal government is less relevant than ever. Debate on the Hill is often like ratifying Kyoto under the Liberals—who really notices?

Other things happened in that decade, too. The Parti Québécois went from hateful rants against immigrants to embracing new Quebecers. More power is shifting west. And every party in politics today accepts that the deficit and debt were problems that needed to be dealt with. That's all happened since Rae left the NDP—as if change happened everywhere but the NDP, which Rae calls a party of protest.

What he means is that the NDP *he* knew is a party of protest and I can't quibble with it all. New Democrats in the West, however, have won some of Canada's most progressive policies. And both the party he knew and the party he now derides have acted responsibly and pro-ductively in minority Parliaments. No matter.

Then he called the Liberal Party a movement. No, not that kind, but the type that asks what kind of a country we'd like to be and works to build it. The Liberal Party is many things, but that's not one of them. Movements—Martin Luther King's kind, as well as Tommy Douglas's—include protest. But listening to Rae, you'd think all the NDP did was bellyache about a budget, not make it better.

What he means is Liberals don't protest, but women did it to win the right to vote; queers protested, too. You may have done it to keep Canada out of Iraq or Vietnam; and environmentalists squawked, too, as Canada made a climate crisis worse. Heavens, Howard Dean's campaign that enamoured Liberals so much was born of protest. No Liberal leadership candidate supported Star Wars, but they have the Bloc and NDP to thank for kicking up a fuss about it. Maybe it's only me, but that can't just be written off.

Liberals like what reframed politics brings, but history shows that the public is well ahead of them on some big questions. The NDP is, too, and sometimes it daring to outline and demand more helped bring about some of the wins that Liberals now value.

That wheat board? Prairie socialism from the Depression. Universal health care? Pensions to address abject seniors' poverty? Left-wing ideology both. Equal marriage? The product of protest, and also in NDP platforms for years. Women in politics? The NDP is way ahead.

To Michael Ignatieff, however, the NDP is stuck in a ghetto of ideological rigidity. Indeed. Four years before Ignatieff came back home, there was a party talking specifics—involving private enterprise—on dealing with the climate crisis. Say what you will about Layton, but he wasn't playing catch-up on global warming. And it says something about our politics that the crisis we agree we face couldn't get traction only two years ago—raised eloquently by many, in different parties or non-partisan circles.

After 13 *years* of Liberals, Canada ranks 27th out of 29 industrialized countries on global warming emissions, with both the Liberal and Green leaders saying the Kyoto plan they called good enough in 2005 isn't in 2007. We've got a small problem when there isn't enough political space to put things on the agenda—whether Liberals like it or not—and a bigger one, if we do a backward Oliver Twist again, politely asking Liberals once more, "Please, Sir, can I have some less?"

This all brings me to Stéphane Dion, the new Liberal leader, who like Rae glosses over the decade since he became an MP. When Dion's federalism is described, it's with adjectives like principled or courageous, but ideological would work, too. But just as Dion himself challenged separatist logic in his famed Cartesian logic letters during the dark years for federalism, why shouldn't we now ask if the Liberal Party—and Dion's—ideology is wise.

Ah, I hear you saying, but he *is* right. And Dion and Chrétien proved it by increasing Liberal seats in Quebec during the get-tough years. True enough. Liberal seats did go up in Quebec but that horserace isn't interchangeable with having a stronger Canada. Maybe, just maybe, it's time for progressives to ask if things matter beyond what kind of Liberal we send to do battle with the separatists in Quebec.

When do we get to look around and ask where the country that Liberals tell us they built is? Donald Rumsfeld shouldn't be the only ideologue on the continent asked to explain the gulf between his articulately argued, consistent beliefs and, you know, facts.

In Liberal lore, they are the great foreseers. If a problem is on the way, we are assured that the Liberal Party will see it coming and prepare for it, so that whatever century we're in will be Canada's. But it's just not true. Liberals were behind the global pack in building social programs after the Depression. Behind the times on a woman's right to choose. And oops, they've done it again, letting Canada fall behind the global pack on sustainable economies—all in the name of the future.

If all that mattered was having more Liberal MPs from Quebec, we'd be a stronger country now. But we're not. And what struck me, watching the Liberal leadership race, was that the natural governing party seemed to think it wasn't running the show as all those problems they had solutions for just grew. To Dion, it's inconceivable that there could be solutions to problems that aren't Liberal. To Elizabeth May, he's "one of the best ministers of the environment we've ever had."

Talk about a low bar to clear. And even then, not clearing it. Under Dion, the environment ministry morphed. Chemical companies were given a say in the hope that regulation wouldn't be necessary. Imperial Oil—whose parent company, Exxon, funds some of the more virulent global warming sceptics—was invited to write energy policy. It was so bad, environmentalists boycotted the consultations. After a decade of letting pollution rise as usual, Dion still couldn't find the stomach to regulate much. Bloc and NDP MPs, along with environmentalists trying to cut pollution more, were left outside. That's not the balance the Liberals tell us they represent, nor is it respectful of the Parliament that voters elected.

There could be enough oil in the tar sands to fill 600 billion SUVs. Each barrel of oil takes two barrels of water to make. And every two days, enough sand is displaced to fill Yankee Stadium—as we drill for natural gas in the Arctic to power the excavation. Dion said he couldn't do much because there is too much money involved. The British government agrees, saying global warming will cost $7 trillion, but that's not what Dion meant. Like Liberal opponents of public medicare before, he meant that vested interests were at stake.

This ideological ghetto of thinking regulation can work drives Michael Ignatieff wild. But it's worked on acid rain and the ozone layer; in other forms, it brings minimum wages or stops children working. But until the problems get too big to ignore, Liberals delay regulation, and write off progressive critiques as just being old-fashioned. As environment minister, Dion didn't fire off *one* Cartesian logic letter to any polluter, dissecting opposition to regulation in the same way he dissected the separatists' logic. If we only look at fights he wanted to pick, without asking why not more, we'll keep being stuck in the Liberal Party's twilight zone.

So back to the fights that Dion wanted to pick, which we're told—because Liberals won more seats—built a stronger Canada. If that's true, why the unease about what Canada means and where we're going? Recapturing a sense of purpose was the foundation for each Liberal leadership candidate, but each also managed to avoid any contrition for any of the problems that they all agreed needed to be fixed. It was just like Enron. Facts just couldn't disrupt the mirage.

When's it time to check if the mirage is real? After a decade of allegedly building a stronger Canada to compete in a globalized world, we actually have a more fragmented Canada that has fixed a deficit problem but let others grow.

Facing a globalized world, Canada doesn't even regulate the stock market together. As corporate accounting scandals rocked the United States and new laws were passed to stop the shell games, Canada couldn't follow suit. For all our puffery about preparing for the 21st century ready to compete, stock trading is provincially regulated.

As demographics age Canada, our economy needs foreign talent more. But after a decade, our immigration system can't speak to provincial bodies that regulate the professions. In effect, we lure talent from abroad and then use them as cab drivers. Neither makes much sense but despite years of promises, a Liberal Party supposedly building a stronger Canada in a globalized world didn't spend much political capital on the project. Why bother, if, at the end of the day, all that matters is having more Liberal MPs?

It's time to rethink progressive because we can't let the Liberal Party hit the reset button whenever it's convenient. History says that cozying up to the Liberal Party delays—not enables—change, and it's time to stop pushing the past aside when Liberals are weak. That was true in the Depression facing social injustice and it's true today. Alliances with Liberals—labour ententes before, environmental today—don't help win the changes we need.

Waking up to that climate crisis isn't our only shock after the globalizing decade when we got e-mail. We have twenty somethings in Montreal talking about visiting Canada and provinces trying to cope with global challenges alone—on a continent where we're already in bed with a pretty big elephant. Hitting the reset button now, on a voting system invented before the telephone, doesn't seem that strategic.

We built medicare during a time of flux when Liberals were weak and change was underway in Quebec. As we rethink progressive, facing a twenty-first century whose challenges we are unprepared for, maybe it's time to do it again. Knowing that the Liberal Party hasn't voluntarily won much—and more forward-looking, realistic progressive politics that have changed since the Rae days. When do we get to ask if Stéphane Dion's unwavering loyalty to the Liberal Party isn't an asset, but a liability? Heresy, but if we don't rethink progressive, who will?

Ridings within 5,000 votes west of Quebec

THREE-WAY RACES

WINNER	RIDING	RIDING TYPE
NDP (Lib 2nd)	Burnaby-Douglas (Vancouver), BC	Big city
Lib (NDP 2nd)	Esquimalt-Juan de Fuca (Victoria),* BC	Medium city
Con (Lib 2nd)	Fleetwood-Port Kells (Vancouver), BC	Big city
Lib (Con 2nd)	Kenora, ON	North
NDP (Lib 2nd)	London-Fanshawe, ON	Medium city
Con (NDP 2nd)	Newton-North Delta (Vancouver), BC	Big city
Lib (NDP 2nd)	Welland, ON	Small city

NDP-LIBERAL RACES

WINNER	RIDING	RIDING TYPE
Lib	Algoma-Manitoulin-Kapuskasing, ON	North
Lib	Beaches-East York (Toronto), ON	Big city
NDP	Burnaby-New Westminster (Vancouver), BC	Big city
Lib	Churchill, MB	North
NDP	Hamilton East-Stoney Creek, ON	Medium city
NDP	Hamilton Mountain, ON	Medium city

NDP–Liberal races cont'd

WINNER	RIDING	RIDING TYPE
Lib	Nickel Belt, ON	North
NDP	Parkdale-High Park (Toronto), ON	Big city
NDP	Sault Ste. Marie, ON	Small city
Lib	Sudbury, ON	Small city
Lib	Thunder Bay-Rainy River, ON	Small city
Lib	Thunder Bay-Superior North, ON	Small city
NDP	Trinity-Spadina (Toronto), ON	Big city
Lib	Vancouver-Kingsway,** BC	Big city
NDP	Western Arctic,*** NT	North

NDP–Conservative races

WINNER	RIDING	RIDING TYPE
Con	Edmonton-Strathcona, AB	Medium city
Con	Kamloops-Thompson-Cariboo, BC	Rural
NDP	New Westminster-Coquitlam (Vancouver), BC	Big city
Con	Oshawa, ON	Small city
Con	Palliser (Regina), SK	Medium city
Con	Pitt Meadows-Maple Ridge-Mission (Vancouver), BC	Big city
Con	Regina-Qu'Appelle, SK	Medium city
Con	Regina-Lumsden-Lake Centre, SK	Medium city
Con	Saskatoon-Rosetown-Biggar, SK	Medium city
NDP	Vancouver Island North, BC	Rural

LIBERAL–CONSERVATIVE RACES

WINNER	RIDING	RIDING TYPE
Con	Ancaster-Dundas-Flamborough-Westdale (Hamilton), ON	Medium city
Con	Barrie, ON	Small city
Lib	Brant, ON	Small city
Con	Burlington, ON	Small city
Con	Charleswood-St. James-Assiniboia (Winnipeg), MB	Medium city
Lib	Desenethé-Missinippi-Churchill River, SK	North
Con	Edmonton Centre, AB	Medium city
Con	Essex (Windsor), ON	Medium city
Lib	Etobicoke-Lakeshore (Toronto), ON	Big city
Con	Glengarry-Prescott-Russell, SK	Rural
Con	Halton (Toronto), ON	Big city
Lib	Huron-Bruce, ON	Rural
Con	Kildonan-St. Paul (Winnipeg), MB	Medium city
Con	Kitchener-Conestoga, ON	Medium city
Lib	London West, ON	Medium city
Lib	Mississauga-Erindale (Toronto), ON	Big city
Lib	Mississauga South (Toronto), ON	Big city
Lib	Newmarket-Aurora (Toronto), ON	Big city
Con	Niagara Falls, ON	Small city
Lib	Nipissing-Timiskaming, ON	North
Lib	North Vancouver, BC	Big city
Con	Northumberland-Quinte West, ON	Rural

Liberal–Conservative races cont'd

WINNER	RIDING	RIDING TYPE
Lib	Oakville, ON	Small city
Con	Ottawa-Orléans, ON	Medium city
Lib	Ottawa South, ON	Medium city
Con	Parry Sound-Muskoka, ON	Rural
Con	Peterborough, ON	Small city
Lib	Richmond (Vancouver), BC	Big city
Con	Sarnia-Lambton, ON	Small city
Con	Simcoe North, ON	Rural
Lib	St. Boniface (Winnipeg), MB	Medium city
Con	St. Catharines, ON	Small city
Lib	West Vancouver-Sunshine Coast-Sea to Sky Country, BC	Rural
Con	Whitby-Oshawa, ON	Small city
Con	Winnipeg South, MB	Medium city
Lib	Winnipeg South Centre, MB	Medium city

* Former Alliance leadership candidate Keith Martin, an open opponent of the Canada Health Act, is the Liberal MP. Progressive? Hardly.

** The winning Liberal, David Emerson, became a Conservative Cabinet minister within two weeks.

*** All three seats in the territories were decided within 5,000 votes, but Nunavut and Yukon were convincing wins albeit with extremely few votes. Western Arctic had a margin of 1,000 votes—compared to 50 in 2004—and a healthy number of votes cast.

Acknowledgements

NEW DEMOCRAT STAFF don't have it easy. They have all the crap other parties do, with fewer numbers and without that Senate. But despite it all, they still hit above their weight. Progressives are the better for them, and so am I. Thank you for teaching me a lot and hanging tight during the dicey spots, foremost to the small but spunky research and communications shop: Karl Bélanger, Ian Capstick, Kevin Dorse, Tanya Graham-Doucette, John Hall, Cicely McWilliam, Gaby Senay and Greg Shouldice. Christina Lopes was a brilliant lifejacket and to her, deepest thanks. And to the very brave Monia Mazigh, an apology. I'm sorry that job wasn't a great fit.

Brian Topp's 2006 election team was also pretty special, and Heather Fraser, Bob Gallagher, Eric Hébert-Daly, Brad Lavigne, Anne McGrath and Sue Milling are good friends. Appreciation as well to two NDP caucuses for putting up with me; Bill Blaikie and Alexa McDonough most of all. And Jack Layton, for asking again.

Grovelling thanks to those I bothered during this project for your generous patience, in particular to George Nakitsas and Johnathan Schmidt for extremely helpful feedback. Appreciation, too, to Don Loney for taking a chance, Lindsay Humphreys for saint-like patience, as well to the good folks on Alex Munter's mayoral campaign. And to Alex himself, for getting equal marriage passed. Finally, to all the thoughtful people who do good work in Ottawa. They're in every party, the civil service, lobby groups and the press gallery, too. The city doesn't *have* to be synonymous with problems. There are plenty of folks there itching to really get some things done.

But there's more to life than politics, as a rethink finally figured out. My parents are wondrous, adventurous people who spark free thinking, as are some of my best friends, whom I leaned on pretty hard. Thanks to Jeff Atkinson, Marco d'Angelo, Jo Dufay, Bruce Gillespie, Karin Jordan, Michael Khoo, Ryan Lanyon, Peter Nogalo, Rick Smith and Jen Story who along with Mum and Dad, were there when really needed.

Index